Fulham:
THE PREMIERSHIP DIARY

Also by Harry Harris

Ruud Gullit: The Chelsea Diary
Vialli: A Diary of His Season
The Ferguson Effect
Pelé: His Life and Times

Fulham:
THE PREMIERSHIP DIARY

Harry Harris and Danny Fullbrook

ORION

First published in Great Britain in 2002 by Orion
an imprint of Orion Books Ltd
Orion House, 5 Upper St Martin's Lane, London WC2H 9EA

A CIP catalogue record for this book is available
from the British Library

ISBN 0 75285 144 6

Typeset in Great Britain by Selwood Systems, Midsomer Norton
Printed and bound in Great Britain by
Butler & Tanner Ltd, Frome and London

CONTENTS

Acknowledgements   vii
Foreword by Mohamed Al Fayed   ix
Introduction   1

PRE-SEASON

Promotion   11
Tigana . . . A toothpick instead of a cigarette   18
The Harrods Owner . . . gold bars and videos of the
    championship parade   31
July   37

THE SEASON, 2001–02

August   51
September   71
October   84
November   98
December   117
January   134
February   153
March   173
April   196
May   214

ACKNOWLEDGEMENTS

Thanks to Fulham Football Club, in particular Mohamed Al Fayed, Chester Stern, Sarah Brookes, Juliet Slot, Carmelo Mifsud and Stephen Rose; Jim and Sylvia Fullbrook and Gordon 'Ivor' Davies for being a hero.

FOREWORD BY MOHAMED Al FAYED

What an extraordinary first season we had in the Premiership. After such a stunning First Division promotion campaign everyone at the club was breathless with excitement and brimming with optimism when we took to the field at Old Trafford on the opening day. They call it the 'Theatre of Dreams' and we all had to pinch ourselves to make sure we weren't dreaming when Louis Saha put us ahead against the champions after just four minutes. The joy was shortlived. Eventually we lost by the odd goal but not before our stylish, adventurous play had won us many new fans among the millions who tuned in on television.

In many ways that first match against Manchester United was a microcosm of our whole season – a bright start, some brilliant goals, some dubious refereeing decisions, some costly defensive errors, some wonderfully entertaining creative play and defeat in a game from which we might have expected more.

Before the season began I had spoken of my vision to make Fulham the 'Manchester United of the South' and based on those declarations perhaps some people's expectations were a little too high.

Make no mistake, those are still my ambitions, and I see no reason why we cannot achieve them. But I was under no illusion that the Premiership was going to be an easy step up for us. We knew that both Jean Tigana and his players were being plunged into a new learning experience and that it was going to take time to adjust.

Some of our fans, I know, were disappointed that we did not achieve our stated goal of finishing in the top half of the table. There were times during our long run of poor results after Christmas when I, too, was disappointed and more than a little frustrated. But looking back I think most Fulham supporters would accept that maintaining our Premiership status, reaching the FA Cup semi-final and getting into the Intertoto Cup represents a more than satisfactory first year in the top flight. We now have the basis of a squad and the residue of experience from which to build a solid foundation for future success.

During the season I was able to make my views on referees, on support for poorer clubs, on television deals, and on players' contracts, known to my fellow chairmen and to the FA and Premier League. As a result there are new initiatives moving forward in all these areas for the better of football altogether.

We all also learned that football is pricing itself out of business if it continues to rely on television revenue and allows itself to become a slave to the unreasonable demands of players.

I hope that you enjoy reading this book. It is a fair reflection of Fulham's first season back in the big-time for thirty-three years. One thing is for sure. Football fans are the life-blood of the game and there are no finer supporters anywhere in the world than those who follow Fulham through thick and thin.

Come on you Whites!

INTRODUCTION

Dear Diary ... Going up, staying up, and an uncertain future

The Diary traces Fulham's promotion path and details their historic first season in the Premiership. However, things are not all that they would seem. Politics, controversies, insecurities and policies, from the boardroom to the dressing room form a fascinating seam that runs alongside the big money transfer wheeling and dealing and the involvement of agents in the quest for glory in the FA Cup and eventual survival in the Premier League. Among the usual ups and downs – players breaking curfews, a drink-driving offence, FA disciplinary hearings, success and failure – is the chairman's concern about his manager's excessive transfer activities involving French players and agents, and particularly whether the club overpaid for Steve Marlet, the record £11.5m signing who failed to score goals.

Eventually the club surprisingly hired another legend, Franco Baresi, to work alongside Tigana, but the Italian announced on his own website that he would become coach after the final year of Tigana's contract. Baresi's impact was instantaneous. Instead of French imports, Baresi began talks with Parma's out of contract 34-year-old defender Antonio Benarrivo and put Antoniono Asta and Filippo Maniero on his wanted list.

The director of football and coach combination was a partnership that smacked of Gerard Houllier and Roy Evans, and that didn't last long.

But Baresi assured Tigana that he was not after his job and that they could, indeed, work together. Baresi said: 'Jean has the total and full responsibility for the team. It's totally his decision when it comes to buying and selling players. I'm here for advice.'

However it did not start that way with South Americans, striker Facundo Sava and goalkeeper Martin Herrera bought while Tigana was on holiday. 'He was not best pleased,' revealed an insider. 'He was on holiday, had nothing to do with Sava's signing, and, in fact, was not even consulted, but he says he will give him a chance and do the best he can with him.'

Then, as *The Diary* went to press, came the dramatic news that Franco Baresi was leaving the club by mutual consent after just 82 days.

'I have decided that it would be in my own professional interests, and also a sensible outcome for Fulham, to terminate our brief relationship,' he said. 'While all parties have worked constructively to develop our respective roles, I am disappointed that the nature of my position is not as I had envisaged it. It makes sense to recognise this sooner rather than later, and particularly before I make commitments which involve not only myself but also my family.'

The club thanked Baresi for his efforts, wished him, well and expressed a hope that they could work with him on player transfers in the future. It emerged that Baresi and his assistant, Danielle Martinelli, had only been signed on a six-month probationary contract. Director of Corporate Affairs, Chester Stern, said: 'The Chairman always saw this as an experiment. He believes in experimentation in football as well as in business but he also accepts that some experiments don't work.'

However, the significant signings of Junichi Inamoto and Martin Djetou were as a result of the Tigana-Baresi team effort, although they were disappointed when the £3m deal for Victor Sikora collapsed just before the start of the new season.

When Tigana unveiled Inamoto at a press conference his comments about his future at Fulham did little to convince anyone that there was harmony behind the scenes: 'This season is the last year of my contract. I don't know if the chairman wants me to stay or if I want to stay. It's a long way off. I've only a year left on my contract and I don't know what's happening inside the club. I need a meeting with my chairman about that. It's not a meeting about the building work only about what is happening around me.'

To add to the intrigue the club had explored the possibility of building a new ground at White City because of escalating costs at Craven Cottage, with the concern that the two-year ground sharing at QPR might become permanent in the absence of a redevelopment scheme.

However, despite the chairman's new financial restraints, there were promising new arrivals. Exciting prospect Inamoto joined on a one-year loan from Gamba Osaka with an option to buy at £2.5m. Released by Arsenal prior to the World Cup, the blond bombshell certainly made an impact that left Arsène Wenger red-faced.

Inamoto was used as a bit part player in the Worthington Cup and failed to make a single Premiership appearance for Arsenal but two goals in the World Cup pushed him into global prominence and guaranteed Fulham a valuable marketing tool in Japan. Cruelly labelled T-shirt at Highbury, Tigana urgently needed Inamoto's invention and goals from midfield, and his arrival was described as 'one of the close season's transfer coups'. A successful season would ensure a contract to keep him at Fulham until 2006. The hero of Japan's World Cup campaign said: 'London still appeals to me, I have decided on my future.

I will go to Fulham where they will play me. I have always thought it would be difficult to make it in England. It is very physical, but I can cope.' Inamoto accepted the modest pay of £400,000-a-year as Fulham balked at the salary demands of Juninho, who also had his problems negotiating a deal to return to Middlesbrough.

Inamoto had his own following of Japanese media while at Arsenal, mostly turning up disappointed that he wasn't even on the bench. But his arrival at Fulham guaranteed that all the club's games would be live on Japanese TV.

Tigana said: 'Inamoto will definitely play in the Premiership this season. Arsenal have a big squad, but at Fulham it will be easier for him to play more games. He is not a discovery to me. Eighteen months ago I met with Philippe Troussier, the Japan manager, and tried to take Inamoto on loan, but Arsenal got there first. You know how difficult it is to fight with Arsène Wenger! But now he is our player and I know he has the capacity to play at the highest level.'

Asked if the temporary nature of the Inamoto deal was a result of the financial restraints, Tigana answered: 'It's difficult because of my own contract only has a year to go.'

Tigana wanted Inamoto even though a multitude of midfield players were on offer. Matt Holland was offered to the club, but despite his outstanding World Cup with the Republic of Ireland, again Tigana and Baresi preferred Inamoto.

Dutch winger Sikora was a major target but his move from Vitesse Arnhem stalled after several weeks of advanced talks for a £3.5m deal. Sikora said: 'The English league is the best to play in. I have spoken to Ruud (Van Nistelrooy), to Jimmy Floyd Hasselbaink and to Boudewijn Zenden. They have all given me a few tips.' Naturally enough he also consulted Edwin Van Der Sar.

So, off he went to sign for Ajax! Fulham should have known because before they thought they had his signature he was quoted on Dutch radio: 'I want to go to Ajax. Vitesse Arnhem have made mistakes and I will take them to court if I have to.' An insider at Fulham described Sikora as 'the new Marc Overmars', so it was a big loss.

As compensation, Tigana finally got the defender he wanted for the start of his Premiership reign. Martin Djetou joined on a year's loan from Parma. The 27-year-old centre-back snubbed Fulham a year earlier when he joined the Italian club from Monaco for £6.5m, but he suffered a disappointing debut season in Serie A and missed out on the World Cup squad. Djetou spent four seasons with RC Strasbourg before joining Monaco in 1996 where, under Tigana, he helped his side win the French Championship in his first season at the club. He had six international caps making his first appearance for the national side in the 4–0 win against Turkey in October 1996. The Ivory-Coast-born defender can also operate as a holding midfielder. Tigana moved for a player he knew so well after the on-off deal with Antonio Benarrivo was finally off after a medical showed up an ankle condition that required surgery, and at the age of 37 that was too great a risk. Even attempts to lower his wage demands yet again failed to resolve the issue to the point that the Italian considered legal action for loss of earnings and called on Baresi to resign! Benarrivo said: 'While I was waiting to sign for Fulham I lost three teams because of them, I refused to renew my contract with Parma, said no to Birmingham, and also Bolton. Now here I am, out of work.'

Talks also broke down with Martin Keown, as Fulham were not prepared to match his Highbury salary.

Even though the club were desperate for a goalscorer, they would not pay silly money. The mighty 'Batigol' was apparently 'desperate' to come to Fulham. But on wages of £4m a year NET, there was no chance, with the chairman revising his transfer policy on wages as well as fees. Fulham spokesman Chester Stern said: 'In the early part of the year one of our directors was approached through a third party representing Batistuta. We were asked if we would be interested in signing him. Jean Tigana was asked and we immediately responded with a "thanks – but no thanks." Jean didn't give his reason but his policy is to maximise profits on young players rather than buy older ones who might be very expensive and not have any sell-on value in the four years after their contract.'

Betfair.com announced a new one-year sponsorship deal worth £600,000 rising to £2.2m depending on performance, on the day the club unveiled Inamoto.

Mohamed Al Fayed commented: 'The Club is very excited about the sponsorship agreement with Betfair, a brand that is emerging as one of the brightest new names in the betting industry. The rise of this football club is the result of my vision for us to achieve great things both domestically and internationally. I am always happy to be involved with brands that share my drive and passion, and I am sure that it will be a very successful combination of two ambitious organisations which I believe makes it the right choice of partner for us.'

By June 2002 Arsène Wenger and Gerard Houllier were the obvious names being thrown forward for the job of French national coach, with Roger Lemerre tipped to offer his resignation after departing the World Cup with the worst record of any defending nation in history. But Tigana was another early possibility with just one more year left on his contract and Fulham not likely to stand in his way, just as Al Fayed accepted the inevitable when the FA came calling for Kevin Keegan. But, eventually, the job went to Jacques Santini, who took Lyon to their first French title in 2002.

But as the preparation for a new season got under way in remarkable circumstances, *The Diary* concentrates first on the promotion campaign and then, day-by-day, the first season with the big boys in the Premiership.

Tigana is the central character in an unusual examination of a club with a reputation for being 'humble and friendly' but which, in reality, is ultra professional and ambitious. But with Mohamed Al Fayed as chairman and a manager who has a vineyard in Provence, who sucks a toothpick in the dugout and who came to Craven Cottage after working as an agent, it was never likely to be any other way. Bankrolled by Al Fayed and with a dressing room directed by a highly controlled French coach, Fulham shed their homely 'little club by the Thames' image. While Tigana's reign began with promotion, the club's first season in the Premier League was played out in a decrepit relic of a stadium that is a throwback to the days of black-and-white television, but plans for a new all-seater luxury stadium illustrate the club's aspirations.

Tigana's idiosyncrasies and aloofness bordering on the reclusive make him a fascinating subject. After being crowned champions of the First Division with more than 100 points, only just short of Sunderland's record of 105, Tigana made no secret of his desire ultimately to land the Premiership title before quitting. After a thrilling and highly successful debut season in English football he said: 'Winning the First Division is a fantastic story but it is only one step towards what I want to achieve. My dream is to win the Premiership or the FA Cup. I always work towards my dream.' Tigana keeps his passions under control when he concentrates on the game from the dugout, but even he couldn't hold back his emotions at the precise moment when Sean Davis, the London boy among his cosmopolitan team, scored the late winner for ten-men Fulham at Blackburn to guarantee Premiership football. Tigana explained: 'It was the first time in my career as manager that I have jumped out of the dugout to celebrate. John Collins told me he had never seen me react like that before. But I was so happy.' There were high hopes for Davis, the kid who dreamed of playing for arch rivals Chelsea. Tipped as one of a large group of promising youngsters earmarked for international stardom, he was rejected by Wimbledon and West Ham and recalls: 'I was at Wimbledon for a year and they said I wasn't good enough, and West Ham only took a week to say the same and show me the door. Initially I was a bit disillusioned after the rejections. I kept playing local football at Battersea youth centre, but there were times when I thought my dreams would never be realised. I was extremely lucky, though. The coaches at Battersea, Ray Henry and Andrew Beadle, recommended I gave it another shot and told me to go for trials at Fulham. I've never looked back.'

The 'happiness factor' continued when Fulham secured the championship with a 93rd-minute equaliser against Sheffield Wednesday at the Cottage. William Hill immediately installed Fulham as 25–1 shots to win the Premiership in their debut season. And when Al Fayed, whose personal wealth was listed at £750m, pledged he would do 'whatever it takes' to make Fulham champions of English football, he meant what he said. Whatever the Tractor Boys could do, the Cottagers could do even better.

Tigana was given a formidable transfer budget and in August alone spent virtually £1m a day, but the big question became whether he had spent his chairman's money wisely. Joining Arsène Wenger and Gerard Houllier as the latest French coach in the Premiership, he is arguably a bigger name in his homeland, and certainly more flamboyant. Part of the great French team of the eighties and early nineties, he played alongside Michel Platini, and instead of going straight into management became an agent and ran his vineyard. When he joined Fulham he introduced a system of discipline that included a rigid ban on alcohol – yet his own brand is, fittingly, on sale at Harrods! Domaine La Dona Tigana sells at £8.50 and is made at his vineyard in Cassis, Provence. A full-page advert appeared soon after Tigana arrived at the club describing the wine as 'full-bodied as Chris Coleman, its floral aroma is as beautiful as a John Collins free-kick, and as lively on the palate as Fabrice Fernandes is on the ball'. Not bad, apart from the fact that Fernandes was loaned out to Glasgow Rangers after a few months.

Premiership football guarantees £50m in TV rights, extra sponsorship and increased attendances. With the club benefiting from the first year of the unprecedented £1 billion TV deals, it was imperative Fulham retained Premiership status and the funding that went with it. Yet Fulham were in Division Three in 1997 and on the verge of going out of the League and out of business. The revival began under the chairmanship of Jimmy Hill and former manager Mickey Adams. The club has ridden the rollercoaster of Al Fayed's arrival, Adams' dismissal, Kevin Keegan's influence and subsequent departure for England management. Although Al Fayed favoured Eric Cantona, he recruited Tigana. Fulham are also the first club since the Taylor Report into Hillsborough and the subsequent mandatory policy of all-seater stadia to play in the top flight with terraces at their archaic Thames-side ground, Craven Cottage. In fact they had 13,000 standing places, two-thirds of the Cottage capacity at a time when Minister of Sport Kate Hoey had opened up the controversial debate about whether there can be a designated 'safe' standing sector in Premiership football grounds based on a German model. Fulham had special dispensation because the authorities were aware of their plans to rebuild their stadium. Fewer than 6,000 seats were available for the club's first Premiership campaign. On police advice the club cut the away allocation from 6,000 to 1,700, half of which is standing. Chief Superintendent Anthony Willis, responsible for policing all matches at the Cottage, said, 'Clearly, we would have preferred not to be still in the days of terracing. But we have worked out the best solution in the circumstances.'

Tigana embarked on his debut season in English football with limited English and used John Collins to act as interpreter. Having announced a five-year plan to raise Fulham from the Second Division to the Premiership, Al Fayed had achieved his aim a year ahead of schedule.

The club, synonymous with Johnny Haynes, George Cohen, Bobby Moore, Rodney Marsh and George Best, now had £11m players that the fans had never heard of (in the shape of Steve Marlet). Fulham have had their moments in the past: they were the first club to pay £100 a week, to Johnny Haynes, made a Cup Final appearance with Moore and Mullery which ended in defeat to West Ham in 1975, and in the late seventies, with a side that included Marsh and Best, there was glamour without tangible success. Under Malcolm Macdonald in 1982 the club just missed out on a return to the big time on goal difference when they failed to win on the last day of the season.

The last time Fulham graced the top division in 1968 Bobby Robson arrived midway through the season but was unable to save the club from relegation.

The wall on Stevenage Road that leads to the quaint old ground lorded the names from the past: 'Alan Mullery is God', can be seen; 'Ray Lewington and Jimmy Hill out' was beginning to fade. Back in the big time under Tigana, with an array of expensive imports, fans were hoping the club would repay their patience and support throughout the difficult times by securing a place in Europe for the next season. Tigana and Al Fayed, desiring more than mere Premiership survival, shared that hope.

PRE-SEASON

PROMOTION...

On 14 April 2001 Fulham had clinched promotion with a 2–1 win at Huddersfield and on Easter Monday celebrated the Championship against Sheffield Wednesday at Craven Cottage. There were the expected enthusiastic celebrations to mark their momentous promotion season, back in the top flight for the first time in 33 years, and ready for their first ever season in the Premiership. Fulham might have the only ground in the top flight with terracing, but with a new home planned and Jean Tigana in charge, there was an incredible air of expectancy, particularly with Ipswich Town having been promoted a year earlier and battling for a place in the Champions League, proving that the Premiership is not simply the domain of the Establishment.

Tigana looked a touch sheepish at Huddersfield's McAlpine Stadium when asked to pose during the on-pitch celebrations clutching a bottle of bubbly with the sponsors' Nationwide label. He was in no mood to lift the drinks ban, even on the occasion of Fulham's historic return to the big time. 'Alcohol? Why?' he said when asked about the players having a drink to celebrate. 'Okay, one beer!'

Most likely he was joking. Lee Clark said: 'We have training on Sunday morning but, if we do it on Monday and win the title, he might let us have a half.' Rufus Brevett said: 'A beer? I wouldn't have thought so. He might give us a glass of his wine, but I don't know about a beer.' Mohamed Al Fayed missed the promotion 'party' but passed on his good wishes in a telephone call to Tigana, and made him laugh by asking how many more millions he would want. Michael Fiddy, said: 'Mr Fayed is very, very proud. I have just spoken to him. He wants to thank everyone who has helped with Fulham since he's been here – Kevin Keegan as well as Jean Tigana. It has been his dream to get Fulham into the Premiership and he is very pleased, as you can imagine.' Yet the *News of the World* carried what appeared to be a lengthy interview with Al Fayed which read as if he was actually there. The story reported Al Fayed as saying:

'It's a wonderful day for Fulham. It has taken us 33 years, so I'm absolutely delighted for everybody connected with the football club and Craven Cottage. A lot of people have put a lot into this and we've a long way to go. But it's marvellous we're now up there playing in what is one of the best leagues in the world. It's something I was determined to give to the loyal supporters of what is surely one of the friendliest clubs in British football. Manager Jean Tigana's contribution this year has been superb. He has been the conductor of my orchestra, quietly turning Fulham around, laying the seeds for our success this season and, hopefully, for even greater things to come in the next five years. I have a great relationship with Jean. When you have as good a manager as him, you let him do his job. Whatever Jean needs, he knows he has my full support. Money is no object. I've already spent close to £60m and whatever my manager asks for, he will get. All I want is for the club to be successful. Our message to Manchester United, Liverpool, Arsenal and the rest is, "Watch out for Fulham". The plan is to be at the very top in the next five years. Jean and I have a dream – to win the Premiership. Our immediate plans are to adjust to the new league first. But we're also looking to enjoy success. It's fantastic that we have won promotion within a few weeks of getting permission to build our new 30,000-seater stadium. Having the stadium was crucial to our long-term plans and the future of those plans. It's all a great achievement for the club and fantastic for the supporters, who have had a lot to do with our current success. We have massive support in the area. It has given me the strength to fulfil the dream for everyone of getting Fulham back in the Premiership. We started very well with a great player and manager of Newcastle, Kevin Keegan. He joined us but then unfortunately left to manage England. He did a fantastic job. Then we were lucky to find Tigana, who has a completely different type of technique and imagination. He promised to deliver – and he has done superbly. All the managers are like maestros, great artists. If they have the support but no interference from the top, they really deliver.'

It might easily have come directly from Al Fayed's own lips, but it didn't. It didn't sound quite like him, although all the sentiments seemed accurate enough. It seemed that the quotes had originated from the fertile mind of Al Fayed's personal PR guru Max Clifford. 'Yes, you're right, it was me,' confessed Max. 'I was actually on holiday in Spain when the papers called me and wanted some comments from Mohamed. I speak to him regularly and the understanding is that I can speak for him as I know what he has said, what he is feeling and what he is thinking.

'I've done it many times in the past. The papers would put the questions to me and I would answer for Mohamed. I've been doing it in rock 'n' roll for thirty-five years! Do you think Jimi Hendrix gave all those interviews? Hardly, when he was so full of drugs and booze! I used to do it for him all those years ago.'

The *News of the World* published a smiling picture of the chairman alongside one of his many 'quotes'. Al Fayed goes to virtually all the home games, and to as many away matches as he can, which are few and far between, as he has understandable pressure on his time.

With only five defeats in forty-one league games, Fulham recorded their fourteenth away win at Huddersfield. Clark had achieved a personal hat-trick of promotions, having done it with Newcastle and Sunderland. He said: 'It's terrific. I've been lucky to do it three times now and it's a special feeling. The club has come a hell of a long way in a short time. Now we will mix it with the cream and it's a fantastic achievement. But we don't just want to make up the numbers in the Premiership. We want to show other teams that we will be a force and deserve to be mixing it with the best. You get your rewards and that's what we have done. There is a lot of ambition at this club, from the chairman, the board, the officials, the players and the fans. Everybody wants to succeed at the top. The club has come a long way in the five or six years since nearly going out of business, and now we can take our place among the crème de la crème.' But under the Tigana regime, it was training the next day. 'There won't be any celebrating yet, though. We are training tomorrow for Sheffield Wednesday and we will be totally focused on that. I don't think we'll really be having a drink until the end of the season. We certainly won't be taking our foot off the gas.'

Tigana's first season in charge was nothing short of phenomenal. An illustration of Premiership potential came with a series of cup contests. Fulham eliminated Derby from the Worthington Cup and took an emerging Liverpool to extra-time at Anfield. Sir Alex Ferguson was full of admiration for their FA Cup performance in defeat at the Cottage. On that day Al Fayed walked across the pitch waving a Fulham scarf, and shook hands with David Beckham. His team's display was almost as good. The pace up front of Louis Saha and Luis Boa Morte was frightening. Both players had stayed only a short time with their previous Premiership clubs – Saha at Newcastle and Boa Morte at Arsenal then Southampton – and are still fresh and young.

As the confirmation day for promotion grew ever closer, the discussion revolved around what was to happen next. Former Chelsea defender Neil Clement came to the Cottage with West Brom and after a goalless draw was sure that Fulham would assess their progress in the battle of SW6. After failing to establish himself at Stamford Bridge, Clement had dropped down to the First Division with WBA for a £100,000 fee. The 22-year-old observed: 'My brother is youth team coach at Fulham and I have popped along to the training ground to see them. They are a Premiership club, not a First Division side. They are Premiership class in everything they do. The club is run the right way and they have a chairman prepared to back them all the way. He says he wants to make them the best team in the world, and if he puts his money where his mouth is then the future can be very good. I can definitely see them being a better club than Chelsea. They have some great players at Stamford Bridge but it is all about playing great football and Fulham are doing that. They can definitely overtake Chelsea. Money talks and he [Al Fayed] has got plenty of it, so I'm sure they can. The manager they have at Fulham is spot on. He is a massive name in France where they have some terrific players so he could easily attract first-class players to the club if he wanted to. Fulham have got some good players who have adapted to the way Tigana wants them to play football. As long as they keep the manager and the way he wants to play football, they have a great chance.'

Fulham defender Steve Finnan harboured thoughts of how Jack Walker and Blackburn were crowned Premiership champions just three seasons after promotion. Finnan discussed the internal blueprint for the future: 'The chairman wants us to do what Blackburn did. It would be great if we could do the same thing. The chairman will obviously spend money signing some big players in the summer, but we already have a lot here who deserve a chance anyway. The main objective would be to stay up, and then to consolidate we would have to be looking for a top-half finish. But then we want to push on with a title challenge in the next couple of seasons. The one thing we don't want to do, though, is follow Blackburn's example by getting relegated again a few years later.' Ironically, the next stage of their early promotion confirmation came at Ewood Park where, despite losing Rufus Brevett to a red card, the ten men came from a goal down to win 2–1.

Eyal Berkovic had been rescued by Graeme Souness from his latest problems at Celtic, but he had one eye on a move back to London and behind the scenes there had been overtures to Fulham. Little wonder the Israeli international was out to impress. Both Fulham and Blackburn were battling out a contest within a contest, as to who might be the more powerful new Premiership side. Fulham emerged on top, confirmed their Premiership status at Huddersfield and then celebrated at the Cottage. Al Fayed performed a lap of honour before the game while Fat Les, alias Keith Allen, was on the pitch as match sponsor. Sean Davis popped up with the late equaliser after Wednesday had threatened to be party poopers. Davis stripped off his shirt and threw it to the ground as he rejoiced in the goal forty seconds from time that earned the point which secured the Championship. 'I Love Sean Davis' proclaimed a banner as the 21-year-old from down the road in Lambeth received the obligatory yellow card from referee Eddie Wolstenholme for removing his attire. During the on-pitch celebrations Davis gazed glassy-eyed into the cameras and provided the usual in-depth analysis: 'I'm buzzing, buzzing!' But for a club synonymous for romance rather than ruthless success there was a feeling all that might change.

'Welcome to this potentially historic day,' 'Diddy' David Hamilton enthusiastically bellowed over the PA system before kick-off. He had been the country's top DJ when Fulham were last in the First Division back in 1968. Hamilton told the expectant fans that the last time Fulham were promoted to the top flight was back in 1958–9, coincidentally beating Sheffield Wednesday 6–2 on Good Friday. Expectations couldn't have been higher, and disappointment loomed until the equaliser was scored.

The 33-year-old John Collins, who'd had such an influence as player-coach, said, 'It's a special day. I've played for Scotland many times and won the French league with Monaco but this means just as much to me. We dominated the game but, at times, they had ten men in the box and it was difficult to break them down. We kept passing the ball and it was a fantastic goal by Sean. He can go all the way. It was fantastic for the club that it was a local lad who has come through the youth system who scored such a vital goal.' Wednesday manager Peter Shreeves commented: 'We weren't uninvited guests, but we wanted to be gatecrashers. It was their party and they got their reward not for today, but for what they've done all season. It was just marvellous to come here and get a point. Congratulations to Fulham. They've played magnificently all season and they're well equipped to make the step up.'

John Collins continued: 'I'm looking forward to getting back into the Premiership myself. We've proved we can match Premiership teams when we've played in the Cup against both Manchester United and Liverpool this season, and now we'll have to do it week by week. We will stay up. We will not be overawed. We have lots of good players in the team who are more than capable of holding their own in the Premier League. But no doubt we'll strengthen in the summer because every team needs to improve, even Manchester United and Arsenal. There's still plenty of hard work to do and I am sure Jean is already thinking of next season.

'We are looking forward to enjoying it and believe we can do well. We have nothing to fear. It will be a terrific challenge. Obviously it is stepping up a level from what we play week in and week out in the First Division but it will be a great experience for everyone involved with the club. But every team needs to improve and in the summer we will need to do so by bringing in players.'

'Fulham, the new champions of the First Division,' bellowed 'Diddy' David Hamilton as Al Fayed, injured skipper Chris Coleman, who had hobbled on to the pitch, and just about everyone else celebrated to a combination of Queen with the obligatory 'We Are the Champions', Andy Williams and The Monkees' 'Daydream Believer'. Mohamed Al Fayed certainly wasn't holding back either; wearing a preposterous red wig, draped in his black-and-white scarf, and holding up a Fulham shirt with No. 1 and Al Fayed on the back, this was not going to be an anonymous chairman!

'Bring on Chelsea!' chanted the jubilant crowd.

Despite a full Premiership programme, their exploits and the memorable goal celebrations made the top half of the front page of the next day's *Independent*.

With 96 points Fulham needed 10 more points to beat Sunderland's Division One record. It was within sight after beating Wolves at the Cottage for the first time since 1964. 'The players aren't talking about it but the manager is!' said Collins. But a draw against Wimbledon made the target impossible. However, the on-pitch celebrations were on again as the Championship trophy was presented and paraded. Guess who was in all the papers over the next couple of days? Yes, it was the chairman, with baseball cap and scarf, never too far away from that precious piece of silverware. Defender Andy Melville, who was twice promoted with Sunderland, observed: 'The result was bitterly disappointing but today was about more than just winning or losing for us. We wanted to win in style but we've been playing with style all season so no one can complain. It's a magical day for all of us and we're looking ahead to many more in the Premiership. We fear no one and we can prove we can hold our own against teams such as Liverpool and Manchester United.' As for missing out on breaking Sunderland's record Melville added: 'The lads are pretty disappointed about that but we've had too many draws recently and we've made it just that bit too hard for ourselves.' Wimbledon manager Terry Burton might have been fuming about the penalty decision that effectively ended his club's chances of reaching the play-offs, but he was full of praise for Tigana's side. 'It was their party day and they were determined to show why they are champions. They have set the standard this year. They are very professional, their passing is out of this world and their shape is very good. They are the best team to go up for some time.'

Despite the constant speculation of transfer targets, Tigana was going to give many of his players their chance in the Premiership. In the Wolves programme he wrote: 'We have almost the same team as last season. They are different players now. They have different vision, different bodies, different philosophy.' Despite all the hype and expectancy, there was realism. Several newly promoted clubs have been immediately relegated since the Premiership was formed in 1992. The record of newly promoted sides illustrates the degree of difficulty when joining the big boys:

1992–3
Ipswich 16th
Blackburn 4th
Manchester City 9th
Middlesbrough 21st (relegated)

1993–4
Newcastle 3rd
Swindon 22nd (relegated)
West Ham 13th

1994–5
Crystal Palace 19th (relegated)
Leicester City 21st (relegated)
Nottingham Forest 3rd

1995–6
Bolton 20th (relegated)
Middlesbrough 12th

1996–7
Derby 12th
Leicester 9th
Sunderland 18th (relegated)

1997–8
Barnsley 19th (relegated)
Bolton 18th (relegated)
Crystal Palace 20th (relegated)

1998–9
Nottingham Forest 20th (relegated)
Middlesbrough 9th
Charlton 18th (relegated)

1999–2000
Sunderland 7th
Bradford 17th
Watford 20th (relegated)

2000–01
Charlton 9th
Manchester City 18th (relegated)
Ipswich 5th

TIGANA...

A toothpick instead of a cigarette

Born in the West African nation of Mali 47 years ago, Jean Tigana worked in a spaghetti factory and as a postman before becoming a professional footballer. The following anecdote captures his attitude to Fulham: 'In Bordeaux I rebuilt an abandoned property,' he said. 'I improved it bit-by-bit, by my own hand, until I was proud of what I had done. I'm not tough, merely professional. I take command from the start. My idea is to build a good club at Fulham. It is very good for me to put down good foundations by developing young players and promoting our youth academy, because that is the way forward, as Manchester United and Leeds United have proved. When I have finished my job at Fulham, I want to leave behind a great club, one that can produce its own talent and stand alone. I want to create something special.'

Tigana is a footballing recluse. Rarely seen in public and hardly ever interviewed, he spends the majority of his time in his office at Fulham's Motspur Park training ground, just off the A3 outside London. The site used to be owned by the Bank of England and was bought by Mohamed Al Fayed during the Kevin Keegan reign, and then developed under Paul Bracewell. It is the type of facility that so-called bigger London clubs like West Ham, Chelsea, Wimbledon and QPR envy. There are acres of space, with five different pitches, one with a grandstand, which is being extended. The youth teams and reserves train at the site. There is also an astro-turf facility which helps during the winter, as well as a gym house containing saunas, and a state-of-the-art medical unit for the physios to work from. Fulham also have Harrods' personnel resources which offer the very best facilities and medical expertise to all of the players and staff. The offices are in an old manor house which has been converted into an operating training ground. Michael Fiddy, who began the season as MD before surprisingly quitting halfway through, had an office there, as do the rest of the media staff since most of the press events are held at the training ground.

While Tigana is obsessed with football, Roger Propos, one of the most respected trainers in French football, is obsessed with fitness. This is why so many of the Fulham players are the lightest they have ever been in their careers. Propos was so concerned to make sure his players were in the right condition that he had a training hill built at the side of one of the pitches so he could work the players harder. Nevertheless, Tigana and his coaches realise nothing is gained from grinding players into the ground. 'A lot of coaches in this country think that if you train lots then the players will be fit, but that's not necessarily the case,' says captain John Collins. 'What we do at Fulham is not too much but not too little. It's a science. Everything is done for a reason, it's not just to kill time.'

Tigana's office at the training ground is unextravagant with a desk, chair, telephone and picture of his wife and three kids. In pride of place is the television with which he keeps up to date with every football programme and can watch videotaped games featuring opponents or players he wants to buy. His best work, though, is done on the training pitch with the players. He works in a similar way to former Spurs, England and Monaco midfield genius Glenn Hoddle in as much as he is prepared to prove to his players that he can do anything he asks of his squad. He is ready to train as hard as any first-team player, and then join in a game to show them his skills by example. Head of Communications Sarah Brookes described Tigana's typical working day: 'He is always there about 9 a.m. if they are training at 10 a.m. He will always arrive in a suit and go into his office. He will then get tracksuited up and deal with paperwork and any calls he has to make. He is out on the training pitch before anyone else. He is so hands on. On a Thursday there is a head tennis session that goes on and he plays and is always laughing and joking with them, but he hates to lose. He is a winner at the end of the day and he hates losing anything. There is a staff game every week, which Jean instigated and right at the very beginning Christian Damiano started to play but then he took the mantle of referee and Roger Propos played. Every Thursday throughout the season there is an important hour which begins at 12.30 p.m. Right at the beginning only about four staff turned up and played five-a-side because nobody thought they could go and play with the great Jean Tigana. But in a matter of weeks everybody was turning out. It was like the cast of *Ben Hur*. It was just ridiculous. All the French players would stand and watch. Some of us used to wander down and watch to see the genius of Tigana. Patrick Mascall, after playing on a Thursday, would always be on the telephone to one of his mates, saying, "Yes, well, I blocked a shot from Tigana and then shimmied up the wing against John Marshall and shot against Gerry Peyton [former Fulham and Republic of Ireland goalkeeper who is goalkeeping coach] and stuck it in the top corner." They all play. It is a good spirit, and when we held the staff game at Craven Cottage at the end of the season the girls had a game as well, in a five-a-side competition on half a pitch. Jean watched the whole game and was shouting instructions. I got christened Sarah Boa Morte because I took the ball from one end of the pitch to the other and then fluffed the shot.'

Tigana is certainly not too proud or pompous to fold and hand out bibs while his assistant Christian Damiano, who has been chief scout and assistant coach of the world-beating French national side, and who was the force behind France's football academy Clairefontaine, takes the players through their paces. 'A player at this level is like a Formula One racing car,' says Damiano. 'If you put diesel in the car instead of the right fuel it will not run as well.'

Throughout all the procedures there is one common factor – the trademark Tigana smile. Instead of patronising his players, he instils confidence in them, mainly by relaxing them. Tigana does this by creating a sense of unity and loyalty, and backed this up by refusing to go above £8m for Anderlecht's Czech striker Jan Koller and declining to meet Teddy Sheringham's £50,000-a-week wage demands – even though he admired the former Manchester United striker who came off the bench to dump Fulham out of the FA Cup. Subsequently, the mood around the training ground and among the office staff is good, with laughter often heard rolling out of the doors of the manor house.

To discover the innermost thoughts and philosophy of Tigana is not easy, but when this man of few words opens up, he is always worth listening to. In his first season in English football he rarely gave an interview, often delegating one of his players, usually John Collins; Tigana himself was hardly on TV, feeling that media interaction was not something for the coach. Head of Communications Sarah Brookes remembered how she had tried to advise Tigana on giving interviews:

'I tried to explain to him how the press in this country worked. It was not just about the Sky games, where the revenue was important. I also tried to tell him that managers in the Premiership in this country speak before a game, say on a Thursday. He just looked at me with this wonderful expression on his face and said, "Never, never I speak with the press, even when I was playing with Monaco." He just could not understand what was interesting about what he had to say before a game. He said he was happy to speak after a game, but he could not get to grips with speaking before.'

As the season unfolded, it became clear that the enigmatic Frenchman would choose to speak only at selective times, and certainly not before and after every game. Sarah Brookes again: 'He and Christian took it in turns, but it is slowly, slowly with him and the fact that he did not speak once in the course of a nineteen-game spell in the season made it incredibly hard.'

However, after winning the First Division title, Tigana was in reflective mood in his one major concession to be interviewed before embarking on the much higher-profile Premiership. Tigana is not a man who is given over to emotion, and he tends to take a laid-back attitude towards life. The reason for this is that he naturally expects to be successful. Not a man used to failure, he explained that he fully expected Fulham to be promoted to the Premiership.

From the instant he arrived at Fulham, Tigana slowly but surely began to get his philosophy across to his players. A good example of this, towards the start of his reign, is when he encountered a pre-season testimonial match against Tottenham for their longest-serving player, Simon Morgan. Five minutes before kick-off Tigana sat with Michael Fiddy on the balcony at Craven Cottage. Fiddy leaned over to the new manager and made a very gentle observation: wasn't it about time he went down and talked to his players before kick-off? Tigana replied: 'I have been a coach for fifteen years, and these players have been in the game for at least ten. If they don't know how to prepare for and play a game now, I can't teach them!' It was certainly a surprise, a change from the British-style up-and-at-'em approach before kick-off.

Mohamed Al Fayed knew that former boss Paul Bracewell was not to his taste as early as Christmas 1999, so he set about getting a new manager. Bracewell was never enigmatic enough for Al Fayed. Although he was Kevin Keegan's suggestion as boss, Al Fayed quickly lost patience with him, especially when Fulham looked like they would not make it to the play-offs. Club captain Chris Coleman had to persuade Al Fayed not to sack Bracewell just after Christmas.

Al Fayed flirted with the idea of appointing his friend Eric Cantona but was advised that, while the enigmatic Frenchman was a brilliant footballer, he was a loner and not a good people person. He would not motivate players well. The pair discussed Fulham over dinner at the Ritz hotel in Paris, but the idea went no further. Instead the chairman commissioned research into the best potential managers available world wide, and a shortlist of five, including Jean Tigana, was drawn up. Fulham directors Mark Griffiths and Tim Delaney were dispatched to the south of France where Tigana was working as an agent and living on his vineyard, and the vision for Fulham presented to him at that first meeting was exactly what Tigana was looking for. Delaney said: 'We brought him to England and smuggled him incognito in to watch a match at Craven Cottage. Nobody recognised him. Fulham were 2-0 up at half-time, and he turned to me and said, "This team is awful, but I can work with them." I was a bit nonplussed, but at that point we knew we had our man.'

Having arrived in this country, his main aim now is to leave a legacy at Fulham. Tigana has said he will give up football when he is 50; by that time he hopes to have produced a number of international players for England, leaving behind a foundation for a new era at Craven Cottage that every Fulham player and fan will be proud of. He is not prepared to compromise his philosophy of playing good football. Tigana is only interested in the beauty of the game, and he is convinced and has been proved right that the best style of play is a creative, passing game.

It does not matter what level a team is at, or what division they are in, his philosophy is that the football is always the same. He explained: 'Football is my life. I love it. In France I took a lot of young players and developed them for the national team. People like Thierry Henry, David Trezeguet, Fabien

Barthez, Emmanuel Petit and Lilian Thuram, all players who are known to Premiership fans. It is this that gives me the ultimate pleasure in football. It is what I would like to do with English players at Fulham. That is my dream. If I have the good young players I know exactly how to turn them into international stars. I can assure you that if I get hold of a player at sixteen or seventeen and he works with me for two years he will progress. I know what to do because that has always been my main aim. At Fulham we have Sean Davis who played for the England Under-21s against Finland and Albania. Him achieving that has given me as much pleasure as winning the First Division title. It is good for him and for the club. It is progress. But equally I am just as happy when I see players like Rufus Brevett and Kit Symons, who are both over thirty, start to play proper football. I saw the videotape of Symons last year and now he may be the same man, but he is a different player altogether. He is confident, passing the ball around and is doing things he never did before. Again that gives me pleasure.'

Sean Davis said at the time: 'I've been fortunate with Tigana. He's been like a breath of fresh air. He used to play in my position, so that helps, but Damiano has brought my game on as well.'

Searching for an insight into how Tigana goes about changing his players is futile; even he is not quite sure. Perhaps it is about attitude and confidence, and the fact that, as he considers himself to be the best, every player under his guidance should also strive for that. It comes from a coach telling a player that mistakes are okay, as long as everybody is pulling in the same direction.

He said: 'I don't know how I change them. It is not just down to me, it has a lot to do with my staff. When I saw Rufus last season I spoke to him after watching him and told him I did not understand why he kept kicking the ball high in the air. It was not only Rufus. It is all down to what you do on the training ground. But it is not about me; it is the players. If they make mistakes I have told them not to worry, just keep playing football. I get angry if we lose the ball by kicking it up in the air. But if they are playing football I do not get angry with them. Losing possession is not just about the player who gives the ball away. It is about the movement around the player. He needs two or three options, and if he does not have that then you give the ball away. When I arrived I tried to put them at ease, and if they made a mistake I would just say, "Keep playing, keep playing." Sometimes a player gets down after making mistakes, but I just told them not to worry, and slowly that sunk in. There is always another game to put things right. When you have the ball you are strong. And also if you play football by passing then over the long term you will always succeed. If you watch any football in the world the team that wins is the one which plays football. At the start of the season people tried to tell me it was not possible to play a passing game in the First Division, and I asked them why. The football never changes at different levels. In the Premiership who always wins? Manchester United, of course; and why? Because they play football. Barcelona are the same, as have Liverpool been at different times. They all play football. It is the same with Chelsea and Leeds.

'For me, I have a different vision than just to spend money. When I first arrived people said I would be able to spend as much money as I liked. But I kept the same team pretty much because I knew we needed to progress step-by-step. My philosophy is not always to solve things by keeping buying more and more players. I want people to communicate and air their views and work hard and understand my ways, because they will never change. I want players who will fit into my way of thinking. But at the same time it is not possible for me to buy players that the likes of Arsenal, Liverpool or Manchester United would be interested in because they play in the Champions League and UEFA Cup. If you buy players all the time, and then they leave just as quickly, you are never really building a club. What will make me most proud and happy is that when I finish, Fulham will be a big club. I am delighted by what we have achieved so far, but it is just the start. If I do my job properly there is no reason why we can't be as big as Arsenal or Manchester United. All my career I have managed at the top level in football apart from this season, and it did not take long to get there.

'I have played and managed at the very top, so I have the experience. For me, the best example of what I am talking about is Sir Alex Ferguson. When he eventually leaves Old Trafford, he will leave a huge club and legacy behind him. That is what I want to do with Fulham, although it will be difficult to do it on the same scale as Ferguson. For me, Ferguson is a fantastic man. We played against Manchester United with Monaco four years ago and knocked them out of the Champions League. But look at the progress they made and the trophies they won. They are always the best, and if they aren't then they are disappointed, as they were last season when they were knocked out of Europe. I have always been impressed by him and the way he has dealt with his players.'

The Fulham players did not quite know what to expect from Tigana when he arrived. He came and watched a few of Fulham's games before the end of the 1999–2000 season to see what he thought of his playing staff. It was a nervy time for a lot of the players at Fulham who had been brought in by Kevin Keegan and Paul Bracewell. Nobody knew quite what style of football he would play. The Fulham coaching staff was cleared out and he brought in two Frenchmen who were pretty well unknown to English football; many players felt they would follow their former coaches out. One of those was Barry Hayles, who had been bought for £2m by Keegan from Bristol Rovers. Bracewell had told Hayles that his Fulham future would be limited, but Hayles was not prepared to give up and has flourished under Tigana, who has always been impressed by his pace.

Tigana spent the last six games of the 1999–2000 season assessing the Fulham squad while Karl Heinz Riedle was in charge. He quickly decided that Paul

Peschisolido was too small, and Geoff Horsfield was too lumbering as a centre-forward, with not enough pace. There was also never a look in for the likes of Wayne Collins and Paul Trollope. Tigana was faced with a large squad: several members of that squad, like Alan Nielson and Steve Hayward, who had been a Fulham stalwart, were eventually ditched. But Tigana knew what he wanted and created an axis around John Collins, Sean Davis, Luis Boa Morte and Louis Saha which worked – in the First Division at least.

Hayles, though, was surprised he remained in the new manager's plans. The striker said: 'I must admit that I never thought there would be a place at Craven Cottage for little Barry Hayles when Jean Tigana arrived. I thought that he would be bringing in a lot of his own players and that a few of us would go. But that has not really been the case.' However, that was before Tigana invested a record £11.5m in French international striker Steve Marlet from Lyon after only a few games in the Premiership. However, Hayles was still involved in Tigana's rotation system.

Hayles wanted to improve under Tigana. He explained: 'Bracewell used to tell me that I needed to run into the channels and I should concentrate on holding the ball up and bringing other players into the game. By comparison Tigana just told me to go out and play my own game. I was not allowed to worry about things because he just wanted me to express myself. He said that if I tried something and it did not come off then not to be put off by it. I should just get on with it and try again. He gives you incredible confidence.' Hayles pinpointed the difference between Keegan and Tigana. 'Kevin Keegan showed more passion, he was more of a get-behind-the-lads type. Tigana's more relaxed, more chilled out.'

Tigana swept into Craven Cottage for his opening press conference with an English teacher at his side. He would never give interviews to journalists in France, so he was reluctant to tell too much when faced with an English press marvelling at another French manager in English football to rival Wenger and Houllier. But the one message he did get across to those gathered was that he was prepared to give almost every player a chance to prove his worth to the squad, apart from a couple whom he had already targeted as weak links in the side.

One of the few players to go immediately was Fulham hero Geoff Horsfield. He was considered by Fulham fans to be the lynchpin of the side, but it was clear that Tigana did not want a battering-ram, typical English centre-forward in his team. Instead he bought the fleet-footed Louis Saha for a bargain £2m from Metz, and was repaid with 32 goals, making him the top scorer in the First Division. Saha observed: 'Everything Tigana has taught me has given me a better mentality and made me a better player. He has given me a lot of confidence and taught me the main things, like how to score goals when I am a striker and how to pass when I am a midfielder.'

Saha was one of Tigana's clients when he worked as a players' agent. The players were full of admiration for Tigana's methods. Lee Clark said: 'Everybody's got strengths and everybody's got weaknesses. The manager will put people in for their strengths and make sure they cover for other players' weaknesses. You might have a quick player lined up with somebody who's not so quick; a good passer with somebody who likes getting their foot in.' Clark was impressed with one of Tigana's late summer signings, Steed Malbranque. 'Steed's a very good passer, sharp and strong. That's the way the manager likes football to be played in the midfield; one-and two-touch passing. But it's a blend. In a team, you need all kinds of players.'

John Collins, who had worked with Tigana at Monaco from 1996–8, came in from Everton. Tigana, using Collins as his interpreter, quickly got his thoughts over to the squad, although some of his techniques were not quite what the players were used to. At times they would train three times a day, and have to go through tougher sessions than most of the players had ever experienced. The stringent medical each player underwent was also a surprise, as were the regular blood tests. Each player also had their teeth checked as there is an increasing understanding of the correlation between the positioning of teeth and a player's posture. 'It's not a Jean thing, it's a French cultural thing,' explained Collins. 'They expect players to look after their body. It's just professional, good preparation.'

The fact that Fulham were told to report back two weeks before most other teams tested the players' patience. 'What happens on the pitch is only sixty per cent of the game,' says Tigana. 'The rest is taking care of what you eat and drink, making sure you stretch, resting and so on.' His credentials suggest he should know: as a player he won the European Championship with France in 1984 and collected five French championship medals. Since then he has coached Monaco to the French title and taken Fulham to the top flight for the first time since 1968. 'We've had a doctor and a dietitian telling us what we can and can't eat, how to eat, how to drink,' Chris Coleman said shortly after Tigana's appointment. 'Nobody's ever gone into that sort of thing in the same depth.'

Teaching footballers how to eat and drink is a means of ensuring the body gets maximum benefit from food. Water sipped rather than gulped, carbohydrates definitely in the diet, with food to be consumed within an hour of the end of training so the body can absorb more energy from it. Plenty of pasta, potatoes and rice can be found in the training-ground canteen, where breakfast cereals and toast are also laid on. The importance of rehydrating and refuelling before, during and after training has been clearly stressed. Water is taken before a session and at fifteen- or twenty-minute intervals throughout. Lucozade is saved for after, to avoid blood sugar levels rising and dropping suddenly mid-session.

Collins sums up the difference he found when he left Celtic for the Cote d'Azur six years ago. 'At Monaco the one thing you immediately noticed was how disciplined they all were, very serious about their football, and how fit and athletic. Things like diet and how they prepare themselves for every match are up a level from British players.'

Arsène Wenger, speaking a little over six months after his arrival in England from coaching in Japan, stressed that what he found was not wilful disregard on the part of English professionals but a reflection of the culture and environment most players grow up in. Old dogs in particular are benefiting from new tricks. 'It is not the players' attitude which is the problem; it is the culture of the country,' Wenger said. 'The whole day you have tea or coffee with milk and sugar and cakes. It is the worst, it is not conducive to a high sports diet. In the morning, eggs and bacon and then tea and coffee with milk and sugar and cakes. Cakes every day, the whole day.' Then there is the 'traditional' English footballer's habit of liking a drink or two. Tigana, realising the importance of setting the right example, does not even indulge in the wine that bears his name. 'It is not possible to drink or smoke or go to nightclubs if you are going to ask the players to avoid these things,' he says. 'What I ask of them I do myself. I have the same attitude as when I played. When I find myself putting on a kilo or two of weight I immediately diet.'

This is not to suggest that Tigana spent his highly successful career with Toulon, Lyon, Bordeaux and Marseille living the life of a Trappist monk. 'People have been suggesting he never touched a drop but that's a fallacy,' says Chris Waddle, the former England international who played with Tigana at Marseille. 'I can guarantee we used to sit at the back of the plane and have two or three beers. He wasn't on it every day but he did drink after a game.'

However, attitudes have changed with the advancement of the game in terms of speed and fitness. 'Fat tests are taken regularly and blood analysis is taken so the boys know that the lifestyle of even a decent player is not enough,' says Steve Kean, Fulham's youth academy director, who has worked closely with Tigana. 'We need top players. We're talking seven and eight per cent body fat, which is very low, so the players are lean athletes first and foremost. If you look at a typical team you might find the average was nine to ten per cent. The boys look after themselves because they know what is required.' Blood is tested every six weeks or so. The value of this is explained by Alex Court, Fulham's first-team exercise physiologist: 'From the blood tests you can see the levels of fatigue. The doctor will look and see if they are too fatigued or if they need more work, and increase or reduce training accordingly.'

The tone was set as Tigana arrived, with pre-season training in Clairefontaine. There they faced 6.30 a.m. wake-up calls and three training sessions a day on occasions: at 7 a.m., 10 a.m. and 2.30 p.m. 'It's been a big culture shock,' Coleman said at the time. Yet the training was calculated and gradual rather than gruelling. Rest is as important as hard work, and those who need a break get one. Swimming may be used for post-match recovery if there are fixtures in quick succession, and the day before a game low-intensity training is held as close as possible to kick-off time to mould the players' body clocks. 'The intensity level of training is controlled,' Kean says, 'so the players are peaking for each game and their bodies are screaming to get out there come kick-off.'

Fulham's success has been based on more than diet changes and helping the players to relax with massages. Tigana, Damiano and the rest of the staff are excellent coaches, too. The fluidity of the team's passing football has been impressive and the improvement in the technique and confidence of players has been notable. It stems in large part from a carefully planned training routine in which ball-work is paramount – few players will have as many touches per session as Fulham's. Drills are repeated until the pattern becomes second nature, and everything is done with the match in mind.

'We do not do exercises for the sake of it,' Damiano says. 'It is always so it can be transferred into a game.' The idea is to build instinctive understanding and passing patterns. Players work in their natural positions, and respect for Tigana is huge. As a member of the great French midfield of the 1980s alongside Platini, Giresse and Fernandez, his players realise he knows what he is talking about. 'Jean has gained the trust of every player,' Kean says. 'Even the guys who are not in the team are happy because they know they can look in the mirror and say they are better footballers.' And doubtless fitter ones as well. Under Roger Propos, everything from strength to agility, flexibility and balance is worked on. 'The training programme put together by Roger is detailed to a level I've never seen before,' says Kean, who played at Celtic and in Portugal and has coached at Reading. 'The benches they jump from in some of the power sessions are measured in centimetres. People might think, okay, you just go in the gym and go round a couple of times, but there will be a personal programme for everyone and when we induct the young players in the gym, the angle they sit at when they are on the machine is important to build up a muscle in the right area. The way they push the bar up is important so they have full control. Nobody's allowed in the gym unless there's a member of staff there to take them round so it's not a place where they go and spend the time talking. There's a very big emphasis on the fact that you are in a workshop, be it, say, for speed or power.' Nothing is left to chance. As Damiano says of his boss: 'Jean knows that at the highest level you win on the smallest details.'

Nine months later it all ended up in the ultimate success: the First Division Championship and promotion to the Premiership. Tigana said: 'Being successful in my first season was very important, but quite honestly it is more important for the players. When I arrived at the start of the season my only focus was to get promoted. I am happy, but it is only the first floor. One year is good to have done this. It has meant a lot to me because the chairman came looking for me and put his trust in me. He has also worked very hard for this. But for me this success is normal, because if I never win then he would sack me. I never feel pressure because this is my job. I never felt pressure as a player. I know myself. I work very, very hard, but I am not a god. I work full-time. All the time I am focusing on my players and the team. After you win, okay, I am very happy, but I know it is not possible for me to work any harder than I am doing now. I work all the time, seven days a week for my club. Sometimes I am not here but I am still working for the club, from first thing in the morning to last thing at night. But I have always been like that. But then again it has always been important for me to be the best right through my career.

'When I played and I was thirty-six I always wanted to run faster, train harder than anybody else. Football is my life and I want to be the best. I have tried to pass that on to my players, but you always need good co-operation from them on that. The player needs to know exactly what I want and feel the same. But this season has been a fantastic discovery for me. At the start of the season after only fifteen days the players knew what I wanted from them and understood my philosophy. They worked very hard for me, and there was a huge transformation in almost all of them. I thought it would take longer but they were eager to change their philosophy, their bodies and general attitude. At Monaco I needed six months to sort the team out because there were a lot of different factions and in-fighting when I took over from Arsène Wenger. It did not annoy me, but there was a lot of trouble. But here there is an incredible togetherness and a great atmosphere which is so important. If you don't have a good atmosphere it is very difficult to work. I had no intention of coming into Fulham and then sacking a load of players. It is not my way. I wanted to keep them together and drag them slowly forwards because I knew where I could get them to.'

The Fulham players discovered their manager is very single-minded in the pursuit of excellence. He does not like being messed about, and he will not mess people about either. Although he would not admit it, he is considered to be ruthless by those people who have worked around him. He was very aware that coming into English football he would have to deal with the game's drinking culture, which is not as bad as it was, but certainly still exists, especially in the lower leagues. The Fulham players were told categorically what to expect from Tigana, who as a player cut out drinking and smoking to improve his game. Any player who was suspected of having had a drink soon found themselves training with the kids.

Nor does he like lack of discipline or players who do not buy into the team ethic. Fabrice Fernandes was a young French player brought over on loan by Tigana from Rennes. He was a sensation on the left wing and scored some fantastic goals, especially the one against Manchester United in the FA Cup. But he did not listen or play for the team, and eventually ended up having a couple of dressing-room bust-ups with a number of players. Tigana's answer was to get rid of him straight away because he was too big for his boots and felt he should already be in the Premiership. Although Fulham certainly missed him after his departure, Tigana was happy to pack him off to Scottish side Rangers because nothing would be allowed to disrupt the team. Tigana said: 'In terms of discipline I only ever want my players to respect the team and each other. It is very, very important. When a player does that there is no problem.

But if they show any disrespect then he will work with the reserve team. But every player is always given a second chance. After the second chance, if a player has not changed his attitude then he is out. In terms of drinking too much, I have not had a problem with the Fulham players. I know that in England people do talk about that. I was very surprised when I first arrived at Fulham and I got into my hotel room and there was a bottle of champagne. I did not understand. I gave it away. How can I drink if I ask my players not to. It is possible sometimes that I may have half a beer, but that is all because your attitude has to be right all of the time. I think the players have listened to me because the trust is there. Absolutely, I think that trust is there. But then again I play with them sometimes in training and show them what I can do. That is the best example. It was the same at the start of the season in pre-season. I ran with the players and took part in games to show them I was prepared to do things. I always demand maximum effort from my players because it is so important, and they are happier when they have given that.'

To draw Tigana away from football is almost impossible. Just like Sir Alex Ferguson he lives and breathes the game. Arsène Wenger is the same. He relaxes by watching videos of other games! They share a common denominator: dedication leading to a will to win and be the best. But at the same time he does not need any particular time to relax, because he is naturally so laid back. He rarely shows emotion from the touchline and does not get carried away because he simply expects to win. And if that does not happen then there is always the next game. Though he can handle that, not everyone around him always can, and he admits that it drives his wife mad. His idea of a good family day out is to go and watch football, and you can imagine how that goes down in the Tigana household.

He explains: 'I have a toothpick in my mouth because twenty-six years ago I used to smoke. I always think about football, which is my big problem, especially for my family. If I wanted a day out with my family, it would usually be to watch a game. I never read books, I just watch television and only football. It drives my wife mad; she does not like football. It is a huge problem for me. This is my life though and we just all have to adapt. People keep asking me if I enjoy London. I say yes, but all I have seen of it so far is my house, the training ground, Craven Cottage and of course Harrods. I don't know where Big Ben or Buckingham Palace is. I have never been to a theatre or a museum. It is possible I will stay in London during the summer and have a look around and do some sight-seeing.'

Before the start of Fulham's first season in the Premiership, Tigana was very aware that he would be seen as a rival to Houllier and Wenger, and that having three French managers in the English top flight is unprecedented. But once again Tigana is unassuming. He realises that with the teams his two opponents have in Liverpool and Arsenal, they are on a different level, for the time being. However, that will still not put him off when it comes to trying to be the best. Although Tigana will be judged by them and their achievement, he does not feel Fulham are in the top flight just to make up the numbers. Tigana said: 'I respect them because I am friends with both Gerard Houllier and Arsène Wenger. I speak to them on the telephone and they have co-operated with me. But I do not feel any pressure to live up to them. Why should there by any pressure, because I have a great life. For twenty-six years I have a had a great life being involved with football. Everything I do now is just a bonus. What Houllier has done is fantastic, but Houllier and Wenger are a few years ahead of me and I need to run quickly to do some catching up in the Premiership.'

Tigana is very aware that in Al Fayed he works for a man who wants immediate returns, so promotion was exactly what was needed. It was only to be expected that the Harrods boss demanded the Premiership title in one or maybe two seasons. But Tigana knew exactly what the fans wanted, and before the start in August said his main aim was 'to beat Chelsea, of course!'

Statistically, the promoted clubs struggle when they make the leap to the Premiership. But there were such expectations created by Tigana at Fulham that it acted as an inspiration for Luca Vialli to try to emulate him at Watford. The day before being paraded at Vicarage Road, the sacked Chelsea manager met Tigana, and was convinced he had made the right decision to manage in the First Division. Vialli said: 'I met Tigana and what he has done with Fulham has impressed me so much. You know, when Jean left Monaco for Fulham people in France couldn't believe it. But he has proved a very skilful and successful manager in the First Division and won promotion straight away. I had had many unofficial approaches from clubs in England and Italy, but nothing official until Watford. I came to them with an open mind and I was very impressed with what I saw.'

Vialli stoked up the hostilities with Chelsea when he suggested that it wasn't much fun anymore at the Bridge. He said: 'I have nothing against Chelsea and I still have great friends at the club like Dennis Wise. I had some happy times at Chelsea and other times which were not particularly happy. At Chelsea the job of the manager could not really be fun because of the responsibilities which came with the job. Here at Watford we will of course work extremely hard for success but I hope we can have some fun as well.'

Back at Fulham, Tigana's future with the club rested to a large extent on his first season in the Premiership. He said: 'Fulham is my last step. I have two years left on my contract plus the option of another two if I want. After that I will spend time at my home in Cassis, fishing, having a good time and resting. I've been in football for twenty-six years with just five weeks' holiday. I love football but I'm repeatedly being told at home that football is not the only thing in life.'

Al Fayed reacted typically to this comment. As he sat at the head of the boardroom table on the fifth floor in his Harrods suite of offices, he smiled and said: 'Let's see about that! People all the time say that kind of thing, but don't really mean it when the time comes. In any case . . . he can't retire!'

THE HARRODS OWNER...

Gold bars and videos of the Championship parade

Mohamed Al Fayed was relaxing in the boardroom of his suite of private offices on the fifth floor of Harrods, in an open-necked shirt, on a sunny afternoon. He enthused about his love of football and his aspirations for Fulham. The private audience with him had taken plenty of organising and much coaxing from PR guru Max Clifford. Al Fayed can be charming and persuasive and uses earthy language to illustrate that he too can be one of the boys. He possesses a disarming smile and a passion for the game that perhaps few suspect.

With our usual scepticism, *The Diary* asked Al Fayed when he had first become fascinated with the game.

'At the age of fourteen I had my own club,' he replied.

'Oh yes? What position did you play?'

'Centre-forward.'

'How many goals did you score?'

'Hundreds of goals,' he replied with a chuckle.

Al Fayed sensed that we didn't believe him, so he sent for the evidence and it duly arrived: a snapshot of a very young and sprightly Mohamed, clearly in his teens, posing with a football.

'There,' he said, and duly accepted the invitation to autograph the fading black-and-white photograph. He then left the room and returned with gold bars and videos.

'I hope it's real,' *The Diary* ventured with a touch of humour.

He smiled. 'No, they are chocolates.'

The video was of the victory parade moving along the Fulham Road, led by the open-top bus, drawing up outside the Town Hall.

Yes, we told him, we recalled seeing the pictures while away in Valencia with Leeds just before the Champions League semi-final second leg. Didn't he tell his adoring public that he promised to deliver the Premiership trophy in a year?

'Yes, that's right,' Al Fayed confirmed.

Max interceded: 'It's a five-year plan, though ... the title within five years.'

'That's right,' said Al Fayed, 'but we are going to win the Premiership in two years ... no ... one year!'

Not even one of the country's top PR men could halt the ensuing runaway train. His sheer enthusiasm was unstoppable. Al Fayed explained: 'I want to build Fulham up to be as big an institution as Harrods because I want them to be number one. I want them to be bigger than Manchester United. Next season ... Okay, the season after next. That is why I have told Tigana that I want to win the Premiership next season because we want the best at this club. I have always loved Fulham. It has been in my heart since I arrived in England. My first home in this country was near Craven Cottage.'

He went on to explain how he came into football, and how he planned to develop Fulham. 'I have been a Fulham fan for a very long time. It was always my club. I was very concerned that one of the oldest clubs in England had suffered such a long period of misfortune. When the previous owner approached me for help I was glad to invest in the club. From the beginning it has always been my vision to make Fulham the Manchester United of the South, and to do that I needed a footballing figurehead. I was fortunate to persuade Kevin Keegan to join us and was later proud to give him to England as manager. After that I wanted to appoint the best coach in the world to take my vision forward. We did a great deal of research and discovered that Jean Tigana is one of the five best coaches in the world. I am delighted to have him with us. Fulham has the potential to become a global brand. My ambitions over the next few years are for domestic and European success, followed by recognition as one of the major players in the football industry in this country and, ultimately, worldwide.

'Football is like no other industry in the way it creates a brand loyalty among its fans – its customers – which is unique. Although the industry is already huge, its potential remains enormous. As a working environment, it cannot be compared with any other industry. The redevelopment of Craven Cottage is an integral part of my vision and it is vital that Fulham remains in the borough from which it takes its name. Our new stadium will be state-of-the-art because I want to create a unique footballing experience for Fulham fans to enjoy.

'I want to make funds available to Jean Tigana that he will need to build a successful football team. I have also made a significant investment in the academy to ensure a substantial return over time. Jean believes in developing the young players to become the foundation of the future of the club. Creating future Michael Owens and David Beckhams is the aim and, of course, we already have our own Sean Davis. Jean is on a contract with the club and is enjoying the challenge of creating a team which will fulfil my dream to make Fulham as big as Manchester United. When the time comes to discuss his future, I know that my investment will have been nurtured wisely, and that the club can continue to be successful in the long term.

'Although our core supporters have remained loyal through the lean years when the club was struggling in the lower divisions, we lost a whole generation of potential supporters. Now we have the most sophisticated marketing structure of any football club in Europe. We are developing and building the supporter base through investment in the community department, so that we can give something back to the community from grassroots level. We have more than two hundred and fifty thousand children coming through our football courses in six boroughs throughout the year.'

Al Fayed's heart has certainly ruled his head when it comes to football. And it could well be that other clubs in the lower divisions will benefit from his passion in the way Fulham FC and its supporters have. Al Fayed has promised to shake up the Premiership in the corridors of power as well as on the field; he plans to attend the big pow-wows of club chairmen and intends to campaign on behalf of smaller clubs. The Harrods tycoon has already taken on the Establishment, but in the shape of the Government and royalty, and while these ventures have brought him little success, Al Fayed never shirks a challenge: football won't hold any fears for him. The newest recruit to the Premiership elite certainly doesn't plan to play the timid new boy.

He went on: 'I will go to as many Premiership meetings as possible. I will be the new blood around the place, and I intend to make my mark in the chairman's office in the way the Fulham players have on the pitch.'

Al Fayed has a manifesto for the improvement of the game as a whole. He doesn't want the Premiership to be known as the League of Greed, but for it to have an awareness of the welfare of other smaller clubs. He will fight for their cause, remembering that once upon a time Fulham was a lower-division club. 'I will make sure I get the message across to everybody in the game that this country is the home of football, and that it should maintain standards that the British public can be proud of. In my view there needs to be real encouragement among the big boys of the game to help others who are struggling in the lower divisions. More financial aid should be given to the First, Second and Third Division clubs because they are part of the fabric of our national game. At least seventy or eighty per cent of the lower-league clubs are suffering, struggling to make ends meet and begging for handouts like Fulham did in the past.

'If I had never rescued Fulham, they could quite easily have closed. Football is the game of the masses, a game for ordinary people, not just the rich, and I think that some of the Premiership chairmen need to realise that. To me, it appears that the chairmen of the top clubs only think about the Premier League, but of course it's the league teams who often help provide the players and managers of the future in the Premiership. That is why I intend to enlist the support of other club chairmen to help the smaller clubs. Not enough money is passed down. More money should be spent on grounds and academies, on creating great managers, great players and trainers for the benefit of the game. Instead, all we hear about is the number of clubs that are in danger of closing down.'

Al Fayed believes it is time to put something back, not just take from the pot of gold that now exists in the Premiership. He funds the National Disabled Five-a-Side Championship, and froze Fulham season-ticket prices for the inaugural Premiership season. He said: 'I also subsidise supporters' transport for every away game because I want Fulham fans to be able to afford to follow their club. There are billions coming into the game through TV sponsorship but no money is set aside to keep ticket prices down. More should be done, and I will try to do what I can by enlisting the support of other Premiership chairmen to my cause.'

One prominent Premiership chairman immediately pooh-poohed such radical thinking, insisting Al Fayed will be defeated by 19 votes to 1. He even doubted Al Fayed would turn up. That kind of attitude didn't deter Al Fayed; it inspired him. He shocked the Premiership Establishment when he turned up for a chairmen's conference in London twenty minutes after his absence had been noted. The noise of an approaching helicopter drowned out the speakers as the chairmen began to guess who was dropping in on them.

Following his fight with the Government over British citizenship, Al Fayed now wanted to take on the Establishment in football. His bond with Fulham intensified with his feeling that the Establishment was opposed to his son's liaison with Princess Diana. He recalls how the Fulham fans rallied: 'I will never forget the warmth and kindness they showed me in those dark days when I lost my son. Men, women and children came up to speak to me, and the comfort they gave to me was so important. Therefore, I get so much pleasure from Fulham's success because I see the pleasure that it gives those fans. I get an awful lot from the supporters, and I want to give back as much as I can. I've said that my aim is to make Fulham great again, and I'm prepared to stay there until that happens.'

Al Fayed has also instituted an active anti-racism programme. An audit of crowd attendances showed an increase in ethnic minorities visiting Craven Cottage, albeit a minimal one, over the previous season. The object was to 'make our stadium a friendly and welcoming environment for all members of the community'. The club continues to work to attract ethnic minorities to 'reflect the multicultural society in which we live'. On 7 April 2001, the Nation-wide game with WBA was the focal point of that year's anti-racism event. In the mid- to late seventies, WBA fielded three black players, Brendan Batson, Cyrille Regis and the late Laurie Cunningham, who are widely regarded as outstanding pioneers in the fight against racism in football. A host of celebrities, including the ex-Celtic manager John Barnes, and dignitaries such as the Mayor of Hammersmith and Fulham and former Minister for Sport Kate Hoey, appeared alongside Al Fayed. The 'Black & White Help Fulham Unite' Working Party is committed to promoting equal opportunities at every level within the club. Fulham recognises the need to reach a section of the community that is under-represented and employs a community officer with a special interest in ethnic minorities. Fulham are actively encouraging increased participation by blacks and Asians through the soccer and adult education courses that are being organised by the 'Football in the Community' scheme. The objective is to redress the lack of representation at coaching and administrative levels.

Despite the untimely departure of Andrew Beardall, who was very influential during his short stay as community officer, the work continues. Dereck Brown has been promoted from within the community department, and he has been quick to acknowledge that there is no easy solution to a long-standing problem. 'We don't expect to change people's perceptions overnight, nor are we paying lip service to a subject that is controversial. However, slowly but surely, by liaising with people who have expert knowledge in this area, we will instigate change for the better and it will be the community of Fulham FC which will hopefully reap the benefit.'

All around the ground there are signs which state that racial abuse of any kind will not be tolerated, and indicate the penalties that offenders can expect to face. There are training programmes and workshops planned for all members of staff so that they are better prepared to face any racially challenging situation in the course of their work. To attract more ethnic minorities into the ground the community department has also given free tickets to youth clubs and other local organisations so that groups can sample the atmosphere generated on a matchday and not feel isolated. There are also plans to offer a variety of cuisine at the ground to cater for cultural differences.

More recently the financial difficulties experienced by another London club has led to Fulham taking over the running of a 'Football in the Community' scheme in the borough of Lambeth. This is one of the poorest boroughs in London, and comprises a high ratio of ethnic minorities and a varied cultural mix. It is the intention of the club to give as many of the children within the borough as possible the opportunity to experience football in an organised environment. The club has already donated playing strips to local teams and there will soon be job opportunities on offer within the region.

Fulham can claim to be a unique club as from the boardroom down there is a good racial mix providing a relaxed and friendly working environment. In 1975 there were fewer than twenty black professional soccer players in the Football League. Now that number has increased significantly. However, the number of Asian players in the professional game is no greater than it was in the seventies and the proportion of ethnic minorities in the crowd does not reflect those who are interested in and play the sport. The club has noted this imbalance and is playing a positive role in trying to redress it.

The redevelopment of Craven Cottage ignited opposition, but with planning consent granted the club looked at a variety of options for a temporary home – even Wembley at one time. The grounds at QPR and West Ham were the most realistic proposals. A short-term ground share at Loftus Road was always on the agenda, with QPR chief executive David Davis saying: 'If we were approached by Fulham we would welcome it. We could talk to the local authority together and I think we could put the arrangements in place quite quickly.' After a period in administration resolving the issue of rugby union club Wasps (who were based at Loftus Road) finding a new home, a move across West London was set in motion. Initially, in an open letter on the Fulham internet site, the fans were asked for their opinions and former MD Michael Fiddy said: 'The club have made initial inquiries to various stadia and I would like to invite all supporters to comment on any relevant issues that should be considered before the ultimate decision is reached. Securing a venue that will benefit all involved will clearly be a difficult process. Its convenience to our fans is of immense importance. But we will also have to satisfy the relevant League regulations, and ensure that the temporary home will be agreeable in terms of facilities and as a commercially viable proposition.'

Little seems to have changed at the Cottage over the years. The stroll from the nearest tube station, through the park, past the tennis courts and terrace houses seems so familiar. Sarah Brookes, the club's Head of Communications, recalls her feelings when she went to interview for the job: 'I was an Arsenal fan and used to be a season-ticket holder at Arsenal, in the Clock End. I desperately wanted a job in football, because there is something about the game that gets under your skin, so I applied to about four or five London clubs and I got a call from Fulham. I was driving down Fulham Palace Road and I had never been there before so I had my *A–Z* out. When I turned into Finlay Street I saw the Cottage with "The Fulham Football Club" standing out in big letters. The hairs stood up on the back of my neck because it was just the cutest, loveliest, most beautiful thing I had seen. There is something so unique about it. There are all these wonderful houses that you know cost millions. There is this complete affluence of wealth and I drove down to this ramshackle Cottage, as it was about four years ago, and it was so lovely and poetic it was just incredible. I had the interview, then walked around the ground and looked out on to the Thames. It was a nice day, about June-or July-time, so the sun was shining on the pitch, and I went on to the riverside and imagined Saturday afternoons there looking on to the river and then watching a great football game. I just thought it was fantastic. I came and watched on a Tuesday night just before I took the job. I simply fell in love with the club. I stood on the Hammersmith End: it was a Second Division game and I just stood there with the floodlights on and said to myself that I wanted to be a part of it.'

Times have changed dramatically. Those terrace houses now fetch £1.2m, and Mohamed Al Fayed is the new owner. Surprisingly, the affection for Al Fayed is so tangible you could almost touch it. He makes a theatrical entrance from one side of the pitch, waving constantly to the fans who chant his name religiously. Fulham may no longer be a small, modest club, but it's still a popular one.

JULY

New arrivals and departures ... Pre-season health checks – and Pizza Hut

SUNDAY, 1 JULY

Jean Tigana realises the priority is to find a striker. While there are other areas he wants to strengthen in the team – central defence and midfield in particular – to finish off the kind of stylish passing football Fulham play he requires a top-line striker. He narrowly missed out on the Czech Jan Koller, whose club Anderlecht had agreed an £8m fee before Borussia Dortmund lured him away with the attraction of Champions League action. However, the Germans would crash out in the first phase, and the centre-forward was soon offered around on a loan deal.

Koller himself explained: 'Although I have always said I would be interested in coming to England, I now have some doubts. It looks as though Dortmund will play in the Champions League next season and that makes them more interesting to me from a sporting point of view.' The 6-foot 8-inch centre-forward was not telling a tall story – he duly signed for Dortmund! He would have been the tallest player in English football, bigger than Kevin Francis of Hull City and Peter Crouch (both of whom are 6 feet 7 inches) then of QPR.

There are conflicting stories on the transfer. At one point, Koller announced he was definitely signing for Fulham. In a statement from Belgium he said: 'It has taken a long time for Fulham to give me a contract, but I have finally reached an agreement.' Tigana was so fed up that at one stage he wanted to call off the deal, suspecting the agent of playing off the two clubs to hike up the personal terms. 'After long discussions, we are delighted this fee has been agreed and we now look forward to discussing personal terms with the player,' announced MD Michael Fiddy. Although it all ended in tears, there were no public recriminations from inside Fulham.

Bayern Munich's giant centre-forward Carsten Jancker was an alternative target following the failure to land Koller. He was also coveted by Sunderland. Bayern's general manager Uli Hoeness said that they would listen to offers for

Jancker if he could find a suitable club. The fee was reported to be anything from £4.5m to £10m!

Tigana also made a move for Frederic Kanoute, since the gifted forward wanted to evoke a get-out clause in his contract with West Ham. With Glenn Roeder recently installed as Harry Redknapp's successor, Fulham were joined by Villa and Spurs in the chase for the £15m-rated Frenchman. In the middle of the first week of the Wimbledon tennis championships, the story broke that Kanoute had suggested he was ready to quit West Ham for Fulham following a reported bid of £8m. 'I have to admit I'd like to play for them because it is a club that I like, I like how they play,' Kanoute said. 'I know the coach Jean Tigana very well, because he used to train Lyon when I was younger, so I know him and how he works. And I know it is a club where I would feel good.' Despite denials from the Hammers, Michael Fiddy confirmed the offer: 'Kanoute is a player whom Jean knows very well and, hopefully, it will be possible to bring him to Fulham.' However, the Hammers placed a prohibitive £15m price tag on his head and Kanoute abandoned his plans to join Fulham. He explained: 'It was a serious thought and at the time I did want to leave. But after I spoke to Glenn [Roeder], I wanted to stay. I thought about it a lot and now I am happy.'

Inter Milan striker Hakan Sukur was linked to both West Ham and Fulham. Sukur, who is 29, had been unable to command a regular first-team place at the San Siro, and was available for £4m. Again, the trail went cold as Sukur changed his mind and chose to stay in Milan following the arrival of his former Galatasaray team-mates Emre Belozogulu and Okan Buruk. Parma's 30-year-old African Player of the Year Patrick Mboma was linked to a £6m move after Tigana saw the powerful striker score both goals in Cameroon's 2–1 victory over France in a friendly. (Much later in the season he signed for a desperate Sunderland.)

Tigana's transfer targets also included Teddy Sheringham. Although Tigana's strategy was to seek young players to build for the future, he also needed a short-term kick-start to the Premiership campaign which Sheringham, still a valued member of Sven Goran Eriksson's England squad, could bring. But his wage demands became prohibitive and the England striker left Manchester United to return to Spurs on a two-year package worth £3.5m. Tigana had decided not to disrupt dressing-room morale by bringing in an outsider on significantly higher wages than the rest of his promotion side. George Burley had shared an identical view as manager of newly promoted Ipswich a year earlier.

Tigana had the same feeling about Emmanuel Petit. He was convinced he could get Petit to love the game again and regain his appetite for football at club level after a miserable season at Barcelona. But Tigana was only interested if Petit particularly wanted to play for the manager who was once his mentor at Monaco. For it had been Tigana who helped Petit flourish and earn his move to Arsenal. However, Tigana was not prepared to have Petit with him again with the player on a huge salary. On learning this, Petit decided against a move to the Cottage. The highest wage, in fact, was just £20,000 with the arrival of Alain Goma. This was at a time when salaries were into six figures, with the Bosman-ruling move of Sol Campbell from Spurs to Arsenal and the arrival of £28.1m new record-signing Juan Sebastian Veron at Manchester United indicative of this.

Atletico Madrid's 21-year-old Portuguese playmaker Hugo Leal was added to the list of targets. Atletico's technical director Paulo Futre said: 'Fulham contacted us to check on the availability of Leal. I informed them that the price is £5.5m and we are waiting to see if they make a bid.' The most galling transfer saga involved John Arne Riise, who agreed terms with Tigana only to renege on the deal and move to Liverpool for £4m. (Little wonder he was booed every time he played against Fulham!) The move for 'one of the best young players in Norway' ended in a U-turn by the 20-year-old left-sided midfielder. He passed the medical which would have completed a deal from Monaco, the club where he was originally purchased by Tigana, only to find complications arising from his original move from little-known club Aalesund. They were demanding a 25 per cent cut of the fee, which in turn stalled the deal from Monaco, providing Liverpool with the time to intercede.

Fulham needed a left-sided midfield player since Frenchman Fabrice Fernandes had moved to Glasgow Rangers. Riise had met Tigana in the Fulham manager's house in Marseille and agreed a four-year contract. He said: 'I have agreed personal terms with Fulham after meeting with Tigana and my agents. We met in his house for just over an hour-and-a-half and we agreed on the personal deal. Tigana is a really nice person, with lots of good humour, just like he was when he brought me to Monaco. Tigana showed his faith in me and I was already a regular when I was aged eighteen. He has told me that he will give me a chance if I go to Fulham, which is important for a young player like me. The team has a lot of young players and I believe that the club will challenge for the Premiership title within four or five years. It would be fantastic to be part of it – if the deal goes through. I am still keeping my options open, but I want to play in the Premiership. It was rumoured that Liverpool would make an offer and if that happens I will consider it. Liverpool are a big club, and Fulham are a team full of promise. Both clubs are ambitious, and I am excited about it. Last year I was close to joining Leeds, but that deal fell through, so I won't take anything for granted. Everything looks bright, but I'll wait with the celebration until everything is done.'

Riise added insult to injury when he finally confessed that he had no intention of joining Fulham and had only used the Cottagers to secure his move to Anfield. Riise told Liverpool's official website: 'I was always determined to join Liverpool. I first spoke to Mr Houllier three months ago but Liverpool had so many important games that he couldn't discuss a transfer. He told me he would buy me, but I was hoping things would happen more quickly. When Fulham came in I talked personal terms because I knew if I did that I would get what I wanted and Liverpool would make a bid. Mr Houllier called me from his holiday and arranged the transfer with Monaco the next day. I wanted to join Liverpool so much I even gave up fifteen per cent of the transfer fee I was entitled to. This was not about money for me. Liverpool is the place I have always wanted to be.'

Riise agreed a five-year contract. He said: 'I followed Liverpool closely for the last month of last season. I watched all their games on TV. They are fantastic. I supported Spurs when I was a boy in Norway. Now it's Liverpool. I've won the Championship with Monaco, and my aim now is to do it with Liverpool.' Pictured in the *Daily Express* holding up a Liverpool shirt, he then delivered what the paper 'spun' as a barbed comment aimed at Fulham. 'Liverpool have a better reputation. It is a safe environment to join. I feel it is a better alternative. They have shown that they are good with young players. Fulham are newly promoted and could find themselves in trouble.' However, Riise did take the trouble to contact Tigana personally. Riise revealed: 'I talked to Tigana on the phone and explained what had happened and why I wanted to play for Liverpool. It was good to talk to him and I can assure people we still have a good relationship.' Although they retained their cordial relationship, Riise appreciated that the Fulham fans might not be so full of bonhomie, adding: 'I am ready to get some comments from Fulham fans when the teams meet in the autumn but that's part of football and I'll handle it.'

Tigana was also eager to recruit a top-class winger. Portuguese international Simao Sabrosa, the former Sporting Lisbon player then at Barcelona, was unhappy with his number of first-team appearances at the Nou Camp, but Benfica were also interested and the winger took the chance to return to his homeland. Paris St Germain winger Laurent Robert admitted that he was approached by Fulham, but Bobby Robson signed the coveted 26-year-old for £9.5 despite interest from Spanish club Valencia. Robert revealed: 'I have spoken to Fulham and their manager Jean Tigana – although I have not been to England to see them, or Newcastle, as some reports have suggested.' Tigana was also linked with Kaiserslautern's Jeff Strasser, the 26-year-old Luxembourg international midfielder, German wunderkind Sebastian Deisler, a creative midfielder, and Antoine Sibierski, available in a £3.5m deal from Lens.

The signing of Luis Boa Morte for £1.7m from Southampton came as little surprise, since the striker had spent the promotion season on loan. But he did consider going back to Portugal with Benfica, and also had the option of a move to St James's Park. He said: 'One of the biggest clubs in England, Newcastle, revealed an interest, but I preferred to be with Fulham and remain in London. In truth, I am perfectly accustomed to life in London and this influenced my decision. Also the squad is good and the team has technique. We have to fight the best without fear. Everything is possible. We only need to believe in ourselves.' Boa Morte signed for Fulham on a four-year contract, adding: 'I feel very well in Fulham, always very well, as I was treated like this since the first day.' The 23-year-old admitted Benfica had been close to signing him. Indeed, sources from Lisbon insisted a deal had been struck to take him to Estadio da Luz. 'This is a situation that must be clarified,' he told *A Bola*. 'I travelled with Antonio Simoes in the same plane, from Lisbon to London, but we did not speak about anything. By the way, I never spoke to any officials at Benfica, not even with Filipe Luis Vieira. Jesualdo Ferreira did ask me if I wanted to play for Benfica. I said "yes", I would like to represent Benfica. Perhaps we lacked the time to negotiate. I believe time became scarce.' Boa Morte confessed to being upset that the proposed move to the Portuguese giants had not materialised. 'In part, I was a little sad,' he admitted. 'Because, in my soul, I counted upon returning to Portuguese football. I believe that it could happen in the future, if I continue to progress.'

Boa Morte was an important summer signing. Yet Southampton received none of Fulham's £1.7m. He had gone to the south coast on a pay-as-you-play transfer deal from Arsenal, but Southampton never needed to pay even the first instalment of £400,000 because he failed to play twenty games. Instead he went off to Craven Cottage on loan where he scored twenty-one goals on an all-season loan arrangement. So the money headed off to Highbury.

Perhaps the most significant summer signing proved to be that of one of the country's most promising youngsters. Sean Davis signed a new four-year deal and the England Under-21 star said: 'I'm glad everything has been sorted out. I've signed for four years and, hopefully, we can win the Premiership in that time. I want to improve as a player so Jean and Christian played a big part in my signing. I can't wait to get back to training now and hopefully we can start the new season with a home win against Chelsea for our fans.' Michael Fiddy commented: 'We are delighted to have agreed a deal with Sean for the next four years, he is an integral part of today's squad and is constantly improving as a player. Sean's dedication to Fulham from his early playing days is a testimony to both the club's academy system and to Sean's talents and we look forward to seeing him reach his full potential in the Premiership.'

Republic of Ireland defender Steve Finnan signed a new five-year contract. The 25-year-old, signed by Kevin Keegan for £600,000 from Notts County, said: 'Fulham is a club that's going places and I want to be part of that.' One of the club's brightest young stars, striker Calum Willock, signed a two-year contract. The prolific 19-year-old striker hit two hat-tricks towards the end of the promotion season for the reserves and scored a number of spectacular goals in their Championship-winning campaign. Willock said: 'Obviously I am delighted to have signed for two years. I can now settle down and look forward to concentrating on my Fulham career. This is such a big club and it's a dream come true to be a part of it. My ambition is now to go on and break into the first team. I have been friends with Sean Davis for a long time and I'll be looking to follow in his footsteps.'

MONDAY, 2 JULY

Most of the squad return to Motspur Park for the start of pre-season training, less than two months after the old season had finished. Latecomers are those who have been on international duty in the summer, like Boa Morte. It is a surprise there are no new faces as yet, but Moroccan central defender Abdeslam Ouaddou is on his way from French Second Division side Nancy. The 21-year-old arrived in England for talks and the club is sorting out a work permit that will allow him to start his four-year, £10,000-a-week contract. Dubbed 'the French Rio Ferdinand', his style is considered perfect for Tigana's team strategy. He was also linked to Arsenal, Bayern Munich, Bordeaux, Lens, Monaco and Ajax. Fulham agreed a £2m fee while the player was away on international duty, and as part of the deal played Nancy in a pre-season friendly in the town of Epinal. If Ouaddou was the breakthrough, then the signing of Steed Malbranque, who made his debut for Lyon at the age of 18 at the start of 1998, was the follow up. Malbranque twice won the French Championship at under-15 level (1994, 1995), the French Cup in the Olympique Lyonnais under-17 side and the Amateur French Championship with the reserves in 1998. He was also a member of the France side that finished as runners-up in the 1996 Under-16 European Championships and captained France at the 1999 European Under-18 Championships under the guidance of Fulham's assistant manager Christian Damiano.

First day back is all about getting the needle! The health checks by the medical staff are among the most stringent in football. They consist of a series of blood tests examining the toxins in the body, checks on players' hearts, teeth and muscle strength. Most of them looked like they had kept themselves in good shape during the summer. In terms of training there was nothing too demanding but the players are expected to train up to three times a day in short bursts in order to improve their stamina. In France players do not get anything more than four weeks off in the summer, so despite the early start date, no moaning was tolerated. The previous pre-season, the Fulham players were annoyed by the early start date and also by the strenuous regime, but after reaping the benefits of promotion and the First Division title there was no grumbling in the ranks this time.

TUESDAY, 3 JULY

A big slice of sponsorship action: a lucrative shirt deal with fast-food chain Pizza Hut. No doubt none of Tigana's squad were allowed to take home a stuffed-crust pepperoni as they knuckled down to pre-season training. The £2m one-year contract established the company's logo on the black-and-white shirts as the club entered the Premier League for the first time. Alain Goma observed that the new logo reminded him of the Citroën marque!

WEDNESDAY, 4 JULY

New home kit launched with a redesigned club badge chosen by Mohamed Al Fayed. The chairman wanted to celebrate the club's return to the top flight with a new crest. The reason for the change is that the crest which had adorned the shirt for just over fifty years did not belong to the club; it was the crest of the London Borough of Fulham and Hammersmith. It will be kept on and used for a selected range of heritage merchandise, but the new one, a unique badge based on the FFC badge used from 1973–7, will be used solely by the club.

THURSDAY, 5 JULY

There is further frustration for Tigana in the struggle to snap up a striker to lead the line with power and presence. Although Fulham have extensive funds at their disposal, spending the cash remains a problem. Top stars want the bonus of being able to play in Europe if they are going to sign for a new side, and Fulham couldn't offer this. Experienced German striker Oliver Bierhoff continued to be linked to a move to Fulham. The 33-year-old saw his first-team opportunities at the San Siro restricted and believed a move to England, where he would be guaranteed first-team football, would enhance his chances of making the German squad. 'If I want to achieve my goal of playing in next year's World Cup finals, I cannot waste my time just sitting on the bench in Milan,' he said, and added: 'I've had a £2.4m offer from Fulham and the assurance of a first-team place. I'm very tempted to play in the Premiership and I am giving the offer serious consideration.' But the club found it difficult to work out exactly who was the official representative of the AC Milan hitman, and whether the Italian side wanted a fee (of £2m) or whether Bierhoff was available on a free transfer. Hopes of signing him receded after the player admitted that he was most likely to move to Brescia as a last-ditch attempt to fight his way back into the German World Cup side. Bierhoff was happy to accept a one-year deal with Brescia after receiving assurances from coach Carlo Mazzone that he would be a first-team regular – a promise that Tigana refused to make.

Leaving Craven Cottage was former favourite Paul Peschisolido. The Canadian international striker did not get many chances under Tigana and signed for Sheffield United. He was Fulham's first £1m signing when he joined from West Brom in October 1997 and scored on his debut against Northampton Town.

SUNDAY, 8 JULY

One-time crime reporter, Chester Stern, a former head of Scotland Yard's press bureau, was recruited to the club's press office. Media guru Max Clifford was apparently unaware of the appointment until he was informed by the *Sunday Telegraph*, according to the paper's own report, that Stern was being elevated to a boardroom position. The paper's 'Inside Sport' diary claimed it had caught Clifford off-guard by informing him of the appointment and that a few hours later he had called back to say: 'I've just spoken to Mohamed and Chester is going to be appointed press officer for the club. I am still director of media and he will be working under my jurisdiction.' Max explained to this *Diary* that his overall jurisdiction was not being usurped, as the paper had suggested. Clifford said: 'It's an in-house appointment, he is not on the board. He will be dealing with the day-to-day press enquiries relating to the football club.'

MONDAY, 9 JULY

Fulham set off for their training camp in Luxembourg boosted by the encouraging news that Steve Finnan had signed a new five-year contract. Finnan expressed his happiness with the deal: 'I'm delighted to have signed up for five years. Fulham is a club that's going places and I want to be part of that journey. We've got some excellent players and a top-class management team. Obviously it's nice that the management feel I deserve a five-year deal, and personally it's a great confidence booster.'

The name David Ginola had been linked to Fulham for most of the summer. Newly appointed Chester Stern found himself being approached because Ginola's entourage had seemingly failed to persuade Tigana to make a move to contact Villa. Stern told the *Diary*: 'I was at a press golf day and Neil Silver, who had written Ginola's book, bumped into me in the car park. I kind of made a joke when I suggested that if his man wanted to come to Fulham, to give me a ring! The next day Ginola's agent Chantelle Stanley contacted me. I was still the *Mail on Sunday*'s crime correspondent and she tracked me down at the newspaper's offices. She started to talk about figures, personal terms, but I told her I would contact the managing director Michael Fiddy so he could discuss the proposition with Jean Tigana. But I soon heard back that they were not interested.'

Tigana is a great believer in taking his teams away for pre-season training. Assistant manager Christian Damiano explained the decision to journey to Luxembourg: 'It is an interesting change for the players to train in another country. We have a long pre-season in front of us so it's important to change the surroundings for the players so they keep focused and work hard.' While the physical side is taken care of by fitness trainer Roger Propos, Damiano knows and appreciates how tough the pre-season regime can be psychologically and is just as ready to work on the players' minds as their bodies.

The first pre-season game is on Friday against Nancy. Damiano continued: 'We have started to mix the sessions by including technical work along with the physical work we have been doing. Naturally the players have to prepare the technical side of their game. The first three matches are good preparation for us. It is a very interesting situation being in a more difficult division playing teams of higher quality, and we need to prepare properly. Last season the situation was different; we needed to build confidence in the squad and the players needed time to adjust to a new system. Now the players know how we want them to play, we have to improve and help them adapt to playing better opposition.'

FRIDAY, 13 JULY

Fulham make their way from their training camp in Luxembourg to Epinal in France to play Nancy. Signing-to-be Ouaddou was due to play, but at the last minute was called away on international duty. The team entered the pitch to a typically continental welcome of smoke, flares and fireworks, on a mild evening for the hundred Fulham fans who had made the journey.

Louis Saha produced the start they wanted with an early headed goal. Saha managed to leap at the far post to get on the end of a Rufus Brevett cross and steer his header back across the face of the 'keeper and into the net. The second half started with the introduction of Cheriffe Toure Mamam, the Togo midfielder on trial, who replaced Bjarne Goldbaek on the right-hand side. Nancy were in no mood to be pre-season fodder as an incisive attack managed to breach Fulham's defence, allowing striker Laurent Dufresne to fire past Maik Taylor on 70 minutes for the equaliser. However, with 15 minutes left Saha scored again to give Fulham victory. Line up: Taylor, Finnan, Brevett, Melville (Symons 45), Goma, Goldbaek (Mamam 45), Davis (Knight 80), Clark, Collins, Saha, Boa Morte (Betsy 86).

MONDAY, 16 JULY

The senior squad played a friendly against Sparta Prague at a rain-soaked Woking's Kingfield Stadium. The torrential rain spoiled the occasion and limited the run-out for the team, but there was one special visitor, England manager Sven Goran Eriksson, who had come to check out Clark and Davis. The former was one of the few players to shine at Fulham's new reserve-team home. Eriksson saw little to keep him entertained, with Clark's creative free-kicks in the first half providing the most dangerous moments from Tigana's side. Given the conditions, it was hardly suprising that the game petered out into a 0–0 draw.

TUESDAY, 17 JULY

Lee Clark was wanted by his home-town club and the lure to return to Newcastle was becoming overwhelming. As speculation grew that the 28-year-old would return to St James's Park for £5m, Middlesbrough, about to appoint Steve McClaren from Manchester United as coach following the departure of Bryan Robson, joined in the transfer scramble. But speaking after the bore-draw with Sparta Prague, Clark revealed he could sign a new deal in the next four weeks: 'Talks have been going on and lasting a long time. They've been going very well and hopefully in the near future – maybe before the start of the season – we can get something sorted out.'

Clark told of his frustration at persistent speculation that his future could lie away from Fulham, adding: 'When I first came here I signed a four-year contract and I am entering my third year of that contract. I cannot stop what's being written in the papers when I'm on a ride at Disneyland in Paris. It's not something I can do anything about. If people want to write that, so be it – but it never came from me or anyone connected with me.' Clark insisted he remained fully focused. 'It's something I can just put on the back burner. I'm concentrating on doing well for the football club in an important Premiership season. I'm focusing on the last few weeks of pre-season, getting good results, before the big kick-off.'

WEDNESDAY, 18 JULY

Alain Goma was not unduly bothered by the inactivity in the transfer market. The £4m signing from Newcastle said: 'I'm not really surprised because it's a low-profile club. I like the way they don't buy players indiscriminately. The fact that we don't have any more big names is perhaps better. It doesn't make a big difference, for us it's more about team spirit. We're more a collective team than a bunch of individuals, with each player participating in the game. I think we're good enough to perform. I know the Premiership and I think we'll do quite well. We don't really have specific targets, and we know it won't be easy, but we're confident.'

Little did he know about the spending spree about to come.

FRIDAY, 20 JULY

In front of a packed crowd at Celtic Park, Fulham were given a rapturous welcome from the Celtic faithful as Tigana presented Bhoys manager Martin O'Neill with a commemorative trophy in recognition of Celtic's Treble.

For the first time a Fulham game was live on their own internet site. Unfortunately it did not make good viewing as the Scottish champs, at least two weeks further on in their pre-season preparations, won easily. Swedish star Henrik Larsson gave his side the lead with a header, and then scored from close range in the second half after a mix-up in the centre of the Fulham defence; Brevett and Taylor got in each other's way and young Celtic star Sean Maloney scored the third to complete a miserable night for the Whites. Line up: Taylor, Finnan, Knight (Ouaddou 53), Goma, Brevett, Betsy (Stolcers 32), Collins, Davis, Clark (Trollope 74), Saha, Boa Morte (Hayles 62).

Fulham's official website came second in a 'new visitors' report. The Whites finished one place behind a Scottish club who boast a massive worldwide audience. www.fulhamfc.co.uk was launched in 1997 and recently secured the rights to the domains www.fulhamfc.com and www.fulhamfc.tv. The club won a two-year legal battle to secure the rights to the world-recognised .com address in the United States. Former club captain Alan Mullery and ex-player Tony Gale were signed up as regular website contributors for the Premiership campaign. Mullery skippered the Cottagers to the club's only FA Cup Final appearance in 1975, while Gale made 318 appearances for Fulham between 1977 and 1984, scoring 21 goals.

Forty-eight hours before the Premiership fixtures are due to be made public rumours spread that Fulham will face West Ham United at Upton Park in the first game of the new season. Wrong. Instead it is away to Manchester United. Tigana said: 'I was very, very proud of my team when we lost 2–1 at home to United in the FA Cup. That performance has given them a lot of confidence. I am sure we can start with a good display at Old Trafford. Playing against the best teams brings out the very best in a lot of players.'

MONDAY, 23 JULY
The squad had departed at the weekend for their French training headquarters at Clairefontaine for a week of pre-season preparation and will return to Motspur Park on Saturday. Having completed the first half of their scheduled pre-season friendlies, Jean Tigana will be looking to improve upon his side's fitness and tactical organisation.

TUESDAY, 24 JULY
For the first time ever Fulham were targeted by ticket touts in the expectation that every one of their Premiership games would be sold out. The club said it would do everything possible to make sure their tickets are distributed in the correct manner.

WEDNESDAY, 25 JULY
Fulham signed highly rated youngster Sean Doherty, one of the country's most promising youngsters, in a £650,000 deal. The England youth-cap striker, just 16, walked out on Everton. Rated as the 'new Francis Jeffers', his move was a blow for the club who sold Jeffers to Arsenal for £10m. The England Under-17 international joined the club's youth academy set up. Speaking exclusively to www.fulhamfc.com, academy director Steve Kean explained how the move came about: 'Sean's an international left-winger. We were very surprised when he decided that he wanted to leave Everton. Every academy player signs a registration form, and in that form there's a window which allows the player to have a look at other academies. We've been keeping tabs on all international players. As soon as we heard he was available, we scouted him at two England games, then officially contacted Everton and asked if we could trial him for a week. He also went to Leeds and a couple of other clubs, but what was great for us was that he wanted to come to Fulham.'

TUESDAY, 31 JULY
Excitement was generated as Dutch goalkeeper Edwin Van Der Sar revealed he'd signed for Fulham. The 30-year-old was shocked by Juventus' decision to buy Gianluigi Buffon for £33m and wanted to reconsider his career. Van Der Sar is a top-class player and the move had football pundits all over the country suggesting that Fulham had finally shown their real intent ... but there was even more to come.

THE SEASON

AUGUST

From the Stadio delle Alpi to Craven Cottage, a £7m 'keeper ... £32m spent in a month ... Saha shocks Manchester United (for a while)

WEDNESDAY, 1 AUGUST

Odds for the title: Manchester United at 10–11 – inevitably strong favourites. Liverpool 4–1, ahead of Arsenal at 5–1, despite the Gunners' summer spending spree. Leeds are at 6–1, Chelsea at 33s, and Fulham are rated a 50–1 shot.

An illustration of the interest in Fulham's fortunes back in the big time is that three of their first nine Premiership fixtures will be shown live on Sky; the visit to champions Manchester United, the London derby at Charlton Athletic and the match at Aston Villa. The ticket office announced before the end of June that all away season tickets were sold out. With supporters eager to follow the Whites on their travels, tickets had been quickly snapped up. Al Fayed was eagerly looking forward to the opener at Old Trafford: 'You could not have written a better script. We are quite capable of holding our own against the best.' But not everyone was overjoyed. After the initial excitement realism set in pretty quickly, with goalkeeper Maik Taylor complaining: 'I'm gutted. That is the worst fixture we could have had. It might not have been so bad if we had got them at home but to go there for the first game is the worst possible start.'

Tigana's forward planning included a partnership with French side Le Havre, who are coached by his friend Jean-François Domergue. Le Havre have one of the best French football academies and Tigana studies the development of the best young French players, particularly the under-16 side that beat England 4–0 in the European Championships semi-final.

The club recruited scout Bernie Dixon from Stamford Bridge. Dixon left Chelsea critical of manager Claudio Ranieri for failing to gamble on homegrown talent.

Central defender Andy Melville, who skippered the side in Coleman's absence in the promotion run-in, extended his contract by a year until 2003. Melville was delighted. 'I was happy to sign this new contract which keeps me at the

51

club until I'm thirty-four and I've still got lots of ambition to fulfil. With the year we've had and the one ahead it's important to feel settled.'

Although his policy was to sign players for the future, Tigana said: 'My problem is that I have only one player with more than a hundred Premiership matches under his belt and that is Lee Clark. I would like us to make some good signings in line with our ambitions. But we are thirty-three years behind Manchester United, Arsenal, Liverpool and Leeds.'

In any club, during the summer break, there are casualties. Republic of Ireland left-back Terry Phelan was one of them. Just forty-eight hours before his wedding, he received his P45 in the post. 'This is the biggest blow I've suffered in football. To treat a human being like this is a disgrace,' he said. Young players released were James Bittner, Jacopo Galbiati, Sam Keevill, Nicolas Sahnoun and Anthony Tucker. Players over 24 released were Simon Morgan, Alan Neilson, Peter Moller and Karl Heinz Riedle. Neilson, though, signed a one-month contract despite being officially released at the end of the season! The 34-year-old former skipper Simon Morgan had to take a 'substantial cut in wages', according to Mickey Adams, when he opted to sign for Brighton ahead of QPR and Notts County on a free transfer. Morgan said: 'I'm delighted to have signed for Brighton. That's where I wanted to go. Once again I want to thank the Fulham fans for the fantastic years I enjoyed at the Cottage.' (By the end of the season he'd be back, as head of community.)

Tigana made a move for Chelsea centre-half John Terry, who was informed of the £7m offer and considered the proposal, but Blues boss Claudio Ranieri was not willing to part with a player he rates highly. Instead Tigana completed the signing of Ouaddou. International clearance and final paperwork issues were cleared up. Expectations were high for the potential debut of Fulham's latest signing Van Der Sar, but it was French midfielder Malbranque who turned out for the Whites first in a reserve game, with Van Der Sar sitting in the stands watching his new team-mate. Malbranque stole the show, setting up Saha to score the only goal of the game.

THURSDAY, 2 AUGUST

Tigana introduced Van Der Sar to the media at Motspur Park and then admitted he needed 'three or four more signings before the season kicks off'. He had already spent £13.5m, but was looking to spend more of Al Fayed's cash. Tigana spoke of his belief in Van Der Sar's ability, and insisted the aim for the season was consolidation in the top flight. 'He has the habit of playing at the top level and that is very important. I need the players with experience. My vision for this season is to stay at the top level and to progress together. I have many players who have never played at the top level, and I need three or four players at the top level.' A tall, lean, imposing 'keeper with blond hair and pronounced features, the Dutchman used his first appearance before the British media to slam Juve over their attitude towards him. Van Der Sar's destiny had been sealed on the first Sunday in May, in what was effectively the Serie A decider against Roma in Turin when he fumbled a last-minute shot from Hidetoshi Nakata when Juve were leading 2–1. The game finished in a draw, and five weeks later Roma won the title by two points from Juve. Juve had lost only three games all season and the team's only ever-present, their 'keeper, had conceded fewer goals than any of his rivals. But Juve's second successive runners-up spot cost Carlo Ancelotti his job, and the return of Marcello Lippi negated director-general Luciano Moggi's pledge that Van Der Sar's No. 1 spot was safe. Van Der Sar knew nothing of the Turin club's swoop for Buffon, which led to a string of rows with the Italian giants. 'I've got some bad feelings towards Juventus,' he admitted. 'It wasn't a nice ending to my time playing there. We had some arguments and it was a difficult period for me. We had a meeting a few weeks before the end of the competition [the league] and they didn't give any indication of signing another goalkeeper. Sometimes people decide something and, if it's coming from a higher level, it's impossible to fight against it. They didn't say anything about signing a new goalkeeper, so I had to look for another club. There were some possibilities, clubs interested in Germany, Holland and England, but I got this opportunity to play for Fulham. Fulham were the most decisive. Of course, they are not on the same level as my former clubs, Ajax and Juventus, but they are very keen to come up to that standard. It may not happen in two years but we can give it a shot.'

His passion for the game forced him to look for a new challenge, rather then simply picking up a hefty wage packet to sit on Juve's substitutes' bench. 'Nowadays, some big teams have twenty-five players in their squad, and some players who are not playing think, "I'm going to stay here because I'm earning a lot of money. My decision was to play. I have to play – I don't want to be six months on the bench. Of course everybody wants to play in the Champions League, but not everybody can. Sometimes you have to make a decision, not only looking at the established clubs, and I've made a decision to go to a club that is in development in a rather fast way.' Van Der Sar was reassured that his No. 1 status in the Holland camp is not threatened. He added: 'I talked twice in these past weeks with our coach Louis Van Gaal, and he said to me: "The Premier League is one of the biggest and best competitions in the world." I said to him they [Fulham] are not playing European football. That's not the issue – if I can play thirty-eight games in England and international games, I will be playing my matches at the highest level, so for the coach it's no problem.'

Al Fayed pledged to continue to bankroll the star acquisitions. Tigana had no fear of spending £7m on Van Der Sar. But he was still looking to the future. He said: 'I hope next week to buy three or four new players. I need them for the squad. We need a minimum of four new players, in the defensive area, midfield and one striker.'

Van Der Sar met with Tigana and Al Fayed. 'They said they started four or five years ago. They got two promotions and Mohamed Al Fayed bought the club, saved the club, saved the ground. They said they're going to build a new stadium on the place where they have been for the last hundred years. I think that's a good thing – history. I met him [Fayed] when I was negotiating. He's a persuasive man, yeah. I read some things about him, about his life, about things he did. He comes across to me as quite a nice guy. He's approachable.'

FRIDAY, 3 AUGUST

Malbranque officially joined after playing some pre-season friendlies. The former French youth-team captain said: 'I've confidence in myself. Lots of spaces open up during English games, and I reckon I can take great advantage. Although I favour a Latin style of play, I believe I can impose myself in the Premiership. There are plenty of other French players there already, and they are enjoying success. I am sure I can too.' Belgian-born Malbranque, 21, had rejected an approach from Arsenal in autumn 1998, but believed the time was now right to move. He helped Lyon clinch runners-up spot in the French First Division and win the League Cup 2000–01, but grew frustrated at not being guaranteed a regular first-team place.

SATURDAY, 4 AUGUST

Fulham took on Spanish side Espanyol in a friendly in the picturesque town of Le Touquet. The large travelling contingent of Fulham fans were treated to their first look at Van Der Sar. However, it did not go according to plan when in the 12th minute Tamudo gave the Spanish side the lead. On the half-hour mark midfielder Antonio Velamazan nodded home the Spaniards' second after a break down Fulham's left. Barry Hayles pulled one back in the second half as Espanyol started to get physical, but Fulham could not force an equaliser. Tigana, however, was pleased with the attacking nature of his side and with Malbranque in particular.

MONDAY, 6 AUGUST

Van Der Sar spent his first two weeks in London watching videos of the country's leading strikers. Knowing that he would be making his Premiership debut against Manchester United, he quickly got down to work, although he already knew a thing or two about United's new £19.1m Dutch ace goalscorer Ruud Van Nistelrooy. Van Der Sar said: 'I want to learn as much as I can about as many players as I can. I know some of them but I will try to get as much information as possible. It is not just about the way players score, I am also keen on looking at things such as their movement, what players do at every corner and how they react to things. The more you can learn about a player, the better it makes you and when you face them at least you are aware of what they can do and how to keep them out.'

Van Der Sar cannot wait for the chance to play in the Premiership after signing from Juventus where he regularly faced Veron, then at Lazio. He said:

'Veron has not scored past me before and I would like to keep that record. But he is a great player, he can score goals and he has great technique.' He is delighted to be in the Premiership with Holland team-mate Van Nistelrooy and went on: 'I hope he will succeed here but I will be pleased if he waits one week longer to do it.' Amazingly, it was to be Van Der Sar's first game at Old Trafford.

TUESDAY, 7 AUGUST

Tigana's spending intensifies, as he snaps up 21-year-old left-back Jon Harley from Chelsea for a fee of £3.5m, subject to the normal medical examination. It was something of a surprise move, considering he had been linked with Chelsea's John Terry. England Under-21 international Harley is a product of the Lilleshall School of Excellence and made a big impression at Chelsea, making his debut in April 1998. During the 2000–01 season he had a month's loan spell at Wimbledon before being recalled by Chelsea. Tigana said: 'Jon is a very skilful young player with proven tactical ability and we believe that he will be a valuable addition to the squad. I have tried since I have been at Fulham to sign young English players but it has proved very difficult. I am happy now that we can welcome this player to the club.'

Harley was equally delighted with the move. He said: 'I am really pleased to have been given the opportunity to join Fulham as I have huge respect for the manager, Jean Tigana. I am looking forward to being able to play football in the Premiership with Fulham next season. I have happy memories of my time at Chelsea and have many friends there who understand that this is a great chance for me to improve as a player at the highest level.'

This, Tigana's fourth signing in a week, took Fulham's summer spending past the £20m mark.

WEDNESDAY, 8 AUGUST

'There's Only One F in Fulham' fanzine editor David Lloyd cast his prediction in the *Racing Post*: 'We'll be hard pushed to fulfil chairman Mo's declaration that we'll win the Premiership. The highest position we've graced in the top flight was fifth way back in 1960, while our best final position has been tenth. Most Fulham fans would be delighted with that this time around – although the FFC powers-that-be are aiming for the top, as the signing of Edwin Van Der Sar amply demonstrates. Lady Luck will play a part on and off the field.'

THURSDAY, 9 AUGUST

Five Fulham players were called up for international duty next week, the most significant being Sean Davis, who was again included in the England Under-21 squad against Holland. Bjarne Goldbaek will face world champions France, Andrejs Stolcers will line up for Latvia against Ukraine and Steve Finnan was selected for the Republic of Ireland against Croatia. New goalkeeper Van Der Sar was selected for Holland against England at White Hart Lane.

FRIDAY, 10 AUGUST

Racing Post columnist Harry Redknapp observed: 'It's 1,000–1 bar the front five with me and I'd lay 10,000–1 Fulham, yet they are only 50–1 in places, which I find amazing. Yes, they've got money to spend and Edwin Van Der Sar is a hell of a signing. But they've got a big step up to make and there's no guarantee that they will find it straightforward. I know there's a top London club list but if there was one to finish bottom in the capital I'd want to bet them because Arsenal, Chelsea and Spurs won't be involved and there's no reason to think that West Ham or Charlton are going to be any worse. I don't imagine Fulham being involved in the dogfight at the bottom but two teams who probably will are Derby and Bolton.'

Most bookies had Fulham to finish third in London behind Arsenal and Chelsea. Tigana was one of the safest bosses around. Only Peter Reid, David O'Leary and Gerard Houllier had longer odds for the first Premiership manager to lose his job. Glenn Roeder was favourite, followed by John Gregory and Stuart Gray.

SATURDAY, 11 AUGUST

Alaves won a bruising pre-season clash at Craven Cottage 1–0, denting Tigana's build-up to the Premiership. The Spaniards, last season's UEFA Cup finalists, scored the only goal against the run of play on 39 minutes when Ruben Navarro played a one–two with Vucko and chipped Van Der Sar from close range. Team selection saw Tigana working towards his probable starting line-up to face Manchester United.

SUNDAY, 12 AUGUST

Tigana and Christian Damiano took a long trek down the M4 to Cardiff to watch Manchester United take on Liverpool in the Charity Shield. It was a must-see scouting mission. Tigana observed how the pace of Michael Owen troubled the United defence and was impressed with Ruud Van Nistelrooy. 'He is just one player,' said Tigana. 'We will go out there to attack. That has always been my philosophy.'

Tigana knew his rebuilding was far from complete and that a striker was a priority. As he explained: 'I think it is very important for us to sign another striker. It's a long season and we're going to need as much experience as possible. The problem is that the people I wanted all want to play in the Champions League, which is a difficulty. I have bought young players and also Edwin Van Der Sar, but I would like to buy three or four more. I have two players injured and two suspended, which isn't good for my squad. We have many young players and some players who have not played a long time at the top level. I'm impressed by the level of enthusiasm, the facilities, the will-power. The first priority is to stay in the Premiership and build from there, which is why I've bought young players, to work with them and progress with them here in England.'

United eventually lost 2–1 at the Millennium Stadium, but Tigana was gone well before the final whistle. He had seen enough and was well aware what a nightmare it is to depart Cardiff because of the traffic congestion, so wisely left in time to beat the rush home. Tigana had sat just behind the press benches at the wonderful stadium and a few fans took time out to go and speak to the French manager who had his trademark toothpick in his mouth.

Sir Alex Ferguson paid tribute to the progress of Fulham under Tigana, which was a wonderful commendation, but he fell short of believing the West London club could emulate Kenny Dalglish's Blackburn and come straight up to win the title: 'I don't think Mr Al Fayed is putting in the sort of money that Jack Walker did at Blackburn, but they've already got a lot going for them. I know what they are doing at youth level, and it's very impressive. The structure looks excellent and they've shown a lot of ambition already with the signing of Van Der Sar. You have to admire that from a club who haven't been in the big time for many years.' As for 'doing a Rovers', he continued: 'They came up with a powerful, resilient team, but to me Fulham have got what it takes to last longer. It will be hard work, but I think that's what their intention is. What nobody knows is how long it's going to take. I don't think they'll be sensational this season, but they should be all right. They play in the right way. Fulham are the most impressive of all the clubs to have come up recently.'

About Tigana, one of British football's greatest managers said: 'Good foreign managers can only be a beneficial influence on our game. There are possibly too many foreign players, but the good ones are worth having. Tigana's definitely a good manager. I think he's got the lot.'

Sir Alex allowed himself a touch of reflection as he reminisced: 'I remember Fulham in the days of Robson and Haynes but they slipped back as far as you can imagine. When you're in that position you do one of two things: you crumble up and die or do something about it. Quite often after a team have been in the shadows, when they get a chance back in the top league they want to make sure they don't go back there.'

MONDAY, 13 AUGUST

Al Fayed backed the launch of a new-look website. The site went live shortly before midnight. Internet manager Paul Thorpe commented: 'Three months of development, planning and hard work have gone into the new site. As soon as the final whistle went last season we started work. We've only just made the deadline, and it's a huge relief to all of us. I sincerely hope the supporters will enjoy what they find and embrace it like they have our previous efforts. The chairman has been his usual supportive self and the fans have him to thank for what they see.' Fulham were the first club to treat their home page as a daily newspaper. Thorpe explained: 'We wanted to give the supporters, the chairman and the board something a bit different from the usual thing you see around other football websites. We already had a winning formula so coming up with something to beat that wasn't easy. We came up with the 'Fulham Today' concept for the home page. After all, the news section is a news service, and from now on it will be treated more like a daily newspaper than the front page of just another website.' Fulham also became the first club to launch a pay-per-view network for their away fans.

TUESDAY, 14 AUGUST

Sean Davis played a significant role in the England Under-21 side's 4–0 thrashing of Holland. The Clapham-born midfielder played for the whole of the first half, proving that he is at the forefront of new manager David Platt's plans. In the past former Under-21 manager and FA technical director Howard Wilkinson had said Davis can do for England's young team what Steven Gerrard does for the senior side, which is a huge accolade.

Kevin Keegan backed his former club for a top-six finish, although he admitted his tipping is lousy. Last season he backed Manchester City to make the top ten! Keegan said: 'I think Fulham can do what Ipswich did last season.'

WEDNESDAY, 15 AUGUST

Tigana refused to be caught up in any hype: 'I never read the newspapers and whenever TV people speak about Fulham I change channels because they say too many good things about us, they make the expectations around us too high.' Tigana gave an insight into his realistic expectations. 'Last season most people said we did not have the right players to make it to the Premiership. But we're here today and I can tell you we're here to stay. Tenth would be not too bad, and after that to do as well as Ipswich or Charlton last year. It would be a dream to follow Ipswich into Europe. Why not?'

Why not, indeed, with strikers of the calibre of Saha? The Frenchman and Barry Hayles issued their warning to the Premiership. Saha scored 32 goals while Hayles grabbed 19 last season as they took the First Division by storm and the pair felt they could keep scoring in the top flight. Saha said: 'Scoring more goals than last season is a big target for me. To be playing in the Premiership is a dream, playing against excellent players, on good pitches and in nice stadiums. The quality of players is better than the First Division, but I'm confident I can score goals at this level. I'm looking forward to it like everyone, and when you've got a good match to start off with, it's a pleasure to be in the side. Playing in the Premiership puts pressure on you, which is a positive thing. I'm not scared of playing against good players. There are lots of players who would like to be in my position, so I'm not going to waste the opportunity.' Hayles, who will partner Saha at Old Trafford because Luis Boa Morte is suspended, said: 'The boys can't wait until Sunday. We don't have anything to be afraid of and if we play to our strengths, which I think we will do, I can't see too many problems for us. I think the top five teams are going to be Liverpool, Arsenal, Manchester United, Leeds and hopefully Fulham. I'm looking to score as many goals as possible. I'll be aiming for at least fifteen, which I don't think is out of reach. If we keep playing the same way we played last season I can see us creating chances, scoring goals and winning games.'

Van Der Sar enjoyed his first-half appearance against England at White Hart Lane just eighteen days after signing for Fulham and winning his sixty-first cap, which includes a World Cup semi-final. 'I was happy with the forty-five minutes, it was good for my self-confidence. I had a point to prove, it was the first big game in a new country. It's always best if you can leave with a good memory.'

THURSDAY, 16 AUGUST

Fulham held their first press conference ahead of the Premiership kick-off and Tigana didn't wait for his French translator to finish when he leapt to his feet, exclaiming, 'Never!'

The question was whether life in the Premiership held any fears. Tigana explained his 'no fear' ethos: 'My philosophy is that as long as you're strong when you've got the ball, that's what counts. It's the opposition who have to scrap and fight if you keep possession. That was our philosophy last year and I'm sure it will be the same this year, although it will be harder because we'll be playing against better players and teams. Concentration levels will have to be higher. Defensively, if you make mistakes in the Premier League, you will inevitably concede goals. We won't be creating as many chances as we did last year, so we'll have to be more efficient as a team in front of goal. There's no doubt there was, if you like, a revolution in the First Division last year. Everyone said it couldn't be done, that you couldn't pass your way out of the division, you had to roll up your sleeves and fight to win points.' Fulham bucked the trend and believe they can do it one grade higher.

Most of the team conducted interviews, and the same message was delivered by almost every one of them. They made it perfectly clear that Fulham will not be afraid of the Premiership, that the team won the First Division title by playing good football, and that they intend to perform in exactly the same way in the top flight. Playing Manchester United at Old Trafford would be a huge test, but the players were excited rather than nervous. As Sean Davis said: 'The biggest bonus about playing in the Premiership is finding out if we can mix it with the big boys. I watch players like Vieira, Keane and Gerrard week-in, week-out and wonder how I would cope. It is a big test for us, but if we play to our potential we should surprise a few people along the way. Tigana has brought so much confidence to the side. He did not overlook anything and he is very strict, disciplined and innovative. He changed the diets and the training methods and it has prepared us all for the Premiership. It has also helped me get into the England Under-21 set up, which has been a great learning curve. I have great respect for the likes of Vieira and Keane, but I am not intimidated by them or anybody else. Tigana does not allow you to be intimidated. We do not see ourselves as cannon fodder. We know we can play good football, and we intend to show it again in the Premiership.'

Lee Clark took up the confident theme: 'It's about having no fear but, at the same time, playing sensibly. There's no point playing that way and losing 4–3 each week. It's no fear in terms of the lads expressing themselves when they've got possession of the ball.' Saha was also in positive mood: 'We played well last season and showed we had a good spirit. If we can keep that going, there is no reason why we shouldn't do well. We may surprise people.'

Tigana was determined to finish in the top ten, at least, and pointed to Ipswich Town and Charlton Athletic for encouraging signs, but he also admitted: 'The step up is to a different class. I don't know if the players are ready to play at the top level.'

One of the best sights was former club captain Chris Coleman walking across the car park at Motspur Park without any sign of a limp. Given what he has gone through after his car crash this was great news. He was still optimistic that by February he might be playing again, unless, of course, he needed another operation on his leg: 'Things are coming along really well. In the last three or four weeks it's come along in leaps and bounds. I'm now joining in with the lads, although obviously I'm not running around. But I'm doing bits and pieces. I don't want to try too hard and possibly risk overdoing it.'

FRIDAY, 17 AUGUST

The bookies were giving generous odds on a Fulham win at Old Trafford: hardly surprising considering only Liverpool, Middlesbrough and Derby have won Premiership games there in the last three seasons, with Derby's victory coming after the third successive title had already been secured. Equally there was cause for optimism with nine teams having shorter relegation odds – a first for a club making their Premiership debut. 'If you aim low, you can end up finishing lower,' Tigana argued. 'That's why you have to set reasonable targets. I don't expect miracles, but I do believe we can challenge for a top-ten place. After that, anything is possible. We had a good season last year when we dominated the First Division and created a lot of positive headlines but that does not give us any advantage now. All that means nothing as soon as we kick off.'

However, it did help to convince his players of his methods. 'From very early on,' confessed Tigana, 'my players realised the need to be professional. Last season they followed the coaching staff's advice and saw what could be achieved, so I am sure everyone will have the same determination to progress.'

Tigana and Collins know how to come away with a result from Old Trafford, having been involved in Monaco's 1–1 draw in the quarter-finals of the 1998 Champions League, which gave them victory by the away goal. Tigana said: 'I know exactly the way to beat Manchester United, but I have no David Trezeguet or Thierry Henry. So we will have to play in a different way.' On that night

Collins got the better of David Beckham. Tigana said: 'Collins on Beckham? It's possible. We need to beat Manchester United on Sunday but I don't have the same team as I had at Monaco. There I had a very strong team. It wasn't a surprise for me in Manchester with Monaco because after the first leg I told the players we were fifty–fifty to win. Sunday will be different. We are playing against the best team in England and, in my opinion, in Europe. To beat them we need to keep the ball in their half. I don't want my team to stay back. My philosophy is to play attacking football. It's not possible to change that now.'

Collins recalled with relish how he pitted himself against Beckham. 'That's one of my most pleasurable memories in football, coming back to British soil and knocking Manchester United out of the Champions League. That was a special match. To do that, you need to have the whole team playing well and you must keep possession. That night we produced a good team performance and that's what we'll need this time. We couldn't have a tougher game to start the season with, but this is what we worked for, to play against the best. It's a huge season for me personally. I've spent all my career in the top flight except for last season and I'm looking forward to testing myself against the best players. Beckham always plays on my side of the pitch, so I look forward to facing him again, if I am selected. It's a challenge. There's nothing to fear. We've got to respect them but we'll never fear them. If you fear them, you've got no chance.'

SATURDAY, 18 AUGUST

Collins believed team spirit was right. 'As a manager, Jean brings composure to the dressing room. He always keeps calm and that rubs off on his players. He never gets over-excited. When things are going well, he appears quietly satisfied and, when things aren't going so well, he doesn't get down. That's his main strength. A realistic target is to finish in the top half of the league. We've got to take heart from Ipswich last year who came up from the First Division and did fantastically. If they did it, why can't we? The key for them was that they played good football. They did not have many injuries, got off to a good start and believed in themselves.'

Record £28.1m signing Juan Sebastian Veron was back for United from international duty in South America, while skipper Roy Keane was suspended, as were Luis Boa Morte and Rufus Brevett for Fulham. Tigana was relishing pitting his wits against Sir Alex Ferguson again. 'I have great respect for him because he has built a good team not just for now, but for ten years. It's easy to win one year, but every year is very difficult. And I like his strong personality.' Tigana, too, has a powerful will to win and he insisted: 'I don't feel other people's pressure on me. My priority is what happens on the pitch. I watch my players' progress. Also, I've played and coached only at the top level for twenty-six years. I know what pressure is. It's not a problem. I'll sleep well tonight. Don't worry about me.'

SUNDAY, 19 AUGUST
MANCHESTER UNITED 3 FULHAM 2

Mohamed Al Fayed made his grand entrance in the directors' box fifteen minutes before kick-off. The new boys on the block were in bullish mood, from the boardroom to the dressing room. Al Fayed said: 'I am not the most patient man in the world, so I want things to happen as quickly as possible. When I took over Fulham, everyone told me I was mad, that I would spend my money and the club would go nowhere. In my time they've gone from virtually slipping out of the Football League to playing in the Premiership. This rescue operation has been very expensive but hugely rewarding. Anyone who knows me will tell you that I want to build the very best. Harrods is the greatest store in the world, the Ritz Paris is one of the greatest hotels in the world. My dream is for Fulham Football Club to become one of the greatest clubs in the world and I intend to make that dream come true.'

Nothing could have prepared Al Fayed, the fans, the players and indeed the country for such an exhilarating game. Saha and Fulham stunned Manchester United and the Premiership by taking the lead at Old Trafford. Saha ran on to a ball in the fourth minute from Sean Davis, lobbing Fabien Barthez from just outside the penalty area. It was an incredible sight for the 4,000 Fulham fans who had made their way up the M6. David Beckham equalised, but Saha did it again, taking a Steed Malbranque pass in his stride before smashing his shot past Barthez. Twice Fulham had taken the lead, but United's record signing Ruud Van Nistelrooy immediately began to repay his price tag with two goals in three minutes. United escaped, but at the final whistle Old Trafford reverberated to the chant of 'Fulham are back'.

Tigana, delighted with the way his players had performed and their brand of football said afterwards: 'This was a first test for my players. In the first half we had a lot of chances, but it is difficult against a team like Manchester United who, when they have one chance, score. Beckham's goal was great. Many people would have seen this as a very exciting game, but I would have preferred the points. There is no fear in my team, maybe because I am never stressed about football. We will continue to play, not worry about losing and concentrate on the next game. I am not surprised at how well they did against United because I know my team. We played United in the FA Cup last year and lost, we played Liverpool in the Worthington Cup and lost and we have lost this game. We played well, but we do need to win. And to do that I need to add three or four more players to the squad. We need another striker, a midfielder and a defender.'

The Old Trafford experience was very special for the fans, given that it was Fulham's first game back in the top flight for thirty-three years. One amusing and touching account of the magical journey to Old Trafford is related by a Fulham supporter:

'What's that? Oh God, it's the alarm. 5 a.m. Cup of tea. 5.15 a.m. Shower, pack the coffee and sandwiches in purpose-bought backpack, leave the house at 6.15 a.m. Board the coach at 7.20 a.m.; am I mad? No, it's the first game of the 2001–02 season and I am on my way to see my beloved Fulham play Manchester United at Old Trafford. We are the new kids on the block. Six coaches leave from Motspur Park and ten from Craven Cottage. I am nervous and excited and 4 p.m. seems a long way away. Arrive at Manchester 1.20 p.m. My tummy went over as I looked up at a statue of Sir Matt Busby outside the ground. Every Fulham fan you spoke to had a lump in their throat and a tear in their eye. We had arrived. I then had the wonderful bonus of finding myself outside the Copthorne Hotel, looking for a pub and seeing the whole Fulham team come out with Tigana to board the coach. I tell them all how proud and excited I am and thank them all as they sign the shirt I have on. Mr Fulham, Sean Davis, John Collins (such a gentleman), Barry Hayles, Van Der Sar and Saha (so laid back as he was last on the coach), Kit Symons, Melville, Goma, Stevie Finnan. I will never forget Tigana's radiant smile as he said "yes, of course" to signing my shirt. I shouted good luck, waved and off they went. As we all met up under the stands, at the bar, in the toilets, up went the roar "TIGANA, we are *Fulham FFC*". It was good to be back among the faithful again, and I felt so happy. Then up the steps and out into the open. Magnificent stadium full to capacity. There were 4,000 of us but it sounded like 20,000. The teams come out and I cry as the balloons go up, the flutter comes down, the whistle goes. This is it.

'4.04 p.m. SAHA STRIKES, GOAL . . . I, together with the 3,999 explode with joy, jubilation. I can't believe it and jump up and down, laughing and joking with everybody. It was as if time stood still and I was in the middle of the best sixty seconds of my life. I was amazed, surprised, hugging, cheering, and proud, so proud. I thought they would slaughter us, but we were good and I mean GOOD. Van Der Sar gave us so much confidence. I was very surprised to see Scholes, one of my England heroes, have a tantrum and knock the ball out of a Fulham player's hands in frustration. And even David Beckham, my other hero, went crazy when he scored the free-kick, reacting as if he had scored against Germany. They were really angry that "lowly" Fulham had shown them the way in their own backyard. Half-time. Restart . . . SAHA DOES IT AGAIN! Sheer jubilation! We had arrived. I wasn't afraid for my Fulham any more: whatever the score, win or lose, we had come home, we were back and we were flying high. Sean Davis nearly equalised after United's two goals; he wanted it so much that it just would not happen. We should have attacked them more, but the two main positives were Saha, who was brilliant, and Van Der Sar. With all due respect to Maik Taylor, who has been superb, this guy is in a different class. Back on the coach 6 p.m. Depart 6.20 p.m. Motspur Park 12.30 a.m. Home 1 a.m. How did I feel? Tired? No. Fantastic? Yes. It has begun.'

Sarah Brookes gave another perspective on the day: 'I cried during this game. There is a piece in the video when the players get off the coach and Edwin Van Der Sar smiles and waves, and that was at me because I was there grinning like the Cheshire Cat, and wearing the most expensive shoes I have ever bought in my life which I ruined because of the mud. It was a massive special occasion and I was so nervous. I went into the tunnel at the start of the day, and it is so antiquated because a woman has to go all the way out of the ground and up the stairs because you are not allowed through the tunnel. So for the press conference Jean had to walk from his dressing room about a hundred yards and wait for me while I was running along outside. Seeing all these famous people like Sir Alex Ferguson and David Beckham, who was dressed like he was going to a fancy dress party, and Ryan Giggs was incredible. We had played them before at the Cottage, but there is something so lovely about the Cottage that it strips people down. Suddenly we were in the Theatre of Dreams and it was a league game, not a cup competition. I got a wink from Christian and a nod from Jean. Everybody looked elated. There was something so magical about the day. Claire Tomlinson from Sky asked to speak to a couple of players, and to this day I swear Sean Davis was nervous and just switched on the charm for the camera. There were these guys you had seen play on the worst pitch in the world in deepest winter, and all of a sudden they were there on this fabulous pitch on a beautiful day at the beginning of Fulham's first ever season in the Premiership. I don't care how long you have been at the club, it was something magical, and for me, having been there three years, it was like the coming of age almost for the club. It was just amazing.'

Back at Old Trafford, before the official Fulham party left, with the famous 'you couldn't make it up if you tried' routine, Max Clifford used Manchester United's press-conference facilities for an impromptu TV interview in his role as media representative of Neil and Christine Hamilton. I doubt whether the plush after-match press-conference room had ever been used for such a non-footballing media interview. Richard Williams of the *Guardian* wrote: 'Tigana's players have no need of bouffant-haired PR men to make their point in the Premiership. Their excellence speaks for itself.' However, the incredible behind-the-scenes side-issue of the Hamiltons would, indeed, have consequences inside the club . . .

MONDAY, 20 AUGUST

Tigana conceded that his side had learned a harsh lesson about life in the Premiership after leading twice only to be toppled 3–2. Although he seemed happy with his side's efforts, he warned his players that they had to improve at both ends of the field. He said: 'For us it is a good lesson because we need to score more and defend well. It's possible for us to play well at this level but we need to score when we have the chances and to progress together. I am never pleased when I lose. Our next two games are important. My players are very tired – we need time to recover.'

Davis admitted that Fulham were made to pay for lapses in concentration, but still insisted the performance would send them into their next game in good heart. The England Under-21 midfielder set up the first for Saha, but was harshly penalised for the free-kick that saw David Beckham level the scores. He said: 'We came out firing in the second half. Unfortunately we gave away a couple of goals. We defended well today – except for that lackadaisical spell. We've come up against the best team in the country, we've created a few chances and could have gone in at half-time 3–0 up. We'll go into the game against Sunderland full of confidence and we hope to give the fans a win.' Two-goal hero Saha was equally upbeat, despite seeing his double overshadowed by Van Nistelrooy's. He said: 'It was a very hard game – but I think we played well today. It's a dream come true to score against Fabien Barthez because he's one of the best 'keepers in the world. It was a pleasure. We've showed all over the pitch we play good football.'

Sir Alex Ferguson tore into his defence for letting Saha poach his two goals. Though delighted with van Nistelrooy's double strike, he had some stinging criticism about the way his back four were breached at the start of each half: 'There was a casualness about the defending which I hope will improve as the weeks go on. We need to develop an edge to our defending – I would expect us to last more than four minutes before conceding a goal.' That 'edge' would have to be achieved without Jaap Stam, who had just played his last game for Ferguson. Luckily for United, their sloppiness at one end of the pitch was matched by sharpness at the other. Fergie was left drooling at Van Nistelrooy's opening goal that levelled the game at 2–2: 'His first goal was absolutely superb, created out of nothing. It was a goalscorer's goal, which I think won the game for us. I thought Fulham gave us a lot of problems. We did a lot of good things but there wasn't the flow in our game that we expect.'

Rave reviews . . .
Telegraph's 'Scouting Report' by Alan Smith: 'Tigana has fused spirit with technique to create a side who should easily hold their own this year. We should know by Christmas if they are able to emulate Ipswich, a particular inspiration, and challenge in the top half of the table, but they certainly look capable of ruffling some feathers. By showing the audacity to take an early lead against Manchester United, then going on to play with confidence and composure as if this kind of thing happens every week, you knew immediately that Fulham were going to be alright this season. How could they not be with such a fine work ethic, admirable passing game, good organisation and the kind of player up front who will embarrass the most accomplished of defenders?'

Arsène Wenger admits Fulham had wanted Dennis Bergkamp, but denied claims he tried to sell the 32-year-old for £2m before the start of the season. 'He is sharp and keen and knows he's an important player at the club,' said Wenger. 'He signed a new two-year extension to his contract a few months ago and I didn't let him do that to sell him now. Fulham showed some interest and wanted to sign him but I told Dennis this and he didn't want to go, just as much as I didn't want to let him.'

TUESDAY, 21 AUGUST

Lyon's director of sport Bernard Lacombe disclosed that the club had rejected a bid for French striker Steve Marlet. Having already snapped up Lyon midfielder Steed Malbranque, Tigana looked to the French club once again to get his hands on the highly rated Marlet. 'I spoke to Jean Tigana on the phone on Monday morning and he made a large offer,' said Lacombe, who admitted that he was tempted but explained that the club does not have sufficient attacking cover to allow Marlet to leave. 'We simply can't afford to let him go so close to the start of our Champions League campaign,' he said. 'Not only that, but we've just lost Sonny Anderson for three or four weeks to injury and Sidney Govou had to have an operation in July.'

Tigana, who coached Lyon between 1993 and 1995, had been linked with numerous forwards recently as he strived to add a cutting edge to the squad. Twenty-three-year-old Marlet joined Lyon from Auxerre for £3.8m in June 2000, playing an integral part in the club's success. His pace and movement alongside Anderson and Govou caused problems to the likes of Arsenal and Bayern Munich in the Champions League, and he also helped the club secure their first trophy – the French League Cup – for twenty-eight years. He was rewarded with a call-up to the full France side and scored his first international goal against South Korea in the Confederations Cup earlier in the summer.

It was announced that Fulham will take on Monaco in a friendly match on 1 September at Craven Cottage.

WEDNESDAY, 22 AUGUST

FULHAM 2 SUNDERLAND 0

Sylvain Legwinski jetted in from Bordeaux for a medical in another surprise move by Tigana. Although he is linked with so many players, when the boss does make a move it is normally decisive and not many people know about it. Legwinski is a prime example. Tigana had said he needed more players at the weekend, and he proved as good as his word.

Fulham beat Sunderland with Saha scoring again after Barry Hayles had got the first. It was an electric night at the Cottage as Fulham hosted their first Premiership game, a night made even better by victory. Fulham displayed enough swagger to suggest that a fair number of teams will be cautious when they come to Craven Cottage. Although Sunderland themselves had chances that they should have converted, Fulham should have been out of sight long before Saha finally scored with his sixth chance of the night courtesy of a deflection. Saha time and time again worried the Sunderland defence and had the Frenchman been steadier on previous occasions he would probably have got a hat-trick. Hayles scored first, although Kevin Phillips should have already put Sunderland ahead by then, missing a gilt-edged chance. Hayles, the first Fulham player to score a goal at Craven Cottage in the Premier League, paid tribute to the club's supporters for the wonderful atmosphere they created: 'The supporters were different class, they really got behind us. It makes a world of difference to the team and they must take credit for that. Things were pretty even at one stage during the second half but the fans lifted us. And that was probably the difference in the end. I can't remember a better atmosphere at the Cottage. It was electrifying. It's vital that the supporters keep on turning up the volume. If they sense things are tight on the pitch, they can be our twelfth man and help turn things in our favour.'

Max Clifford took his place in the directors' box as normal, but his relationship with the Fulham chairman was anything but normal after the amazing antics at Old Trafford...

THURSDAY, 23 AUGUST

Sylvain Legwinski officially signed in a £3.3m deal. The 27-year-old midfielder played under Tigana at Monaco, winning the French Championship in 1996–97 and reaching the semi-finals of the UEFA Cup during the same season. He joined Bordeaux in January 2000 from Monaco. Tigana said: 'I am delighted to welcome Sylvain to Fulham. I have great confidence in his playing ability as I have worked with him previously at Monaco. I think that he will be a great asset in strengthening the squad and I look forward to him playing for us.'

Legwinski was also delighted by the surprise move. He said: 'I have played under Jean and also with John Collins and I have heard great things about the vision of the club. When I knew that Jean Tigana was manager at Fulham it became a great ambition of mine to work with him again. When the opportunity arose it was an easy decision to leave Bordeaux. I am looking forward to playing football in the Premiership and I have great hopes for Fulham and myself.'

The critics applauded Fulham and Tigana for the win over Sunderland. Under the headline 'Tig Will Be Mister Big', the *Sun*'s correspondent Mark Irwin wrote: 'Move over Arsène Wenger. Make way Claudio Ranieri. There's a new kid in town and he's aiming to become the Premiership's best foreign boss. Jean Tigana is the name and Fulham's delirious supporters have every cause for optimism with the Frenchman at the helm. A sell-out crowd saw a compelling performance from a team with no doubts about their ability to survive at the highest level. England boss Sven Goran Eriksson was among the spectators and the suave Swede will have been impressed by the speed with which Tigana has conquered our game. Fulham, with Tigana's leadership and Mohamed Al Fayed's cash, are going places.'

Chris Davies wrote in the *Telegraph*: 'Four years and four months after playing Doncaster Rovers in the Third Division, Fulham recorded their first Premiership victory as top-flight football returned to Craven Cottage for the first time in 33 years.' He described the game as 'high on excitement and entertainment' and on the evidence of the Old Trafford performance and this one added: 'Fulham will be a breath of fresh air to the Premiership, where they are likely to remain under the shrewd guidance of Jean Tigana. They play with the style of their manager, one of France's finest midfielders of the eighties and, while Mohamed Al Fayed has bankrolled £44m-worth of transfers, the spirit Fulham displayed is something not even the Harrods owner could buy.'

SATURDAY, 25 AUGUST
FULHAM 0 DERBY 0
Fulham endured an afternoon of acute frustration after a doughty Derby held out for a goalless draw at Craven Cottage. The home side had high expectations for their first top-flight meeting with Derby since 1952 following their midweek victory over Sunderland. The Cottagers were given a further boost with the late news that Derby were missing two star men through injury: striker Fabrizio Ravanelli and goalkeeper Mart Poom. But Derby held firm, rarely venturing out of their own half during the second period, which saw Tigana's men throw everything they had at their understrength visitors only to find stand-in Rams goalkeeper Andy Oakes in top form.

Players and fans might have to get used to such tactics. John Collins said about the game: 'It was very frustrating because Derby defended well, but I suppose we should see this as some sort of compliment that after only two games teams are coming to defend against us.'

Max Clifford did not take up his customary place next to Al Fayed. He hadn't missed a home match for a long time and, in fact, he was at this one, but his absence from the chairman's entourage was duly noted...

MONDAY, 27 AUGUST
Steve Marlet's agent revealed that by the end of the day he would know whether the player wanted to see out the rest of the season with Lyon or make the move to Fulham. The 27-year-old was tempted by what he considered a once-in-a-lifetime offer, with the combination of big bucks and a chance to join up once again with Tigana leaving the French forward champing at the bit. Lyon, though, were still holding firm. Coach Jacques Santini, already frustrated by his president's transfer dealings, made a plea for the club to do everything possible to keep Marlet, who was tied to Lyon until 2004. Marlet and his agent, Pascal Boisseau, spent ninety minutes with Lyon president Jean-Michel Aulas and general manager Bernard Lacombe on Sunday. 'If, when he boards a plane for Chile at 8.25 p.m., he hasn't signed for Fulham, he'll stay with Lyon,' Boisseau said.

TUESDAY, 28 AUGUST
The news that every Fulham fan wanted to hear arrived. Marlet agreed to join the club for a record £11.5m. Finally Tigana and Fulham had got their man.

Tigana spent more than £1m a day during August, adding six new players to his first-team squad, a spending spree only topped by Manchester United. Marlet flew to London for his medical and delayed joining up with France in Chile.

WEDNESDAY, 29 AUGUST

Marlet scored five goals in a number of high-profile Champions League games, helping Lyon to qualify for the second phase in 2000–01. First picked for the national team at 26, he has made five appearances for his country, scoring once. A late developer at international level, he is powerful, fast, good in the air and a predator in the box. He previously played with Goma at Auxerre and Malbranque at Lyon. In an official statement Tigana said: 'I am pleased to announce that Steve is joining Fulham. I have said in the past that it is important for me to strengthen the squad and I believe that Steve's striking ability will be a valuable asset to our first season in the Premiership. It is important for the squad to work together to enable us to be successful at the highest level.'

Marlet himself added on the Fulham website: 'I am happy to have signed for Fulham. Fulham is a very ambitious club and the plans that have been put in place by Mohamed Al Fayed and Jean Tigana to establish Fulham as one of the leading clubs in England encouraged me to come here.'

France coach Roger Lemerre fully endorsed Marlet's move. He believed the transfer would enhance the striker's already blossoming career, saying: 'He will progress at Fulham. For me it's a plus for Steve, even though he continued to progress at Lyon. I have been aware of the situation for a while, and I talked to Steve and to Jean Tigana about it. The move doesn't open the door to the France team any wider, but it doesn't close it either.' Despite attempts to keep him at Lyon, Lacombe conceded it was not possible to hold on to the striker, who had been made an offer that was difficult to refuse. 'You can't keep a player against his will,' he said. 'Juventus let Zidane go. It's a good move for Steve. By the time he is thirty-one he will be set up for life. It's hard to refuse that.'

Top French sports journalist Pierre Chamberfort predicted Marlet would be a revelation in the Premiership. He said: 'Marlet has all the right qualities to become the best striker in England. He will put fear into the hearts of defences with his pace and power. I have seen Marlet grow in stature over the last two years. He is a player who is approaching the peak of his career, but at just twenty-seven who knows what is to come, especially when Jean Tigana asks him to play his way. It's difficult to compare Steve to any English striker. He is certainly better than most that come to mind. If you asked me would I prefer Robbie Fowler or Michael Owen, I think we would not want to swap either of these two for Marlet. He jumps very high despite his size. He has power and technical ability which make him difficult to mark. He is like Henrik Larsson at Celtic, but stronger.'

THURSDAY, 30 AUGUST

Marlet joined up with the French squad in Santiago, Chile. Some of his team-mates ribbed him about his move, saying: 'Where is Fulham, is it a big town? Is it near London?' but Marlet was having none of it. He explained how the move came about: 'Fulham contacted me last season but after I weighed up all the advantages and disadvantages I decided to stay at Lyon. Just recently, Fulham came back with another offer and, because of that, I felt the club really wanted me. I had to look at the choices, sporting and financial. But sport is more important and I saw that there was a lot of ambition at Fulham.'

Marlet said he was also looking forward to playing with Saha: 'I learned a lot from Brazilian striker Sonny Anderson at Lyon. He helped me immensely. Perhaps I can now do that for Louis. I don't know him that well but he's obviously a player with great talent. He scored 32 goals last season and I watched on television when he scored twice against Manchester United. He is clearly a very good player and I am looking forward to playing alongside him.'

SEPTEMBER

Not the start Tigana wanted

SATURDAY, 1 SEPTEMBER

The Premiership took an extended breather with World Cup qualifying games taking place throughout Europe. England prepared to take on Germany in Munich, in their now famous qualifier. Meanwhile Fulham took the opportunity to play Jean Tigana's old team Monaco. Tigana is not in favour of big gaps between games, and despite some of his squad being away on international duty, they won in style at Craven Cottage with goals from John Collins and Louis Saha securing a 2–1 victory.

SUNDAY, 2 SEPTEMBER

Following England's phenomenal, historic 5–1 win on German soil, Tigana declined to join the list of managers queuing up to praise Sven Goran Eriksson's team.

MONDAY, 3 SEPTEMBER

Saha set his sights on qualifying for Europe. The addition of Steve Marlet to the squad raised expectations and gave the team some fearsome firepower. Saha said: 'Marlet is an amazing player, our attacking power is going to be extra-ordinary this season. We have so many options and I hope it will help us clinch a place in Europe. I jumped for joy when we signed Edwin Van Der Sar and I could not believe it when we got Steve. He has the qualities to explode into life in the Premiership.'

Marlet is a recognised goalscorer, just the sort Tigana had been looking for. Any side with ambition requires a player who can poach goals as well as score the occasional spectacular candidate for 'Goal of the Month'. Tigana had too many good strikers without any of them being prolific. He hoped Marlet would fulfil that role. Monaco player-coach Didier Deschamps, who played at Chelsea for one season, backed Saha's assessment: 'Marlet is a great buy and I am sure he will create a great partnership with Saha.'

TUESDAY, 4 SEPTEMBER

Full-time player-liaison manager Mark Maunders looks after every need of the club's Premiership stars. The former press officer was appointed when Tigana took over and has been kept busy by so many players joining the club in a short space of time. He said: 'People forget that footballers face the same problems as everyone else and it is my job to make sure they are settled and happy. If a new signing has a wonder game when he makes his debut I would get a lot of satisfaction from knowing that I had played a part in allowing that to happen.' Problems range from finding a new home and a school for the kids, to having the right mobile phone and importing family pets and even cars. These are the practical problems foreign stars face. Harrods Village in Barnes, once part of the chairman's business empire, can often be home while more permanent accommodation is sought. Sarah Brookes gave another perspective on the role played by the liaison manager: 'Jean and Christian needed someone to ensure that when a player came to this country they were integrated completely and that the only thing they had to worry about was what they did on the pitch with their feet and the ball. Mark comes in and whatever the player wants he sorts out. For example, when Edwin Van Der Sar arrived with his wife, they had never lived in the country before. They wanted nannies, dishwashers, dog-walkers – they want the best of everything which is natural, but they also needed someone to advise them on how to do things and on how they would get them. You need one central point of contact. Van Der Sar does not want to get called by seventeen estate agents a week. He wants one person to filter out what he wants and to go and look at the place and then come back and say this is a place you should go and look at. Mark was opening bank accounts for them, sorting out telephones, internet, satellite television and setting up everything any player wants. He would also help the current players as well as the new ones.'

Mark has had to look after Steed Malbranque's dog Pixie, a white West Highland terrier, when the Frenchman has been on international duty. At the same time he was looking after Louis Saha's dog who had gone into quarantine for six months. Everybody was in the canteen one day when Alain Goma came in and called Mark over. He said he had a big problem with his goldfish, which was ill. Unfortunately Mark spotted the wind-up and said, 'I would like to help you, Alain, but I am looking after Maik Taylor's terrapin'. Lee Clark used to go on at him all the time and tell him he should not be walking the players' dogs, even though by this time he was known by everyone as the pet-liaison manager.

WEDNESDAY, 5 SEPTEMBER

Tigana received an indirect invitation to sign David Ginola. Behind the scenes at Villa, the winger's problems with John Gregory were escalating to the point that Ginola had consulted Cherie Blair for legal advice on finding an escape route. A simple solution would have been an instant move. Stuart Higgins, who as part of the SFX agency that looks after David Beckham and Michael Owen was in charge of handling Ginola's predicament, had been in touch with Tigana to see if Fulham were interested if Ginola would lower his wage demands. But Tigana was reluctant to take him on.

Marlet picked up a slight knee injury while on international duty in Chile, Goma was troubled with a hip problem but Clark had overcome an Achilles injury, while Boa Morte was available again after suspension.

THURSDAY, 6 SEPTEMBER

Tigana probably gave Al Fayed a shock by admitting that, despite spending £42m on players in fifteen months, he still wanted to add 'three or four more experienced players' to his squad. He also promised to nurture homegrown talent, revealing: 'My ambition is to take good young English players between the ages of fourteen and seventeen and build a good foundation for Fulham.'

FRIDAY, 7 SEPTEMBER

Enquiries about Max Clifford's absence from Al Fayed's side at the last game were met with shrugs of shoulders all round Craven Cottage. Calls to Clifford's PR offices revealed that he was taking a break in Spain and would not be attending the next match, and perhaps not the games in the foreseeable future, but no reason was given . . .

SUNDAY, 9 SEPTEMBER

CHARLTON 1 FULHAM 1

Marlet was not fit for the London derby where an own goal by Melville prevented Tigana from celebrating his fiftieth league game in charge with a win at The Valley. The Cottagers' skipper inadvertently turned in a Shaun Bartlett header to provide Charlton with a 34th-minute goal. Although Luis Boa Morte volleyed in an immediate equaliser, Fulham could not find the second goal their dominance deserved as Charlton, missing eight first-team players, claimed a point. Saha deserved to win a penalty in the first half after Dean Kiely nearly cut the speedy striker in half with a high challenge that left Tigana seething. 'It was not only a penalty but also a red card.'

Tigana knew Fulham had dropped two points rather than gained one. He went on: 'We had a problem with our finishing but we kept playing, kept playing nice football, and that is what is most important to me. We had many chances, of course we are disappointed.' Charlton boss Alan Curbishley refused to blame injuries for his side's lack of creativity. 'We could keep using that excuse but I don't want to. At times we didn't do things well and when you play against a side like Fulham who like to keep the ball and you keep giving it back to them you are going to struggle. In the circumstances I have got to be delighted with a point.' Saha, fresh from picking up his August Barclaycard Player-of-the-Month award, was named man-of-the-match. He said: 'I played well but missed chances for us to take the lead. I may be winning awards and they are very good for my confidence, but the way to improve is to forget what you have achieved in the past every time you go on to the pitch and to work hard.'

MONDAY, 10 SEPTEMBER

Saha called for more protection from referees in the aftermath of the contest at Charlton, in which he was replaced fifteen minutes from the end by Hayles. TV cameras captured the incident where Saha was caught chest high by the opposition 'keeper's studs. Saha said: 'I am getting used to the tough tackling but I am quite surprised not to get the protection of the referees. All strikers need that because of the way football is so competitive. It is getting harder but I have to accept it. It was definitely a penalty because he did not get the ball. I just missed the target but if he had broken my leg there was no foul, nothing, and I do not think that is right. I would like more protection because that is the right way to play football. The referee made a bad decision.'

TUESDAY, 11 SEPTEMBER

'Out of a clear blue sky...'

So much has been written about events at the Twin Towers, but none of it really gets close to describing such a significant day in world history. Football hardly meant much on such a day. However, for the record...

ROCHDALE 2 FULHAM 2 (5–6 on pens)

Full-back Rufus Brevett was Fulham's saviour with a last-gasp equaliser in extra-time as the expensively assembled Londoners struggled to beat Third Division Rochdale in the Worthington Cup second round. Tigana's side prevailed on penalties at Spotland, with Luis Boa Morte scoring the decisive spot-kick. Boa Morte had opened the scoring only for Kevin Townson to score twice for the Third Division leaders. Brevett's dramatic equaliser came deep into stoppage time in extra-time with a shot across the face of the goal.

WEDNESDAY, 12 SEPTEMBER

Tigana experienced the inevitable fall-out from his midfield signings. The manager agreed to let unsettled midfielder Paul Trollope leave for around £600,000. Unable to force his way into the first-team squad the 30-year-old said: 'I really like being at Fulham but at this stage of my career I need to be playing regularly.'

THURSDAY, 13 SEPTEMBER

Tigana focused on the derby against Arsenal. The game was extra special for Barry Hayles, who had grown up as a Spurs fan. Hayles admitted: 'I've been a Tottenham fan all my life. Sol went for the sake of his career, but if I was still playing non-league football, I'd be bitter and twisted about it. Obviously it would be a bonus for me as a Spurs fan to get the three points.' However, such is the quality of the forward line at Fulham that Hayles was not guaranteed a starting-place, despite notching his first Premiership goal in the club's win over Sunderland. Portuguese international Boa Morte had scored in each of his last two games, while Marlet was fit enough to start on the bench against Arsène Wenger's side. Saha reckoned Marlet would keep the Gunners back line fully occupied if he played: 'He's the kind of player with pace and a quick mind, and he will usually have a chance of scoring. He's world class and will help us to play to our potential. He's also a nice guy. I think Steve will boost everyone in the team.'

FRIDAY, 14 SEPTEMBER
Arsène Wenger praised Tigana and the progress Fulham have made: 'Jean Tigana has done very well at Fulham and I think they will finish in the top seven. In many ways there is a similarity between the way he has come into English football and my own. He has tried to get Fulham to play in the right way and they are always positive. He has also bought well. Yes, he has had money to spend but you have to spend it in the right way and he has done that. He has brought top-quality players to Fulham like Steve Marlet and Steed Malbranque. Marlet is a French international that we know about from playing against Lyon and Malbranque is a young midfielder I looked at while he was at Lyon. But they did not want to sell.' Then there is Sylvain Legwinski, Fulham's signing from Bordeaux. Wenger knows about his talents, having signed him from non-league Vichy when he was at Monaco. Wenger commented: 'I was certain he had the qualities to be successful at a high level.'

In the build-up to the Arsenal game Wenger also paid tribute to Saha, whom he believed could be an outside bet for a place in France's squad for the World Cup. 'I knew about him from a very young age,' said Wenger of Saha, who was in the same year as Thierry Henry at the French football academy at Clairefontaine. 'The coach of the French Under-17 team said to me they had an excellent player coming through. That player was Saha. I am not surprised he has been a success at Fulham. He is strong on the ball, makes good runs and he is not scared. He is able to cope, where bravery is concerned, with English football. He will be a candidate for the French national team for the World Cup, not necessarily for afterwards. I wouldn't rule him out.'

SATURDAY, 15 SEPTEMBER
FULHAM 1 ARSENAL 3
Tigana admitted that his side were given a harsh lesson in how far they need to come to compete at the top level. Arsenal bombarded Fulham in the first half and Ljungberg scored a lucky opener. Fulham were not overawed, however, and were the best side for half-an-hour in the second half, during which period Boa Morte ran Arsenal ragged, setting up Malbranque for his first Fulham goal,

the equaliser. But Arsenal were too strong, and further goals from Henry and Bergkamp gave the Gunners all three points.

Tigana said: 'In the first half the team worried too much and therefore it was not a liberated performance. I don't know why that was because we did not have the same problem against Manchester United at Old Trafford. In the second half we had two chances to kill the game and we played very well. But if you don't take those chances against the big teams then you will lose. In the second half Arsenal had two chances and scored two goals and that is the difference between Arsenal and us. At the top level you must keep your concentration at all times. At half-time I told my players to press Arsenal and to attack them. In the first half we were playing too far back and that shows we were giving them too much respect. If we had attacked and lost then it does not matter. But most importantly, I wanted my team to push forward, play their game and not worry about the opposition. If Legwinski had scored the header that was cleared off the line the game would have been very different, because that would have allowed me to change the tactics. That is the difference in the Premiership. You may only have one chance and you need to score.'

Saha argued: 'I think Arsenal have a very good chance to knock Manchester United off the top and they have the form to be champions this season. They have been close before and they need a bit of luck and consistency but if I had to pick a team now after playing both I would say Arsenal are the stronger team.'

Boa Morte was a huge success, although the former Arsenal player's place was under threat from Marlet, who appeared as a second-half substitute in a contest where Martin Keown and Sol Campbell reigned supreme. Wenger said about Boa Morte: 'I like Luis' spirit and he has just given me his Fulham shirt to thank me for bringing him to England and giving him a chance. I think I'll sleep with it! He was only eighteen when he signed for Arsenal and there was just too much competition up front for him. But I always felt he would be better as a central striker than as a wide player and that is how it looked today. He was very sharp -but maybe the fact he was playing against Arsenal excited him. He had that extra aggression and power which gave us some real problems.'

Fulham were drawn to play Derby County in the third round of the Worthington Cup. The draw, which was made before kick-off against Arsenal, will see the Rams visit the Cottage for the second time in successive seasons.

MONDAY, 17 SEPTEMBER

Van Der Sar warned it was time to stop making friends and start winning points. Fed up leaving the pitch with the praise of his opponents ringing in his ears, he complained after the Arsenal clash: 'We didn't have them really rattled at any point.' He feared that could become a costly habit unless Tigana's Premiership rookies quickly developed a ruthless edge to their play, adding: 'This is the third game in a row where we haven't got the result we deserved. We should have done more than draw with Derby and Charlton and we could have had a point against Arsenal. It's becoming quite frustrating and we have got to do something about it. We didn't play well in the first half but made up for that after the break. We equalised at the start of the second half and, for twenty-five minutes, had them on the back foot. But that was it. The fact that Arsenal could bring on Dennis Bergkamp and Sylvain Wiltord speaks volumes. The biggest difference between the teams was the quality of strikers they could change from the bench. They are also very determined in front of goal. They only need one or two chances and the ball is in the back of the net. That's what makes the difference and it is something we have to develop.'

TUESDAY, 18 SEPTEMBER

Assistant manager Christian Damiano felt Marlet can emulate compatriot Thierry Henry and take the Premiership by storm. Marlet played only fifteen minutes against Arsenal and failed to make a real impact, but Damiano said: 'Steve Marlet is a player who is at the same level as players like Thierry Henry and David Trezeguet and we have high hopes for him at Fulham. At twenty-eight he is older than the likes of Henry but he is just starting to show his full potential now, and playing in the Fulham team in the Premiership will be fantastic for his progress.'

WEDNESDAY, 19 SEPTEMBER

Steve Finnan believes that although Fulham have made a slow start to the Premiership, they have not been overawed by their opponents. 'The football we play is suited to this level,' the Republic of Ireland international said. 'I think you can say that about most of the players at this club. It's pretty much what I expected. You're up against quality players so as soon as you make a mistake, you get punished. We are playing well, we're just trying to keep playing the way we did last year and not change anything. We're creating plenty of chances.'

FRIDAY, 21 SEPTEMBER

Steve Marlet has big ambitions for club and country after his remarkable rise to being a multi-million-pound player. Only eighteen months earlier he was a £3m-rated striker at Auxerre, but one good season with Lyon catapulted him into the limelight and the French national squad. Marlet, ahead of his full debut at Leicester, said he wanted to take Fulham into Europe and make the World Cup squad. He said: 'I was at Auxerre for four years and lost a lot of time there. That is why I've arrived on the scene relatively late. We used to play three in attack and it was hard to shine up front because I was stuck on the wing and had to defend as well as attack. It was very restricted. When I arrived at Lyon I played more centrally with Sonny Anderson so it was a lot easier and I started to score goals. I would never have got into the French side if I hadn't gone to Lyon. When I left Auxerre last year there was contact with Fulham, but they were in Division One at the time. Jean told me he had a project under way to try to become a big club like Manchester United and that I should come over. I refused because I wanted to play in the Champions League and for France. He spoke to me again at the start of this season. We had the same chat but he was able to use Fulham's results from last season to convince me. He said, "I told you so," and I jumped at the chance because now I've achieved my objective of getting into the French team, I want to test myself in the Premier League. The financial aspect was obviously a factor but that was not my real motivation. I like the English League a lot and I want to make an impression on it. French strikers have done well over here – Thierry Henry, Louis Saha and Nicolas Anelka before them. We all play with a similar style and I said if they can do it, why not me?

'A finish somewhere between tenth and sixth would be good, but I think we could push for a European place. My perfect season would be to score lots of goals, reach the Champions League with Fulham and play in the World Cup next summer. I've got my fingers crossed and I achieved all I set out to last year so why can't it happen again at Fulham this season?'

SATURDAY, 22 SEPTEMBER
LEICESTER 0 FULHAM 0

Another frustrating ninety minutes, this time at Filbert Street. Gaining a point away from home under normal circumstances would be seen as a good point, but once again Fulham dominated the first half and should have had all three points wrapped up by half-time. Tigana commented: 'Leicester were worried about us. They didn't press forward, chose to stay back and at the end of the game were very happy with a draw. I personally think that this was because of our reputation. I would prefer that our opponents attacked us rather than sat back defensively, as it makes it easier for us to play our game. But we must find the solution to this.' An average of only a goal a game and six points from six matches so far was not good enough for Tigana.

Marlet made his full debut and young defender Zat Knight also appeared for the first time. Lee Clark thought the draw was another two points lost rather than one gained. 'We need to start winning and soon. But there's nothing to worry about as far as we're concerned. Once we get another victory under our belts, things will become easier. There are new players in this team and they take time to bed in. When that happens I'm sure we'll be more than okay. Our problem is scoring. We run around, help each other and play well as a team, but the fact is we've only one win in the Premiership and that's disappointing. Zat only learned he was in the team this morning but gave an impressive display. The beauty with the reserves and youth team is that they train and play exactly the same way as the first-teamers so anyone can step in and know what to do.'

Leicester boss Peter Taylor was pleased with his side's display even though the pressure was mounting for his dismissal – an exit that wasn't far away as he would become the first Premiership managerial casualty of the season. Taylor said: 'I thought we were very decent because Fulham are a passing side and sometimes it is difficult to get the ball from them. The first half was difficult but we changed one or two things and the second half was much better. We could easily have won the game at the end. Fulham pressurised us in the first half and I had to take Sinclair off because he didn't start well.' For Fulham six points from six matches was a mere third of the points haul they managed from the same number of games last season.

MONDAY, 24 SEPTEMBER

John Sadler of the *Sun* praised Zat Knight to the hilt, suggesting he was the one glowing success of Fulham's game against Leicester. Tigana is not afraid to throw talented players into the action, and he has proved it with Knight. It was his confidence and ability on the ball which the manager liked. Tigana said: 'I was happy with the way he played. I have watched Zat progress very well. Last year he worked very hard and now he can play at the top level. I knew his potential when I first arrived, in the same way that I knew Sean Davis was a good player. But Sean had already played some games and Zat had very little experience. He needed one more year to work very hard and to change the way he thinks about the game. Last season in the reserves I played him in midfield because that is my system. Whenever I manage a young player I try to change their position so that they understand exactly what is involved in different roles. It is an important part of developing the instinct of a player. When Zat makes a pass out of defence to midfield, he will know what is in the midfielder's head, and playing in midfield has also helped his passing and distribution. For me, to change a player's position as part of his development is good schooling. Zat did not have the physical strength to last a full game against Leicester and for him to progress he needs more games. He is a promising talent for the future. Part of my philosophy is looking ahead to the future. As well as the players I have signed, I want the youngsters to have an opportunity too. The door is open for every player who is ready, and this is a good message to encourage young players with. In addition it is also good for the scouts because they can show young players that they would have opportunities at Fulham. This is all part of my vision. In France I managed many young players, and they all made it at the top level. I hope for the future that we will have many more under-21 internationals at Fulham.'

The 21-year-old, signed by Kevin Keegan from non-league Rushall Olympic, is remarkably poised and well balanced for someone who is 6 feet 6 inches tall and he seemed completely at ease surrounded by the multi-million-pound talent imported by Tigana. The Fulham manager confided to his Leicester counterpart Peter Taylor after the game: 'That was one of the most impressive debut performances I have seen from any player. This young lad is sure to play for England one day.' Knight, from Solihull, was just happy to have had his first taste of league football and said: 'I felt pretty confident because of the encouragement I've had from the manager. Funnily enough, despite my height, I was not particularly good in the air when I moved to Fulham four years ago but they have worked hard on me.'

Knight was replaced after sixty-three minutes by Kit Symons as part of Tigana's rotation policy. Rotation was being used up front and particularly in midfield. Lee Clark revealed that there were a number of players still coming to terms with the enlarged squad and the new system. He, of course, had competition with the arrival of Malbranque and Legwinski. Clark said: 'It is quite hard when you are in and out of the side. It is pretty hard to get used to because everyone wants to play all the time. It was tough on Kit on Saturday because he had been one of our better performers against Arsenal last week. The manager will make many decisions like this throughout the season and it was good for Zat to get his chance. Hopefully he will be able to do as well as Sean Davis, who also came through the youth team, because that would give us a big boost. He was pretty impressive, but he will get some stick from the lads because he came off after about an hour with cramp.'

TUESDAY, 25 SEPTEMBER
Tony Gale grew up a Chelsea fan, but fell in love with Fulham. The last time the two clubs played, seventeen years ago, the Capital Gold radio commentator and former Hammer was just a promising young Fulham central defender. Gale said: 'Every Fulham fan has been waiting so long for this game, and I'm no different. Chelsea were my childhood sweethearts. I had a season ticket at the Bridge in the days of George Graham and Bobby Tambling. But Fulham were my first true love and I've considered myself a Fulham fan ever since I played there. The place is special to me. Having been a Chelsea supporter it was strange to make my first appearance as a sub at the age of seventeen in a derby match at Stamford Bridge in 1977. When I warmed up I got dog's abuse from most of the 50,000 crowd – and I used to be one of them.' Former Blues striker Kerry Dixon said: 'It's a passionate fixture and many families are even split down the middle between Fulham and Chelsea. I'll never forget when we went to Fulham during that promotion season of 1983 and won 5–3 in a classic. We were always leading but Fulham kept coming back at us and Gordon Davies scored a hat-trick for them. The atmosphere was incredible. You could tell there were Chelsea fans in every part of the ground but even in those bad old days of hooliganism, there was no trouble. The rivalry is strong but there does not seem to be any malice.'

WEDNESDAY, 26 SEPTEMBER
Marcel Desailly, who was relishing the contest against so many French stars, said: 'There will be so many Frenchmen involved it will be just like playing

Arsenal. Fulham have bought a lot of French players and I am happy that there will be six or seven from France on the pitch on Sunday. I don't know any of the French guys as I left France nine years ago, but I know they are quality. It is a small pitch and the ball will be going very quickly. It will be another test for us.

'The whole of Tigana's generation were very important to me. They were an inspiration. They lit the flame. I played in my second game in the French First Division against Tigana, when I was at Nantes and he was with Bordeaux, in 1986. We were all surprised when he came to London to join Fulham. But you can see how he has changed a lot of things at the club. He has changed their diet and got them serious about training. Now it looks as though Fulham could become one of the best teams in the Premier League. If this year they finish in mid-table, maybe next year they will buy other players and become one of the top teams in the country. They don't just throw the ball forward, they pass it around, because they have players who are able to play.'

Desailly felt there were too many derbies in the capital. 'I agree with Arsène Wenger who said it is unlucky to be a London team because you are always playing derbies. But this one is going to be a great game. The crowd and the team have waited a long time for this day. It's going to be an incredible game to play in. Fulham go into the match on the back of a 3–1 home defeat at the hands of Arsenal. Chelsea, however, are undefeated in six games so far this season.'

THURSDAY, 27 SEPTEMBER

Jon Harley eagerly awaited the first Premiership clash of the West London clubs, even though it might upset his family if Fulham beat his old club Chelsea! Harley said: 'When I was growing up you didn't see any derbies between Fulham and Chelsea because Fulham were struggling in the lower divisions. But things have turned around now and a really good rivalry is shaping up. I was a mad Chelsea fan when I was young and it was a dream come true when I got in the Chelsea team. But now I am determined to succeed with Fulham.'

FRIDAY, 28 SEPTEMBER

Anticipation grew about the first West London derby for eighteen seasons, and the first in the top division since the 1967–68 season. Chelsea have visited Craven Cottage twenty-two times in the league, losing on only four occasions.

For the current Fulham team the missing ingredient was a goalscoring formula, after scoring only three times at home and just six times altogether since chalking up ninety in Division One. Collins argued: 'I am not satisfied with what we have achieved so far. We could easily have won two or three of our games, but we have lacked that killer instinct. We have played attractive football but have not been able to finish the job off. Against Chelsea that must change.' Fulham feel they have been guilty of being over elaborate. Collins added: 'We will never abandon our philosophy of getting the ball down and passing it, but maybe there is a case once in a while for hitting the strikers early.' Pitted against the Premiership's early goalscoring pacesetter Jimmy Floyd Hasselbaink, Saha said: 'I rate Hasselbaink very highly. He is possibly the best striker in Europe at the moment and has a good chance of finishing with the Golden Boot. But I am a totally different player to him.' Both players have the speed and acceleration to frighten defenders, but whereas Saha is wily, tricky, skilful and a little unpredictable, the Chelsea player has power and strength, is more direct and predictable, and has a vicious right-foot shot that makes him a danger from anything up to 35 yards out. Saha is not as experienced as Hasselbaink, who is a full international and has played in Holland, Portugal and Spain, as well as in the Premiership. Hasselbaink is also a more selfish natural goalscorer than Saha. There is not a striker in the game who can hit a ball as well as Hasselbaink, while Saha sometimes struggles with his shooting.

Saha will face his closest friend and next-door neighbour William Gallas when he plays against Chelsea. Saha said: 'William is a nice guy and we're very close, but we will be rivals on the field. He has told me he intends to stop me from scoring, but we'll see. I am determined to start scoring goals again. It's been a little while since my last one, but I am confident they will come again. People say there is extra pressure on me because of my two goals against United, but I don't see it that way. I am doing the same things and playing the same way. Defenders now know about me and are marking me closely, but I will score if I just keep shooting as much as I normally do. I don't think Chelsea can win the title. Manchester United and Arsenal are stronger. Yes, Chelsea have plenty of fine players but if I was to put money on the Championship winners I would not back against United. I've already played against them and scored twice. I have yet to face Chelsea but from what I have seen I think United have the edge, especially with their new men Veron and Van Nistelrooy.'

SATURDAY, 29 SEPTEMBER

Max Clifford would not be attending the West London derby even though he was now back from Spain. It was beginning to emerge from inside sources at Craven Cottage that there had been a falling out between Clifford and Al Fayed.

The Hamiltons case had erupted when Al Fayed was on holiday in the south of France on his luxury boat once used by Princess Diana and his son Dodi. Al Fayed felt that by using the Old Trafford press conference, and by giving a TV interview in which he discussed the Hamiltons immediately after the clash with Alaves, Clifford had somehow implicated him in these events. Time had not proved a healer and Clifford had severed links with the football club although he remained, on the same freelance basis, in charge of Al Fayed's PR.

SUNDAY, 30 SEPTEMBER
FULHAM 1 CHELSEA 1

A noon kick-off did not stop the two sets of fans from celebrating the return of this wonderful fixture. Many West London families grew up watching Fulham one week and then Chelsea the next. For the 21,000 fans at Craven Cottage it was a special occasion; at least it was until Chelsea scored, when a feeling of fear went around the ground. Jimmy Floyd Hasselbaink had already posted a warning by hitting the crossbar, and did not miss on the half-hour mark. But this would be the fans' day after all; fifteen minutes of continual chanting of 'Tigana's black-and-white army' from all areas of the Stevenage Road stand spurred the players on, and eventually Fulham hit back through Barry Hayles after Louis Saha had hit the post with a header. One–one was just about the right result.

Ranieri was having even more problems than Tigana. Despite a summer outlay of £35m, his team had already lost leads against Newcastle, Middlesbrough and now Fulham; if they hadn't squandered those six points they would have topped the Premiership. The Italian coach said: 'We can't maintain concentration for long enough. What do I do? I just don't know. It's very difficult. We speak a lot about this problem, but I don't think it's a mental thing. We have to work at this and I just hope the problem will be solved very soon. We have to sort out our problems quickly but we are still unbeaten and it's important to keep picking up points. Fulham played champagne football at times. They have good players, they are our cousins and I hope they can be as successful as we have been.'

Ranieri was depicted as a figure of fun in the media because of his pidgin English which forced him to refuse interviews until he had polished up his use of the language. Improving his vocabulary with regular visits to West End musicals was one way he did it!

Tigana continued with his policy of declining after-match interviews and indeed was still absent from pre-match press briefings. Although, unlike Ranieri, the Frenchman had escaped any media criticism as a consequence, the season had already reached a defining point with his team in the wrong half of the table. Tigana's 'voice' John Collins said: 'We gave Chelsea too much respect early on. But in the second half, when we equalised, I thought we were the better team. We were relieved to be still in the game at half-time. They outplayed us but then we came back at them. It was disappointing that with Chelsea down to ten men and us at home we still couldn't win.'

OCTOBER

Platini lets slip Tigana's thoughts on his future after Gerard Houllier's heart surgery ... Al Fayed has dinner with his manager to offer a new contract...

TUESDAY, 2 OCTOBER

Fulham have been without their club captain Chris Coleman since his horrific car crash last January. Coleman left his Surrey home in his Jaguar late at night, swerved to avoid an animal on the road, and then crashed into a tree. His wife Belinda subsequently called him on his mobile, which was going off in the car, but he could not reach it because he was trapped. Coleman broke his right leg in three places, shattered his ankle and damaged his knee so badly that eventually he would need ten operations to overcome the appalling injuries.

Now Cookie was on the comeback trail, which was a hard, painful process. The crash had left him critically ill and fearing that he would never play again. About the disappointment of missing Fulham's first match in the Premiership, Coleman said: 'I wouldn't like to say I am jealous of the lads but I was sitting there for ninety minutes feeling pretty glum. I had to turn the TV off when I saw Andy Melville, an old mate from Wales, leading the team out at Old Trafford. I was absolutely gutted and thinking that would be me but for this accident.' He still suffered nightmares and had only recently come off pain-killers. Coleman added: 'I have probably had two or three dreams in nine months when I am back in my car but I wake up each time before I crash it. I am lucky. I could have died in the crash. For four months I was in a lot of pain and on a lot of painkillers. It was a nightmare. Doctors would pump me full of tablets and I would go home and take more. But there are only so many you are allowed. I would be lying bunched up in a ball in tears holding my leg because the pain was so bad. I would have my head in my wife's lap and she'd be crying because I was in so much pain.'

WEDNESDAY, 3 OCTOBER

New signing Abdeslam Ouaddou explained how he received his freak training injury. After being hit by a ball full in the face, he suffered some damage to his eye that has needed surgery to correct. 'The ball hit my right eye during training,' he said. 'It was very painful and there was some bleeding inside so I had to have an operation. Afterwards the doctor said that I have to rest for a month. Fortunately, the operation was very quick and straightforward, using lasers, so I shouldn't be out for too long.' Although remaining upbeat, the Moroccan international was obviously frustrated at being hampered in his fight to establish himself in the first team and he went on: 'I'm very keen to get going again. For two weeks I'm not allowed to do anything, but then I can start to do some running and basic exercises.'

THURSDAY, 4 OCTOBER

Welsh under-17 midfielder Matthew Collins signs from Second Division Swindon Town, despite attracting attention from Manchester City. He opted for Craven Cottage on the request of his parents. Swindon chief executive Peter Rowe explained: 'We made the best offer we have ever made to a youth-team player. We really pushed the boat out but his dad sought permission to look elsewhere.'

FRIDAY, 5 OCTOBER

During the enforced break because of international matches Tigana arranged a friendly against Portsmouth at Craven Cottage played behind closed doors, to help ensure that his players' fitness levels are maintained. Fulham fought back to draw 2–2. Goals from Louis Saha and Luis Boa Morte spared Fulham's blushes.

MONDAY, 8 OCTOBER

Worthington Cup opponents Derby parted company with Jim Smith and Colin Todd took over as manager. A press statement issued by the Rams said that the 'Bald Eagle' was offered the role of director of football but had turned down the opportunity and was leaving the club by mutual consent. An early blow for Todd saw Italian defender Stefano Eranio leave the club in protest.

TUESDAY, 9 OCTOBER

John Collins commented that Zat Knight and Sean Davis are keys to Fulham's Premiership future. He said: 'It's vital for any club to produce homegrown talent. If you can get players coming through the ranks, it gives the team a boost.'

Meanwhile, former skipper Simon Morgan, now at Brighton, said he would be supporting the Whites at the Aston Villa game on Sunday. 'I have no regrets at leaving Fulham because there is no way I would be in the team if I'd stayed,' he said. 'But I do keep in touch with everyone. I've been to see them against

Sunderland and Chelsea so far this season, so I'm a lucky mascot because they got four points from those games.'

WEDNESDAY, 10 OCTOBER
FULHAM 5 DERBY COUNTY 2

Worthington Cup success put Fulham's season back on track with their 'Three Musketeers' getting among the goals as the team finally discovered their scoring touch. Second-half strikes from Legwinski, Saha and Malbranque turned the tie around, catapulting Tigana's side into the last sixteen. Derby twice took the lead in a contest unrecognisable from the league game earlier in the season, when Derby put ten men behind the ball. Craig Burley gave Derby the lead, but Barry Hayles grabbed an equaliser before Fabrizio Ravanelli again put the Rams ahead. But it was not for long as Legwinski scored his first goal for the club. A deflected Collins free-kick gave Fulham the lead in the second half, which saw Fulham go into overdrive. Saha came off the bench to score one of the goals of the season, taking on three defenders from the halfway line and tucking the ball just inside the post. Boa Morte then won the penalty which Steed Malbranque converted to round off the rout.

Damiano paid tribute to Legwinski and Malbranque: 'I'm always glad to see our French players scoring. We have not been scoring enough goals in recent matches.' Such a morale-boosting win would have a knock-on effect, Damiano argued: 'This result will give confidence to the whole squad. We played well and had many chances. Derby had one or two chances and scored, but I think it's a logical result.'

New Derby manager Colin Todd was already feeling the pressure and said: 'We have a lack of mental toughness at this club. We approached the game in the right manner but conceded some bad goals. There is an Achilles heel in the team at the moment. We have ability in the side but we are punishing ourselves. There were positives and we equalled Fulham for the first hour, but games last for ninety minutes. I wanted to get away from being overcautious and wanted penetration up front. I think I got that but it is damaging when you then concede such soft goals. I know I need to strengthen the squad and, if I can, we can give a lot of teams a good game.'

THURSDAY, 11 OCTOBER

Tigana talked to 'Fulham Today' about the start to the season. Despite a relatively disappointing seven points from the first seven league games, Tigana remained upbeat and totally focused, saying: 'I think it is not so bad, although we could have taken four more points. We lost two points against Derby and then again at Charlton. Against Manchester and Arsenal there is a big difference in class and I am not unhappy about those results. I am not disappointed with the quality on the pitch because the team try to play good football and this is very important. It has been difficult because of injury problems with all of the new players. Goma's injury, along with those of Legwinski, Marlet and Ouaddou have caused us some problems. It takes time for new players to settle and integrate into the squad. I have spoken with Arsène Wenger and Gerard Houllier and they have said that the French players will need at least six months to settle into a team, to understand the football played in England and also to understand the referees.'

One of Tigana's biggest summer signings was Van Der Sar. Tigana explained why he went for such a high-profile, top-class 'keeper: 'It was a very important signing for the team. We have two good goalkeepers which gives confidence to a team. I think it was difficult at the start for Edwin because of the differences in English football to the continental game. Players can be very aggressive against the 'keeper in this country, but he has progressed very quickly over here to reach the highest level and I think his signing also encouraged other players to join Fulham.'

Although Goma's early-season injury was a big blow, Tigana was pleased it had given an opportunity to another player, Zat Knight: 'We worked very hard with Zat last year to prepare him for this season and there has been a big margin in his progression, so when he plays it is because I believe that he is ready and that he can play at the top level.' Tigana also revealed that despite earlier reports that he is ready to bring in new talent, he remained happy with the squad, at least for the moment: 'I do not plan any more signings for now. I would prefer that we wait and work with this team. If we have a player injured and I feel that we have insufficient cover, then perhaps that situation will change, but not for now.'

Tigana ended with a message of hope for Fulham supporters: 'This season it is my dream that we stay in the Premiership and progress, and then when we have the new stadium that we will be playing in the European Cup. That is my objective, my dream and it is very important for the club and for the fans that we achieve this. I am very happy at Fulham – there is a fantastic atmosphere here.'

FRIDAY, 12 OCTOBER

Marlet boasted he would break his duck in Sunday's game at Aston Villa. Although Marlet has made just two starts since his move from Lyon, he finally felt ready to make his mark in British football in the game which is live on Sky. He said: 'I promise I will score against Aston Villa. It's very good for the team's confidence to score five goals in a game, and I hope we will play just as well against Aston Villa.' The Villa Park date was also special for Zat Knight, who was spotted by Villa playing for Birmingham Sunday League team Romulus, alongside Darius Vassell as a striker! Knight said: 'I hope Darius plays against us. I keep in touch with him and when I go to Birmingham we have a chat and I am delighted to see how well he has done.' Knight wanted to put one over on Villa after one of the club's coaches told him he would not make the grade.

'Villa were my club, all I wanted was to play for them and I was devastated when they rejected me. I just threw myself into schoolwork instead. This game means a lot to me. It was the first one I looked for when the fixtures were published and it will be nice to go back and prove Villa wrong.'

Legwinski relished the chance of playing against Ginola: 'David is one of the best players in the world and I don't know why he isn't guaranteed a place at Aston Villa. Maybe it's a tactical problem or perhaps he can't work with the management; but he's a great player and should have played a lot more times for France.'

Rufus Brevett felt his team has failed to gain the rewards their attacking football deserved and hoped this would change against Villa, saying: 'We must take our chances, like we did against Derby.' However, Villa manager John Gregory had just been awarded the Barclaycard Manager of the Month award following his team's rise to the summit of the Premiership, which was achieved without the services of Ginola.

SUNDAY, 14 OCTOBER
ASTON VILLA 2 FULHAM 0

Not a good day for Tigana. This game typified the failures of the season so far. Fulham dominated the first half, creating a number of chances, but yet again the strikers could not take them. Marlet's promise to score should have been fulfilled with a first-half header, but instead it was Gregory's high-fliers who took their chances. Darius Vassell gave the Midlanders the lead, before substitute Ian Taylor delivered the *coup de grâce*. Fulham kept battling to the end, and Boa Morte won a penalty after being tripped by Steve Staunton, which Saha missed.

Tigana was a bundle of arm movements on the sidelines. He could not quite believe what was happening to his side. Although his philosophy is to instil confidence into his team, he showed signs of running out of patience, saying: 'We have to start getting things right. It is up to the strikers to score goals. We need to improve our confidence and we will do that on the training pitch. We have been playing good football but we have not been getting results. It can not carry on like this. We need to get some points out of the next couple of games.'

John Gregory admitted he had felt the pressure from the threat of Fulham's talented front-line, despite the Whites' failure to find the back of the net. Gregory said: 'I was concerned about Fulham all through the game. If they had scored a goal at any stage then we would have been under a lot of pressure. I remember looking to see what the time was, it was the seventy-ninth minute, and I was feeling concerned, because a goal, even then, would have made it very difficult for us. There is no doubt that they could have scored goals against us. If they had put the penalty away, who knows what might have happened?'

WEDNESDAY, 17 OCTOBER

Managing director Michael Fiddy did not think that the new signings had fully settled in and adjusted to English football yet but remained hopeful about the club's future. He said: 'Against Chelsea nearly all of our summer signings, Van Der Sar not included, were either injured or on the bench – yet we still put in a magnificent performance, despite having around £30m-worth of players not on the pitch. But I think we've already seen their qualities. At the beginning of the season, Jean said that he'd have a better idea of where we'd finish after ten or fifteen games. We've played very well so far and everyone knows that we deserve a few more points than we've got. It will take some time for the new players to settle and you never know what toll injuries and suspensions could have on the season, but if everything goes well I'm sure we'll finish in a respectable position.'

With a spot in Europe firmly in the club's sights, one route there could be via the Worthington Cup, a competition which offers a place in the UEFA Cup. Fiddy was encouraged by Fulham's progress in the early rounds of the competition: 'The match against Rochdale looked like it was going to be a fairly decent start for us, but as we all know they made a great fight of it. The performance against Derby was brilliant. What was most impressive was that with twenty minutes to go, we were able to bring Saha, Malbranque and Boa Morte off the bench, which certainly reflects well on the strength of our squad.'

Fiddy, the driving force behind the new stadium development, also talked about the faltering progress of the project. 'The stadium development is taking an awful lot of time, there's a huge team of people now working on the construction process and the details of the design. We also have a court hearing next Thursday and Friday, which is a judicial review by eleven residents against the decision of the Secretary of State to approve the development. It could cause us some problems but we're confident that we've got a very good case so we don't foresee too much trouble. We've narrowed down our options on a ground-share to two possible locations but there are lots of issues involved so we can't say what they are yet. We could be looking at a decision being made in about a month's time.

THURSDAY, 18 OCTOBER

Tigana faced a major dilemma over who to play in central defence against Ipswich, with Symons declaring himself fit following a hamstring injury, Goma returning and Knight hopeful of keeping his place. Goma, who had missed much of the start of the season, was optimistic of his team's chances of taking all three points against Ipswich: 'I played against them last season and they were very good. For a promoted team to come up and do what they did was exceptional. But it doesn't matter who you play in the Premiership, all the games are hard. Compared to last season, Ipswich are not doing so well, but I think they are still playing with a good spirit even if they're not getting it right technically. It's now time to start winning points, and after the disappointing game at Aston Villa, it's important to do well at home. The spirit in the team is very good and we have a lot of confidence. I would say that Fulham will win on Sunday.'

FRIDAY, 19 OCTOBER
Fulham defender Alan Neilson left the club to join First Division Grimsby Town. Neilson had been taking part in a short trial period with the Mariners and now a deal between him and Grimsby was reached.

SATURDAY, 20 OCTOBER
Fulham issued a statement to clarify the situation concerning the new stadium plans: 'As you are aware, a number of local residents and interest groups issued an appeal in the High Court against the decision by Government Office for London not to "call in" the club's planning application. This hearing was scheduled for 18 and 19 October 2001. On 18 October the High Court adjourned this hearing without, as yet, confirming another date. The club is disappointed with the delay. However, it is hoped that this matter can be brought before the courts at the earliest possible opportunity. This action is one between the stadium objectors and the Government Office for London, and the club is merely an interested party to the proceedings. It does not come as any surprise that the applicants sought to delay the hearing as they will use any tactic to try to drive Fulham FC from its historic roots. The club is confident that such actions will not in any way hinder the development of the stadium. Our advisors will be seeking a new date for a hearing as soon as possible so that the objectors' submissions can be dealt with. We think it speaks volumes that the applicants have done all they can to avoid this opportunity to have their arguments heard.'

SUNDAY, 21 OCTOBER
FULHAM 1 IPSWICH 1
Yet another game Fulham should have won, but ended up with only a point. On a miserable, wet autumn day, the football reflected the conditions. With both teams near the bottom of the Premiership there were obviously some nervous players on the pitch. Fulham as ever took control, and Hayles gave them the lead. He looked like the one confident striker in the team, Saha having been left on the bench, while Boa Morte was playing on the right. Fulham then won a penalty, which should have put the game beyond reach. However, Boa Morte, who insisted on taking it, screwed his shot wide and was left looking distraught. Things got even worse for him when he was sent off just before half-time. Having already been booked for a foul on Wilnes, when he dived in the penalty box the ref had no choice but to give him his marching orders. Playing for the second half with only ten men put Fulham under a lot of pressure but

when the equaliser came through Jermaine Wright it was one of very few efforts on Van Der Sar's goal.

Tigana was furious with referee Mike Riley at the final whistle, and it was left to defender Andy Melville to comment on the game: 'Jean was frustrated and wanted to get his point across. The referee's only got a split-second to make a decision, but there were some decisions we were a bit disappointed with. The lads thought Herman Hreidarsson might have caught Luis with his knee, but referees have got to make instant decisions. Luis is very disappointed. He's obviously down about what happened. He hasn't said anything, and there's not much you can say to someone who's that disappointed.'

The game was watched by Newcastle scouts, who were following the progress of Lee Clark. Although Bobby Robson had been put off in the summer, having shown an interest in the Fulham player, he felt the 28-year-old might yet be prised away.

MONDAY, 22 OCTOBER

Tigana shocked Fulham by revealing he will step down as manager at the end of the 2002–03 campaign. According to his close friend and former French team-mate Michel Platini, he has already decided against taking up the option of a further two years with the club after his contract expires. With Liverpool manager Gerard Houllier's current health problems highlighting the stress managers face, 46-year-old Tigana confided to Platini his plans to leave Craven Cottage. Platini said: 'Management is a crazy job these days and football has become a difficult world. The financial rewards are good but there is a high price to pay for them. Managers live under permanent stress. It is a job that I could not do. I have discussed all these issues with Jean and he told me: "I will carry on for another year-and-a-half and then I will quit." '

Al Fayed, reported to have summoned his manager to dinner to discuss a potential new contract, was deeply alarmed by Platini's comments. Tigana told his chairman that it was too early to discuss this and that he preferred to keep his options open. Al Fayed said: 'Jean is a man of honour. I know he will fulfil the remaining eighteen months of his contract. After that I hope to persuade him to accept the two-year extension which is available.'

Chester Stern reveals precisely what occurred behind the scenes at the Harrods summit meeting: 'A couple of daily papers, the *Mail* and the *Guardian*, carried the Platini quotes taken from a football magazine in France. The *Fulham Chronicle*'s reporter Paul Warburton, who speaks fluent French, contacted Jean direct via the switchboard and, being the local guy, suggested that, perhaps, he might have been misquoted. Jean responded by telling Paul "what Platini says, Platini says". However, when pressed, Jean didn't deny that he had made his comments to Platini, although neither did he concede that he had. In his interview with the local paper Jean said, "I don't look too far in the future," which seemed to suggest that Platini's remarks might have been a correct version of the conversation with Jean and that he was, indeed, thinking about quitting sooner rather than later.

'Tigana was having a meeting with Mohamed that night. Not a dinner as it was reported at the time. Jean goes to see the chairman at Harrods at least once a week, sometimes twice a week, just for a chat. After their meeting I spoke with Mohamed about Jean's reaction to the Platini comments. Mohamed said that Jean was shrugging his shoulders and saying, "I can't recall the conversation with Platini." But he reassured Mohamed that he was not contemplating moving on and that he was fully committed to the club.'

TUESDAY, 23 OCTOBER

Tigana revealed his belief that his foreign legion were the key to the club's disappointing form of just one league win and insisted it would be another three months before they reached their full potential. He said: 'All foreign players take time to adapt to English football, and that is part of our problem at the moment. Many of our new players arrived at the start of the season and not in pre-season because it was difficult for us to sign players then. For us that is the problem but I am sure the team will progress. Tigana pointed to Arsenal's Robert Pires, who spent much of his first season as a substitute after arriving in summer 2000 and who has gone on to be indispensable in the heart of the Gunners' midfield. He added: 'After Robert Pires signed for Arsenal he spent six months on the bench. He needed time to adjust to the different rhythm of the game.'

WEDNESDAY, 24 OCTOBER

Boa Morte hoped to escape further punishment after being sent off against Ipswich. Some pundits suggested Boa Morte should have been sent off for the foul on Wilnes, which would merit trial-by-video at a later date. But the Premier League have confirmed that, just as in the case of Chelsea's Graeme Le Saux's two-footed challenge on Leeds defender Danny Mills, there was no chance of that happening. FA and Premiership rules state that if a referee sees a challenge and issues a card, then that is the end of the matter. This would mean Boa Morte would miss just one match through suspension instead of three.

THURSDAY, 25 OCTOBER

Tigana refused to panic despite being in the midst of a Craven Cottage crisis. The Premiership new boys have hit their first rocky patch since the Frenchman began his reign on the banks of the Thames fifteen months ago, with Fulham's draw against Ipswich their seventh game without a league win. But Tigana remained characteristically cool, saying: 'The solution is confidence, and goals will come with confidence and nothing else. Points are what we need, and we need to win two or three games in succession to build our confidence. We have begun four big games that are very, very important. They are crucial to the club and I see them as the turning point of the season.' The runaway Division One champions are fourteenth in the Premiership – the lowliest of the three promoted teams.

FRIDAY, 26 OCTOBER

Barry Hayles had a simple message for his team-mates: pretty football was not enough. Time to toughen up.

Hayles, who came through the lower divisions, made this basic point: 'We are not nasty enough at the moment. We need a mean streak. I don't think one of our centre-halves has been booked all season. We need to start tackling more firmly and putting the boot in when necessary. I keep saying to our centre-halves that we strikers get kicked all over the shop, but opposing strikers are treated gently. We need to start roughing them up. I think our niceness comes from Jean Tigana, because he keeps saying he wants to play football. But sometimes we have to be stronger.' Hayles said about Boa Morte's dismissal against Ipswich: 'Boa's a winner. He does have a mean streak, but that first offence was never a head butt. He may have caught the guy but he went down like he'd been knocked out. I've seen it from four different angles and the video doesn't lie.'

Having played at non-league Stevenage, before joining Bristol Rovers en route to the Cottage, Hayles has the background to grind out results in a brutal fashion if necessary: 'I am used to people giving me a kick, coming from Stevenage. I am nasty, I have had to be. My footballing background gives me that edge, particularly with me joining the game late.' Forget the beautiful game, let's get ugly against the Saints, insisted Hayles. 'We are just desperate to get the points. An ugly three points, a 1–0, whatever. Send the fans home bored but happy.'

Surprisingly, for someone who was supposed to be on his way out, Hayles had featured in all but one of the nine league games, starting five and scoring three goals. His eighteen goals in the promotion season was more than both Saha and Boa Morte in open play. Tigana had so far employed six different combinations in attack, but Hayles had impressed alongside Marlet, which would mean an extended period for Saha on the bench.

SATURDAY, 27 OCTOBER
FULHAM 2 SOUTHAMPTON 1

At last Fulham got that vital second win of the season in the Premiership. Okay, it came against lowly Southampton, but Tigana was prepared to take a win whichever way he could get it. And, finally, it was one of his new recruits who came good. But not Steve Marlet, as might have been expected. It was Steed Malbranque. Fulham made about a dozen chances and the two that were taken were both scored by Malbranque. The Saints' new boss Gordon Strachan said: 'There is no question the better team won. Fulham were technically better and much quicker than us. Their failure to take their chances left us with a chance, but we would have had to be very lucky to get something out of this game.'

Malbranque scored first only for James Beattie to catch Fulham's defence napping with an equaliser. But Fulham were back in front within a minute as Malbranque converted a Steve Finnan cross. Tigana's assistant Damiano said: 'Seeing all those chances go begging was very frustrating. We've got a lot of new players here and you can't expect them to come in and make an impression straight away. We have to learn to kill teams off when we are on top. Today was important though, simply because we won. For that, we have good reason to be grateful to Malbranque, who is a complete midfield player. He scores goals as well as makes them and he is doing a fantastic job for us. He always goes into games with a good attitude.'

In fact, Malbranque had been the main success of Tigana's summer buys, alongside Edwin Van Der Sar. He possesses the type of strength and skill to unpick a Premiership defence. Malbranque conceded it has taken a while to get used to the chant of 'Steeeeed' from Fulham fans, at first thinking the fans were booing him! But after his double against Southampton he said: 'It is great to hear the fans calling my name, now that I know what they mean. But it doesn't matter who scored these goals, it was the win that was important.'

MONDAY, 29 OCTOBER

The time-consuming, painstaking and jet-setting lifestyle alongside Tigana in pursuit of new players helped persuade Michael Fiddy it was time to move on from the club. Fiddy surprisingly quit as managing director of Fulham Football Club in order to pursue new opportunities after only eighteen months in the job. The newly appointed director of corporate affairs Chester Stern explained: 'Michael always intended to return to the City, and a new baby and the effort involved during the summer accompanying Jean Tigana in his trek around Europe in search of new players were the reasons behind his decision to leave.' Fiddy had joined the club in March 2000, having established a reputation as a talented young lawyer in the specialised field of insolvency and company reconstruction. He was taken on by Fulham with a double brief: to help win promotion to the Premiership and gain planning permission for building a new stadium. With both aims achieved Fiddy felt that it was time to move on.

Commenting on his departure, Fiddy said: 'It has been a privilege to have been involved with Fulham during the incredible journey that the club has enjoyed over the last eighteen months. I am grateful to the chairman for the opportunity to be associated with the club during this exciting period. I would like to thank the chairman, the board, the players, staff and fans for their commitment and the support they have given me during my tenure. Being managing director of this great club has been an honour but I now wish to pursue other opportunities. Fulham is an extraordinary club and I am sure that it will fulfil the dreams of everyone associated with it.'

Mark Collins of Harrods Estates took temporary charge of the business affairs of the club pending the appointment of a successor. Mark has been an active supporter of the club for over thirty years, and was part of the team advising Al Fayed when he first became chairman.

TUESDAY, 30 OCTOBER

After weeks of talks, an announcement was close on a ground-sharing scheme, with the club awaiting details of the consortium taking over QPR. Fulham's plans were held up by the prolonged takeover at Loftus Road because Tigana was deeply concerned about where Wasps' future lay. Tigana didn't want his team's fluent style of football affected by the state of a pitch that would deteriorate with each rugby game. The club were taking Tigana's concerns into account before going ahead with a link with their West London neighbours, while an option remained to switch to the newly developed Upton Park. Plans to share with QPR were approved by the Football League, with the Premier League expected to follow suit.

WEDNESDAY, 31 OCTOBER

A very mobile-looking Chris Coleman joined in an energetic and competitive game of head-tennis with the rest of the first-team squad. A group of youngsters with their parents visiting Motspur Park saw their hero and responded enthusiastically and very vocally.

Chris spoke about what it was like to be part of the media circus: 'I've been doing some commentating on games for Sky Sports, and I've made a few appearances on programmes like *Soccer AM and Soccer Saturday*. It all came about because one of the PR girls who was at Crystal Palace when I was there now works at Sky Television and she rang me up one day to see if I fancied coming along. She knew that I was going to be out for a long time with my injury, and it seemed like a good thing to do. I enjoy it. Not being involved in the games at the weekend, it gives me something to do. I did get nervous the first couple of times I was on, but I'm okay now. You've just got to be yourself and give your honest opinion about things. You won't be able to please everybody but that's the way it is. It's very interesting though, a great experience. It's all off the cuff. They ask you questions, and you just have to come up with what you really think. Because I'm still playing, although I'm injured at the moment, you have to be very careful of what you say about other players; you can't be too critical about what others are doing. You do get a briefing – they give you some facts and figures – so, say you're watching Villa against Southampton, they'll tell you who's playing, if the striker's in good form and how many goals he's scored, that sort of thing. But basically they leave it to you. It's all very relaxed, especially on *Soccer Saturday*. There's a bit of banter and a few differences of opinion, but that's what everybody's there for really, to bounce things off each other.'

Chris had been primed to slip a couple of key words into his commentary.

'Kit Symons is the one who should be doing all this really, he's very good. But he told me I had to get two words into my broadcast: periphery and pedestrian. And I did, in the Villa–Fulham game. They asked me what I thought of the second goal, and I said I thought our defence looked pedestrian, and then I said our strikers had only been playing on the periphery of the game in the second half. So I got them both in. I was meant to say persona as well, but I couldn't quite fit it in anywhere!

'Being on TV isn't always as exciting and glamorous as it appears. It all depends on the game you're watching. It can be a long day if it's not up to much. And if it's not very interesting, then you tend to listen to the guy next to you and watch his screen, which can be a bit dodgy at times. You have an earpiece, and when they say they're coming over to you in ten seconds, and you haven't been watching your game because it's no good, then you're in trouble and you just have to make it up. I've had to do that a few times! The first game I ever did, Villa–Derby, was awful. After ten minutes hardly anything had happened, and the studio kept coming back to me but there was nothing I could think of to say at all. I really struggled all through that. And another time, Swansea against Northampton, I didn't get the team sheet, so I had no idea who was playing, and when somebody scored for Swansea I didn't have a clue who it was.

'But the more you do the more comfortable you are. I did the Copa America in the summer and I really enjoyed that, even though it meant working from eleven at night until five in the morning. I worked with Tony Cottee; we did two back-to-back games, that was great fun. The only difficult bit was trying to pronounce some of the players' names!'

So has Fulham's inspirational skipper got his sights set on a new career? 'No, no, definitely not. I want to stay in the game. I want to stay involved, be in the thick of it. I'm sure it would be a nice life on the telly, but I'd much rather go into coaching. I've no intention of being the next Andy Gray!'

The pleasure Chris got out of being involved in the first-team training session again left no one in any doubt as to where his heart really lies. Chris said: 'I enjoyed the training very much. I was a bit nervous because it was my first one, but it was just nice to be back with the lads again. It was a brilliant atmosphere because there were a few supporters out there, and I think they enjoyed it as well. It was good to join in today, but I'm only at about fifty per cent of my full fitness, so I'm not rushing around. I'm not really at that stage in my recovery yet. I felt a bit stiff afterwards but I trained again in the afternoon just to get rid of the cobwebs, so I feel pretty good now and I have to say it was a real confidence booster.

'It was nice to do it in front of some of the fans, and afterwards we had a chat and I signed some autographs and I got a lot of good feed-back ... They were brilliant, as everyone has been ever since I had the accident. I can't tell you how much I appreciate that. It gives me a great feeling. All in all, it's been a very good day for me. I am growing in confidence that I will be back soon but if I don't make it for this season, I'll be back for the season after. It's been a long, hard haul and I knew it would take a long time. I've had injuries both mentally and physically.' Coleman finished by saying that he cannot wait to play for Tigana: 'He comes across as a nice guy, but he does have a ruthless streak as well.'

Meanwhile Marlet's injury was diagnosed as a kick on the knee and not a repeat of the internal problem that delayed his move from Lyon, while Gavin Rae, who had been watched by Fulham, made it clear he was happy at Dundee and not interested in a move to the club.

NOVEMBER

First Premiership away win . . . Tigana invites Johnny Haynes into the dressing room where he listens to Al Fayed's extraordinary team talk

THURSDAY, 1 NOVEMBER

Steve Finnan ruled out the chance of a players' revolt wrecking the Republic of Ireland's World Cup dream. Mick McCarthy's men faced a trip to Tehran in their two-legged play-off with Iran despite six Chelsea players refusing to travel to Tel Aviv for a first-round UEFA Cup tie first leg. Leeds' Ian Harte was the first to express concerns about the trip, but Finnan said: 'It was the Chelsea players' decision, and they were given a choice either to go or not. With us it's "we all go or none go". Mick McCarthy's been out there, has said he was treated fine and that everything was OK. I'm sure all the players will trust him.'

On a lovely sunny day at Fulham's training ground, Finnan had been nominated to confront the nation's assembled media. In a gruelling session in front of the television cameras and reporters, he comfortably steered himself through the questions on the upcoming Irish trip, and after that ordeal, discussed life in the Premiership for a full-back who cost £600,000 in 1998 and whose value had soared. 'It's been a big step up,' he said. 'The players you are up against are all quality, everything's a bit quicker and you don't get as much time on the ball, so you've really got to be up for every game. It's pretty much what I expected it would be like, but you're never really sure until you actually get there. Now, having played ten games, we're starting to get used to it.'

He added: 'It's a very different stage now, playing at Manchester United rather than the wilds of Bootham Crescent. It's been superb. Old Trafford on the first day of the season with over sixty thousand people there, that's the sort of stadium you want to play in every week. You can't beat it. Even at the Cottage against the big teams the atmosphere is great. When you're playing against all the big names, the David Beckhams or the Patrick Vieiras, you tend to raise your game. I don't think it makes you more nervous at all. You're just glad to be out there and pleased to be playing against those players. It's more of a motivating factor than anything else.'

FRIDAY, 2 NOVEMBER

Bobby Robson rapped Fulham for refusing to switch Newcastle's game at Craven Cottage. Newcastle had written to the Premier League asking for the game on 17 November to be put back twenty-four hours because they had Irish 'keeper Shay Given and defender Andy O'Brien playing in Iran on the Thursday of the following week. With Fulham having Finnan in the Irish squad, Newcastle thought that it would be a formality, but United were told that the original date stood. Robson said: 'I am sorry they have not played ball with us. Fulham don't want to shift the game and it stays on the Saturday.'

Tigana, meanwhile, was focused on the trip to Upton Park. Little wonder. The *Mail* forecast a third successive win for the rejuvenated Hammers: 'Fulham looked a force on the opening day at Old Trafford but seem to have lost their way. The Roeder revival should roll on.' There were problems for Tigana with Ouaddou out for another week with his eye injury, Boa Morte making his last appearance before suspension and optimism over Marlet's knee proving to be ill-founded.

Malbranque warned of the threat of Frederic Kanoute. 'I have not told the others about him yet but I am sure I will have a chance to do that. Kanoute has the talent to score a lot of goals because he is big, fast and good in front of goal.' Kanoute had wanted to join Tigana in the pre-season but now said: 'I'm happy I stayed here and I'll be wholly happy if we can beat Fulham. Tigana is very tough. He's the chief and he knows what he wants to do and how to achieve it. His three French players are also very good. I played in the same French Under-21 team as Saha and he is very quick. You have to concentrate all the time with him because if you don't, he is away and you won't catch him. He had some kind of problem recently, but I think he has solved that now and he could be back in the team.'

SATURDAY, 3 NOVEMBER

WEST HAM 0 FULHAM 2

The most famous recent meeting between the teams, the FA Cup Final of 1975, was brought to mind by the presence of Bobby Moore's 10-year-old granddaughter as West Ham's mascot, who before kick-off was presented with a Fulham No. 6 shirt. But that was all the visitors gave their hosts.

'Fulham are back,' chanted the jubilant fans from the Cottage as the West Ham supporters drifted silently away. It had taken Fulham two-and-a-half months to demonstrate they are coming to terms with the Premiership, but this convincing away display brought many rewards: buoyed by their first taste of triumph on their travels and first experience of back-to-back wins, you could sense a rush of self-belief beginning to course through their veins. The team

Tigana had constructed began to look the part, with two of his newest recruits, Legwinski and Malbranque, summoning the necessary finishing skills to halt West Ham's mini-revival. With Malbranque teasing West Ham from his position just behind strikers Saha and Hayles, this was a majestic performance designed to frustrate and, ultimately, destroy the opposition.

The highlights of a dull first half were a bout of pushing between Hayden Foxe and Barry Hayles, both of whom were booked, and a comical incident in which Nigel Winterburn slid into Bjarne Goldbaek, one of the Fulham substitutes jogging along the touchline. Glenn Roeder admitted that Fulham, 'though an expensive side to put together, have spent wisely' and envied Tigana his matchwinner Malbranque. 'I don't like to say it, but I enjoyed watching Malbranque play. He's excellently balanced and is difficult to get off the ball. We fought Fulham all the way and tried to play a passing game, but it is disappointing to lose. I cannot fault my players' commitment, they fought all the way and played a lot of good football. My only complaint is that we played too much through the middle and didn't get the ball out wide often enough. I knew Fulham would be dangerous as they are a difficult team to play against.' Roeder was unhappy about Fulham's second goal, which came after he claimed Di Canio had been fouled: 'We should have had a free-kick but instead they broke away on the counter-attack and punished us.'

Damiano was delighted by the result. 'We played very well. It was a very important moment in the game when we scored just before half-time. West Ham then had to attack and take risks. That gave us more space and we could have scored more. Steed is a player with a lot of talent who can score goals. He had a big game for us today.' Collins said about his team-mate: 'He's still unknown but teams will know about him soon enough. Steed is small and reminds me of Gianfranco Zola in the way that he likes to take people on, he plays between midfield and the strikers, likes to get the ball at his feet, turn and go at people and is capable of eliminating them very easily. He is only twenty-one, but he is a quiet lad and has settled in very well.' Rufus Brevett added: 'We didn't know much about Steed, although Louis Saha, who played with him at French under-21 level, told us he is a quality player. He showed that as soon as he came here. And he's also got a great name – with that name he should've been a movie star.'

With a performance that belied his thirty-three years, John Collins showed that he is back on the stage where he truly belongs. Masterminding an outstanding performance from the team, Collins was everywhere, leading by example and showing off his superb range of skills, and his ferocious tackling caught the eye as much as his incisive and creative passing. 'There's still a lot more to come from us,' he said. 'We're playing well enough at the moment. There's no doubt that we can only get better. We've new players in the squad who are still adapting to their new team-mates and their new surroundings, and I think we're just going to get better and better.'

SUNDAY, 4 NOVEMBER

The Sunday papers made an interesting day's reading, with reviews full of praise for Jean Tigana's side. The *Independent* wrote that 'Fulham could easily have doubled their season's total of three away goals, but were happy to settle for achieving a first away victory in the Premiership and climbing back above their rivals from the other end of the District Line.' The *Sunday Times* paid tribute to the style of the team's performance: 'When confidence flows through Fulham, when their players feel at home in the environment and at home with their skills, they are a convincing and soothing sight to see.' Meanwhile, Al Fayed was quoted in the *News of the World* that he would willingly sign England captain David Beckham if his manager wanted him. Al Fayed, who claims to have spent close to £100m on Fulham so far, added: 'I would be prepared to spend an even bigger amount to bring success to Fulham.' Al Fayed also hit out at the Government for not backing young, talented footballers in this country and said he wanted to see politicians put money into the game in the lower divisions. 'A lot of talented players do not have the chance because there are not the facilities,' he told BBC Radio Five Live. With no backing for youth academies at lower-division clubs, many of which are close to bankruptcy, new players were being brought in from other countries because of a shortage of fresh talent, according to Al Fayed. He revealed he has been a Fulham fan since the age of 14, and has set his sights on the club emulating Manchester United by winning the Premiership and the Champions League. 'It's a possibility. I am optimistic and I am sure Tigana will deliver. I will leave it to God.'

MONDAY, 5 NOVEMBER

Damiano welcomed the break in the Premiership as last season's First Division champions adapted to life in the top flight. The Premiership newcomers entered the two-week break for international matches to be played after earning their first away win of the season. Coaching staff were satisfied with the performance that lifted Fulham up the table. 'It was a good game for Fulham,' Damiano said. 'West Ham were pushing us and giving us a lot of defensive difficulties. The best way for us to beat them was by attacking.' He confirmed that Marlet would be out until Christmas with a hairline fracture of the leg, which could give Saha the opportunity to force his way into the French squad.

In spite of the positive signs against West Ham, though, Fulham still were not putting the ball in the back of the net on enough occasions. The pace of Saha, Hayles and Boa Morte had unpicked First Division defences, and although at times this has caused Premiership defences problems, too often they have been closed out. Hayles probably reached his limit at the top of the First Division, but he has managed to play in the Premiership through sheer determination. His touch and composure in front of goal, though, are just not good enough. Saha, on the other hand, seems to have had his confidence knocked out of him. At times he has scored brilliant goals like he did against Manchester United on the opening day of the season, but then again he's capable of missing sitters. There are also occasions when he runs down too many blind alleys. Boa Morte has been used as a winger for most of this season, particularly on the right. The Portuguese international would much rather play on the left, but he was most effective for Fulham in the First Division when he was up front. This season though he has had few chances to play as an out-and-out striker, which could be a mistake.

Furthermore, Saha, Hayles and Boa Morte are similar players. Tigana needs more of a target man to help with knock downs and to hold the ball up. He also needs a natural goalscorer, which Steve Marlet has not quite proved to be, especially with his injuries.

TUESDAY, 6 NOVEMBER
Alan Mullery described the win at Upton Park as 'a fantastic result', saying that 'Saturday's performance was Fulham's best showing of the season. You can look back at the Manchester United, Sunderland and Southampton games and say how they were good performances but when you look at the number of chances Fulham created and the way in which they played – against a side very much in form – it was a great result.' Mullery was looking forward to the clash with the Magpies. 'Newcastle are fourth in the Premiership and are playing brilliantly. After the result at West Ham, the Fulham players will feel that they'll have a serious chance of winning three on the trot, especially if they can score first.'

WEDNESDAY, 7 NOVEMBER
A reserve match against Coventry at damp Kingfield saw a return to competitive action for Ouaddou, who partnered the commanding Tom Hutchison in the centre of defence. Gavin Strachan, whose father Gordon was watching from the stands, carried out the formality of sliding the ball past Maik Taylor for an opening penalty. Kevin Betsy's well-weighted through-ball caught the run of Willock who equalised, but Coventry restored their lead in the 52nd minute. Steve Kean gave his assessment: 'It was disappointing by our standards. Our passing game was a little bit off and we never really got into our flow.'

FRIDAY, 9 NOVEMBER
SOCHAUX 2 FULHAM 0
Tigana and his squad departed early from Biggin Hill airfield in the morning for the near-two-hour flight to Belfort Airport, located on the French–Swiss border. Following a very bumpy flight after which some squad members complained of airsickness, the lads made their way by road to the Montbeliard area. Snow began to fall, much to the anxiety of Saha and Boa Morte who both started an anxious search through kit-man Pudsey's bag for some gloves. Unfortunately they only managed to find one pair, and much to the amusement of the other lads, the suggestion was made that they used one each! At the squad's

hotel, Tigana and the squad were warmly greeted by Sochaux officials.

Sochaux, like Fulham, had a glamorous history up until thirty or forty years ago, but since then have fallen on hard times, until last season when they were promoted back to the French First Division as champions. Sochaux's new stadium, the Stade Bonal-Montbeliard is architecturally very reminiscent of Fulham's planned all-seater arena and Fulham got the friendly under way there in bitterly cold conditions, wearing their away strip of red and black. Santos broke through on the right and was able to fire a low cross into the area which was dispatched into the roof of Maik Taylor's net by Mikael Isabey. With Goldbaek in particular looking dangerous in attack, Fulham attempted to claw their way back into the game. However, their few forward raids mostly failed as a result of a poor final ball.

After the break Hayles replaced Saha as Tigana looked to start the second period of the match with more of a physical presence in attack, but Sochaux managed to make it 2–0 on 51 minutes. Following a quick break down Fulham's left an accurate cross by Crucet fell to the dangerous Argentinian Trapasso to fire an angled drive past Taylor. Sochaux were in control of the game for the majority of the match, showing why they are sixth in the French First Division.

Sean Davis gave the England Under-21 side a lifeline against Holland with a well-taken header for his first international goal as England came back from 2–0 down in a crucial European Championship qualifier in Utrecht to force a draw. His goal came from a right-wing free-kick. Despite being surrounded by players, he was able to find the time and space to direct a header just inside the near post. It was a quality strike.

SATURDAY, 10 NOVEMBER
Steed Malbranque got the only goal of the game for France as they took a large step towards booking their place in the Under-21 European Championship finals with victory over Romania in Bucharest. Malbranque fired home from 25 yards to give his side the lead on 8 minutes. 'It's definitely a good result. Of course I would have preferred to win 3–0, but I'm happy with that,' France coach Raymond Domenech said.

MONDAY, 12 NOVEMBER
Being described by Rochdale manager Steve Parkin as one of the best goalkeepers he's ever seen must come as a great boost if you've been limited to four first-team appearances in the last two years. Offered the opportunity to sharpen his skills with the Third Division high-fliers, that's the situation for American international Marcus Hahnemann. 'I've gone to Rochdale on a month's loan,' he said at the training ground. 'And at the moment I've got one more game left to play. I was reluctant to spend too much time away from my family, but Steve Parkin was happy for me to spend one or two days training down here with

Fulham, and then one day training a day or two before the game with them, so I took the chance. It's been very hectic, but every week is a different schedule. We've had a lot of midweek games, so I've really missed only one training session a week with them. For example, after a game I travel back on Wednesday, train here on Thursday, go back up Thursday night, train with them Friday, play Saturday, come back Saturday night, and so on. That's obviously a lot of travelling back and forth, but it's worth it just to get the chance to get some games. I've played six times for them now, kept four clean sheets, and I've one match left. Rochdale are a very good team, they work hard and play well together as a unit. In the last game I don't think I had a save to make, although I had to come for a few crosses in the last fifteen minutes. After the game everybody's saying: "Great game, Marcus," and I'm thinking that I didn't make a save. But that's a nice situation to be in. The team has been playing very well, has been very organised and efficient, and that's a good environment to be getting the best out of yourself.'

Marcus explained that the reason for the loan spell was an injury crisis at Rochdale: 'Their regular goalkeeper picked up an injury, a cartilage problem, so they needed cover for four weeks. At the moment, though, his injury is taking longer to heal than they originally thought, but I've no idea what's going to happen after my last game. Steve Parkin has been rumoured to be going for the Barnsley job, and I don't know if Fulham want to let me go for another spell or if Rochdale can afford it, so it's all up in the air a bit at the moment.' Hahnemann's case demonstrates that while the loan system has its critics, it can be a situation where everyone wins. 'It's definitely helped me,' he said. 'I will have played seven games in a month, competitive games, two a week, and I haven't had much opportunity to do that for a while. I've really enjoyed it. We won at Luton the other week, it was a really good game and I picked up an injury, but I kept playing because it all meant so much. You can forget what real games are like when you're in the reserves. Another good thing about going on loan is that playing games again is going to be a big help in getting me noticed. I still have ambitions to win more caps for the States. They're going to be taking three 'keepers to the World Cup, so there's no reason why I can't be one of them.'

At the beginning of a season in the Premiership, Hahnemann had to deal with discovering the club had just spent £7m on one of the best 'keepers in the world. 'You definitely have days when it's difficult,' he said. 'You could look on it as a hopeless situation, but you can't take that attitude, you can't go around feeling sorry for yourself. Once you realise that's what you're doing, then you've got to become more determined and get yourself focused. You've got to work hard every day in training because there's always going to be a chance that you're going to be called on, and you can't say you'll be ready in a month, you've got to be ready now. Injuries and suspensions happen and they can happen quickly. When that chance comes you've got to take it.'

TUESDAY, 13 NOVEMBER

Maik Taylor, demoted to second choice 'keeper with the arrival of Van Der Sar, had been restricted to two appearances, both in the Worthington Cup. Although at the age of 30 he had accepted a new four-year contract when the Dutch 'keeper signed, he had an agreement with Tigana to review the situation at the end of the season. He said: 'The manager gave me his word that, if nothing changes, we will sit down and talk again at the end of the season. He made it clear to me he needs a big squad, at least for this season. The fact that I've signed a new deal is good for my family but the bottom line is I'm not playing. That might mean looking for another challenge somewhere else.' Taylor captained Northern Ireland in a 2–1 friendly win over Macclesfield at Moss Road and derived great pleasure from the game. 'It was good to get another run-out and it helps keep me sharp. But it is frustrating not playing. Fulham have had a couple of great results, two wins on the bounce, but it's difficult really to feel part of it.'

In a training session at Motspur Park, some of the players practised shooting from outside the area, peppering Van Der Sar with shots. He dealt with most of the shots fairly comfortably – except for those by Andrejs Stolcers, the Latvian international who had starred in the Champions League for Shakhtyor Donetsk prior to his move to the Cottage. After coming on as substitute against West Ham, his first appearance since the first game of the season, Stolcers was anxious to shoot his way back into the team. 'West Ham was my first match since Manchester United, so it was very good for me to come on and be part of the game. It was late when I came on, but I am happy to take any chance.' With such an influx of midfielders this season, competition for places was fierce. 'It's a very good position for the club to be in, and when the club is doing well that's good for me and all the other players. There are a lot of very good players here, and when everyone trains and practises together, everybody gets something out of it. I certainly enjoy training very much.' Andrejs played a full game in the friendly against Sochaux. 'I enjoyed it because I played the whole game with the first team. It was a bad result but I saw it as an opportunity for me. After the game, as I always do, I was thinking of all the things in the game, the things I did well or badly. It was a good experience for me, but I really need to score a goal. I had a one-on-one with the 'keeper which I missed, and it would have been a good time to score for the team. That was disappointing. As it was, we didn't score at all in the match.'

Andrejs also talked about playing football in a strange country. 'I'm very happy now in London, and so are my family. It's a very different life from what we are used to in our country, but it's been a very good move for us. We like it here. I was on a six-month loan at Spartak Moscow from Shakhtyor Donetsk when Fulham came in for me. It wasn't a difficult decision on the football front to come to Fulham, but there are a lot of other things to think about when moving your family to a different country. The whole business of work permits and visas is all very difficult. I was pleased to come here, even though it meant giving up Champions League football. It's all excellent experience for me. Fulham is a very ambitious club which wants to play in the Champions League itself. It's not going to be easy, but I think we will get there.'

Andrejs was currently in the middle of an international suspension, having notched up more than fifty caps for Latvia. 'We were playing at home against Croatia, we won a free-kick, there was a little bit of pushing and shoving to make space, and the referee suddenly showed me a red card. I couldn't believe it. I asked him what it was for and he said that the linesman had told him I'd kicked a player in the face. I still can't believe it. So that's three games out, which is terrible for me. I missed the game against Scotland, and next year I will miss two European qualifying games. I was a regular with the team, but I don't know what will happen when I'm available again. It might work against me that I'm not playing regular first-team football. International coaches need players who play week in, week out, and I understand that. It's difficult, but once again all I can do is work hard.'

WEDNESDAY, 14 NOVEMBER

Lee Clark battled hard to sort out the knee problem that prevented him playing in the last two games. With the long-awaited match against Newcastle coming up, he was desperate to be fit to play against his old club. The influential midfielder spoke about how difficult it had been for him over the last few weeks. 'It's been quite a frustrating one. The injury came on a couple of weeks ago in training, and when I had it scanned they found there was a bit of bone bruising and a bit of a problem with the medial ligament. But the peculiar thing is I don't really know how it happened. I don't remember getting kicked or anything. It was gradually getting worse and worse and in the end it got so bad I had to stop training. I thought I'd be all right for the Southampton game, and then when I missed that I thought it would just take another couple of days, but it still wasn't improving and now two matches have gone by, which is hard for me because I'm not really used to missing many games.' Having lapped the Motspur Park training complex several times, Lee was hoping finally to overcome his injury setbacks: 'It's started to improve now. I'm back doing a bit of running and it's all about what sort of reaction I might get now. It's not the sort of injury where if you get pain you can play through it. My target is to be ready for selection for Saturday, and hopefully I will be fine by then.'

His love affair with Newcastle is well known. 'It's a game I'd love to play in, a massive one for both clubs. Both teams are coming off the back of good results and good performances so it's a big game anyway, but it's extra special for myself. On the park there's no question of any divided loyalties. I'm very professional. When I go out and play for teams I always do my best. Newcastle are playing very well at the moment. They've had a good start to the season so it's going to be a very tough game, but they all are in this division. They'll come down and try to win the game. They've got some very exciting players, good attackers and they'll be looking to get after us, so it promises to be a very good game.'

Boa Morte played in a farcical international friendly against Angola in Lisbon. The game was abandoned when Angola were left with just six players following four red cards and seven deliberate substitutions. When Helver Vicente claimed he was injured as his side trailed 5–1, the visitors were effectively left with just six players, which forced the 67th-minute abandonment. Boa Morte, who was attempting to establish himself on the full international stage, came on as a 37th-minute sub and scored Portugal's fourth goal. His agent Amadeu Paixco said Boa Morte was stunned by the events unfolding around him. 'He's not very happy,' said Paixco. 'Not because of the football itself, but because the opposition didn't behave themselves. They had three people sent off before half-time and Luis didn't like it because of those scenes. He's never played in a game like that.'

THURSDAY, 15 NOVEMBER

The three-day High Court appeal before Mr Justice Collins by residents opposed to Fulham's new 30,000-seater stadium concluded. Lawyers opposing the scheme said the new stadium would have a 'damaging and massively intrusive effect'. There were also objections to the Government's decision not to hold a public inquiry after the local council gave planning consent. The judge's ruling was expected before the end of the season.

FRIDAY, 16 NOVEMBER

Johnny Haynes was finally able to take up an invitation to return to the Cottage. His scheduled appearance tomorrow had Alan Mullery eulogising about the club's greatest ever player: 'Many Fulham supporters are going to get their chance to see, quite possibly, the best player ever to have worn the black and white of Fulham. Haynes was the instigator of my move to the club back when I was a young lad – he was one of my boyhood heroes. Back then I was a QPR supporter because I lived in Notting Hill. One day I was given two tickets to go and see Fulham play and I went just to see Johnny Haynes. I'd never been to Fulham before in my life, so that was an opportunity to see him close up. Shortly after that match I got the chance to join the club as one of the ground staff, with the opportunity to be around the England captain and one of the greatest footballers I'd ever seen, so I jumped at the chance. The most outstanding memory I have of Haynes was his ability to pass the ball fifty or sixty yards and knock it on to a sixpence. It was absolutely magnificent. I can hardly remember a time when he gave the ball away. I have no doubt that he would have fitted in easily with today's game, purely for the simple reason that he had ability. If he were in the modern game, training with modern methods, he would be a star. I remember when I was on the ground staff sweeping the terraces, I'd watch him come out after training – they used to train at the ground in those days. He'd step on to the pitch from the Cottage, lay his bath towel down near the corner and take a dozen or so balls over to the other side, near the halfway line. From there he'd hit ball after ball and they'd all land on the bath towel. It was amazing.'

The match against Newcastle saw the return to Fulham of another old boy: Bobby Robson. Mullery recalled: 'I played with Bobby for two years. He came back to Fulham in 1962 after Fulham had sold him to West Brom. He played on one side of the half-back line and I played on the other side.' Robson, the grand old man of English football, was just 35 and only nine months into his first job in management when Fulham sacked him one November afternoon in 1968. The Newcastle manager remembered: 'I was driving home over Putney Bridge when I spotted the *Evening Standard* billboard. It said: "Robson sacked". I was white. I tried to think of any other manager in the country called Robson but soon realised it was me. I knew nothing about it. I couldn't believe it. I'd only just left the ground. I stopped the car and bought the paper. I read that I'd been sacked. I didn't know what to do, so I drove home and said to my wife Elsie: "What are we going to do?" We had three children and a mortgage. Christmas was round the corner and I was suddenly out of work. I rang the club. Everyone was embarrassed. They asked me to go in the next morning to meet a guy called Eric Miller to discuss compensation. Tommy Trinder was the chairman then but the real boss was Miller, who later shot himself. When I met him I remember asking to keep the company car. "You can't leave me without a car," I said. I had a three-year contract but they sacked me after nine months, three of which were in the close season. Had they told me I'd be on trial for the first nine months, I wouldn't have signed the contract. I remember walking out to the middle of the pitch. I'd been at Fulham for twelve years as a player. I was really angry and upset. I didn't break down but I shed a tear or two. I remember vowing that I'd never return to the bloody place again.'

Robson smiles at the memory now. In the ensuing decades, he's proved Fulham wrong countless times, with Ipswich, England, PSV Eindhoven, Sporting Lisbon, FC Porto, Barcelona and now Newcastle. He was the Fulham manager when Newcastle last played at Craven Cottage in the top division. Embroiled in a fight for survival at the foot of the table, the Fulham of Haynes, Les Barrett and Fred Callaghan nonetheless beat Newcastle 2–0 in April 1968. 'They were bottom of the old First Division when they appointed me manager and I couldn't save them. We started the following season quite well and were eighth when they sacked me. It obviously wasn't good enough for Mr Miller. I've had no other experience in football to equal that blow to my esteem as a young coach. When I finished playing, I qualified as a coach with Don Howe and committed myself to that path in life. Then they suddenly slammed the door in my face. I was worried stiff. I remember going to the Labour Exchange to sign on the dole but I was too embarrassed to go through with it. I'd promised the kids that we'd have a TV for Christmas and I didn't want to disappoint them, so I went to Radio Rentals in Weybridge. The guy sat me down and we filled out the form. "Occupation?" he asked. I said I was unemployed. I could hear him thinking: "How are we going to get our money?" I remember saying to him: "Trust me. Please." '

The three young Robsons had their TV in place for Christmas and early in 1969 Ipswich asked him to become manager at Portman Road. A year later they were bottom of Division One but, with great foresight, offered him an extension to his contract. 'At Ipswich I had the best job anyone could get. They gave me time to get it right. I was there for fourteen years. I was helped by an understanding board of directors who treated defeat and victory much the same,' Robson said.

Robson also described his time at Ipswich as a 'tranquil experience': 'It prepared me for the England thing,' he said. 'I was reading the other day about Gerard Houllier's illness and realised that I'd never once been to the doctor complaining of stress. I like Gerard. I admire what he's achieved. I wrote to him and told him that I didn't think anyone would repeat his achievement of winning five trophies. When he brought Liverpool to St James's Park he gave me two bottles of French wine and then beat us 2–0. I hope he makes a full recovery, but I do think we make too much of stress in this business. There's always a get-out for those who can't cope: get a job that doesn't give you a headache. I come from a mining village in the north-east and know that the bloke working in drudgery, trying to support a family on low pay, is the one under pressure. I don't think our game has ever been healthier. I'd love to be a player today. Look at what they're earning. A top player can retire at thirty-five and never work again. When I was captain of West Bromwich Albion and England's right-half I had to live in a house near the ground because I couldn't afford a car to get me to training.'

Today Robson is wealthy, famous and rightly regarded as something of a national treasure. 'I can't give up football now,' he said with a grin. 'I've no desire to spend every Saturday afternoon in Tesco. I have a twelve-month, roll-on contract. Every day I've got twelve months to go. Suits me nicely.'

Meanwhile, Saha intended to use the advice given to him while on loan at St James's Park by none other than Alan Shearer. Saha, who made eleven appearances for the Geordies in 1999 without making much of an impact before returning to Metz, said he rediscovered his form partly on the advice he got from Shearer: 'It was a pleasure and a tremendous experience to play alongside one of the top strikers in Europe. Shearer showed me how to gain confidence and to stay confident no matter what. He gave me great advice and I've always appreciated it. I enjoyed it at Newcastle despite it not turning out the way I wanted it to. But it put me in good stead for this season and I'm thankful to Alan especially.'

SATURDAY, 17 NOVEMBER
FULHAM 3 NEWCASTLE UNITED 1

Tigana invited Haynes into the dressing room before kick-off where his chairman was addressing the team as usual. Chester Stern remembered the scene. 'Jean asked to meet Johnny Haynes in his office before the game and took him into the dressing room. He came out chuckling and looked at me. "Blimey," he said, "in my day we never had a pep talk quite like the one the chairman just gave." I was out of earshot but Mohamed likes to say, "We've got to have a result so I hope none of you have been having too much sex, no one must have sex forty-eight hours before the game, and if I find out any of you have been I will cut off your willies!"

Nostalgia was soon in the air on the field with Bobby Robson warmly applauded into the opposing dug-out. Fulham then proceeded to put on the sort of performance to make the occasional observer wonder how they can have been short of goals at home. Some of the passing and movement was a delight, and two of the goals were outstanding. Robson was at a loss to explain his side's woeful record in London which left Newcastle without a win in the capital for four years, a winless streak of twenty-seven games since their last victory, at Crystal Palace. Shearer, who missed a dubious penalty following an innocuous tackle by Goma, was outshone by the irrepressible Saha. After scoring twice in the opening-day defeat at Manchester United, Saha had endured a barren spell and was understandably happy with his performance: 'I was delighted with the goal and it meant a lot to score against Newcastle,' he said.

The third Fulham goal, which properly put the game beyond Newcastle's reach, arrived on 70 minutes, when Malbranque's left-wing corner skidded off the head of Andy O'Brien and was headed in by Hayles. 'You'll never win in London,' cried the Fulham fans and at 3–1 up with ten minutes to go they could be fairly confident that Newcastle would be travelling home without breaking their jinx in the capital. When seconds later Shearer missed the penalty, the Geordie fans knew it too.

For Lee Clark victory over his hometown club was an emotional experience: 'It was a special day. It was the right outcome at the end for me personally because I'm at Fulham now and we wanted the win. Everyone knows how I feel about Newcastle United but it wouldn't be right for me to go out there and not give my best for this club because I've had total support from my first day here from the fans.' On the game itself Clark said: 'It was pretty even for the first ten or fifteen minutes. They pegged us back a little bit but we opened them up, then scored a tremendous goal which changed the game for us. We dominated from that moment. We probably played some of our best football of the season during the first half and with the confidence now flowing there's no telling what we're capable of.'

On the debatable spot-kick Clark added: 'It was never a penalty. I've just been talking to Alan about it and he knows.' Clark insisted that he and the other lads would resist any temptation to dye their hair Saha-style after he hit his wonder goal at the Putney End. 'I don't think so ... but knowing Louis he'll probably be putting on a bit more every week now in the hope that it works every time!'

Tigana was considering adding to his squad ahead of a month featuring games against Leeds and Manchester United: 'December is a big month as we have seven games and we need a bigger squad. I would like my team to finish between eighth and twelfth, but the priority for the club is to stay in the top flight. My vision is to get 41 points. We'll try to get those points and then it's possible to dream about more than that. I'm happy today because we played a very strong team, and when we led 2–0 I was very relaxed on the bench. It was very important to win at home. This was a very strong team performance, and some people have said it was the best so far this season. My feeling is that we got three points and that was what was important.'

SUNDAY, 18 NOVEMBER

More praise for Tigana's team in the Sunday and Monday papers ... The *Independent* wrote that 'Jean Tigana's English may be less fluent than his team's football but, like the players, he is growing into his new status, and felt confident enough to address a post-match press conference for the first time at Craven Cottage.' The *Guardian* reported 'a thoroughly deserved Fulham victory and a scoreline to flatter a Newcastle side which came to London with an outside chance of sharing the lead at the top of the Premiership table – had they won.' The *Sunday Times* described Fulham as 'far the livelier, more penetrative, more inventive team' while the *Sunday Telegraph* wrote that 'Saha has lost a little confidence after his lively start to the season, as a complete mishit after seven minutes seemed to indicate, but the goal he hit after 19 minutes should rectify that.'

MONDAY, 19 NOVEMBER

A number of first-team candidates emerged from a reserve 'trial' with Spurs to put themselves in contention for the Bolton trip. Boa Morte was free from his suspension while Clark played the full game in the 2–1 defeat. Eddie Lewis, the United States midfield player, had only just resumed running after an ankle ligament injury and was still several weeks away from full fitness.

TUESDAY, 20 NOVEMBER

Sean Davis, who has been on top form, despite being overshadowed by Legwinski for the last few games, talked honestly about his season so far, saying: 'I'm only young, it's my first season in the Premiership, and I've still got loads to learn. I'm inexperienced at this level. I've just got to keep working hard on the training ground and keep learning things from the likes of Lee Clark and the Gaffer, and then hopefully it will come right.'

It had taken Fulham, as a club, the first ten or so games to get the feel of the Premiership. Sean spoke about his own experiences: 'The difference is in Premiership players' first touch compared to First Division players, and the way that they keep possession so well. The players are a lot sharper, a lot quicker. You need to think more about what you're doing and be more aware of what's going on around you, but you've got less time to do it, so you've really got to be sharp and you've also got to be really fit. If you're not one hundred per cent fit then you're going to struggle. Arsenal were the best team we've played this season, and really, every player in that side was top class, from Pires through to Vieira. They were so sharp you could hardly get near them, you always seemed to be behind them. When they brought Bergkamp and Wiltord on at the end it showed how much depth they've got. It wasn't exactly a wake-up call to the Premiership, because we've always known it was going to be difficult, but it did show us what we had to do. I think we've done well for a newly promoted team. In some of the games we haven't scored that crucial first goal and we've been punished for silly mistakes, but we're on a run now. We've turned the corner, are scoring goals and winning games, and hopefully we can keep that going and really push ourselves up the table.'

WEDNESDAY, 21 NOVEMBER
Steve Marlet vowed to return before Christmas, insisting he could still force his way into France's World Cup squad. Talking in an interview in *L'Equipe*, Marlet said that the move from Champions League hopefuls Lyon would not cost him a place in Roger Lemerre's World Cup squad. Marlet's injury jinx began almost as soon as he signed. He explained: 'First I got injured with the French team in Chile. When I came back, I took a knock on exactly the same place in training. It was bad luck but I had to wait before I could make my debut. It's the first time since the beginning of my career that I've had such injury problems. It's very difficult to live through, but I don't have the blues. I'm not too depressed, I would be much more bothered and worried if I was suffering from muscular problems.'

THURSDAY, 22 NOVEMBER
Tigana, who cares about everything to do with football, not just how his team does on the pitch, talked about his main problem since coming to England: referees. Last season he had felt they hindered a football-playing side because they did not give enough protection to the flair players and he does not feel things have been any better in the Premiership. Tigana was furious about Boa Morte's red card against Ipswich. 'Luis Boa Morte should not have been sent off and he should have won a penalty. These were not good decisions. I have seen the tape many times now and I am very disappointed about it. It is a big sanction against us. For the game to progress we must help the referees to protect it first, and that is my vision. I want to meet with the referees and the people who work around football to explain exactly what my vision is. I do not

like to speak to them in the newspapers or on the television. I like to speak to them in person and show them tapes and explain to them how I see the situation. If we can achieve this we will be in a fantastic position in England. The priority is to protect the game. Managers make mistakes, and referees make mistakes, and we must also accept that referees are only human. But we need to start a debate on the subject – not only me but other managers too.'

FRIDAY, 23 NOVEMBER

Tigana gave his opinion on France playing Australia in a friendly. While Wenger was against the game, since three of his players had to make two twenty-four-hour flights, Tigana saw it differently: 'My opinion on this reflects what I always say to the internationals at Fulham, both English and foreign. The priority is the national team. I did not understand why many clubs in England did not want their players to go to Australia. If this is the case then you should never buy international players. If you don't want this situation then you should only buy English players. I played at the top level for a long time and the priority for me was always the national team. At Fulham the priority for young players must be the English national team. It is very important to respect the national team.'

Saha was buoyant after his first goal in almost three months. 'This has made a big difference to my confidence and I know there will be many more goals to come now,' he said. Lee Clark was anxious after remaining on the bench in the last match, but hoped he might be used for tough away assignments such as Bolton: 'I know the squad system but I wouldn't like to think the manager would just use me when we are up against it. I'm not happy if I'm not playing.'

Bolton boss Sam Allardyce believed Tigana was paying the price for having too much money to spend. He argued: 'They were the best side in the First Division last season, and having spent such a lot of money to improve their squad Fulham should be a lot better than last year. The possible downside they are facing is that they have brought in all of these new players and are now not so fluent as a team.'

SATURDAY, 24 NOVEMBER
BOLTON 0 FULHAM 0

Tigana was not too despondent with the result, explaining: 'Bolton were difficult to play against because they play very deep, often with nine and sometimes ten men behind the ball. Ricketts was often the only player up front. They do not win many games at home but because of the way they play they are very difficult to beat – they are very strong and were hard for us to manage. It is not possible to criticise their system because it has won them many points but it is a very different system to the one we use. Many managers are happy to draw matches away from home, but I prefer to win. However, we did not have the chances to win this game so I am happy with the draw.' Since Liverpool lost at the Reebok, a goalless draw seems a reasonable result. But after three wins on the trot Fulham wanted to extend their winning run, and the extra two points would have put them equal with Chelsea.

More worrying was the struggle to make any proper chances, although the clean sheet was welcome. Once again Tigana refused to meet the press after the game, so Damiano emerged from the dressing room to talk instead. 'We weren't afraid to play here,' he said, 'but perhaps we needed to take more risks. We arrived with respect and good intentions and I think we played well. We didn't have any good chances to score, but have ended up with a point away from home.'

John Collins insisted Fulham were well worth a share of the spoils, saying: 'I felt that a draw was a fair result because we were playing a very confident Bolton team. Our problem was that we didn't create enough chances to win the game, which you must do at this level.' Collins believes all three newly promoted sides, Fulham, Bolton and Blackburn, all have the capability to retain their top-flight status.

MONDAY, 26 NOVEMBER

Barry Hayles signed a one-year extension to his current contract to stay at the club until the end of June 2004. The £2m buy from Bristol Rovers has become a favourite among the Cottage faithful after a relatively slow start to his career at the club. Despite talk that he would leave in the summer after Wolves and Portsmouth showed an interest in him, Tigana made Hayles feel wanted and he has repaid the manager by scoring five goals so far in this season's Premiership campaign.

Boa Morte talked about his personal anguish surrounding the Ipswich match when he missed a penalty and was red-carded for an alleged dive. He revealed he had desperately wanted to score that day for the sake of a close friend left paralysed by a car crash. Boa Morte said: 'My best friend was in a coma after a car accident. I was wearing a message for him under my shirt and prayed I would get the chance to score. The team let me be the penalty-taker, but the pressure was too much. It ran through my mind as I ran up. That's not very professional. I should have been focusing on finding the net but I wanted that goal too much. After I got sent off I felt so bad. What should have been a special day became a personal disaster. I let so many people down.' Boa Morte is determined to make his mark on the Premiership and has taken advice from Patrick Vieira, who has suffered disciplinary problems of his own. 'Patrick is a good friend, and he gave me some advice about discipline over the summer,' he said. 'I know my enthusiasm can get the better of me and I receive too many yellow cards, this comes from my desire to please and do well for the fans.'

TUESDAY, 27 NOVEMBER

Fulham thrashed Oxford 5–1 in an entertaining friendly reserve fixture at Motspur Park, taking the lead on 40 minutes after a Bjarne Goldbaek free-kick could only be pushed out by the Oxford 'keeper for the watching defender to slam home a bizarre own-goal. Just before half-time, Stolcers was brought down on the left of the penalty area and the Latvian international calmly stepped up himself to make it 2–0. Oxford pulled one back on 49 minutes but any hope of a comeback ended on 58 minutes when Kevin Betsy fired home. The scoring was rounded off by two well-taken headers from Kieran McAnespie, who produced an impressive performance after replacing Eddie Lewis at half-time.

WEDNESDAY, 28 NOVEMBER

Steve Finnan looked forward to the prospect of playing in the World Cup, but said he was concentrating on producing the goods for Fulham. Knowing that good performances for Fulham would not only benefit the Cottagers but also keep him in the forefront of Mick McCarthy's thoughts during the build-up to the tournament, Finnan said: 'I'm very excited. This is a very big season for me. I've worked really hard over the last few years to make the leap from being a Second Division player with Notts County to playing in the Premiership. Now hopefully I can take it a step further and play in the World Cup finals as well.'

Chris Coleman, still recovering from his car crash, would lift the Worthington Cup for Fulham if they win the competition in February. Temporary captain Andy Melville would stand aside to let him hold the trophy aloft at Cardiff's Millennium Stadium. Melville announced the planned gesture, which was a big boost to Coleman in his journey back towards full fitness: 'I am only the stand-in. He is still the club captain and it would be brilliant if we got to Cardiff. He is at the training ground all the time and progressing well. I think he is training more than anyone. He is in earlier and leaves later. He has a presence about him which we still miss. But the lads are seeing him more and more in the dressing room.' Coleman is ahead of schedule in his rehabilitation, joining in first-team five-a-side matches last week, and hopes to be playing again by the end of the season after initially being told he would not be jogging until next year. But Coleman was taking nothing for granted: 'You cannot be too confident because you do not know what is around the corner. In the last few months I have made incredible progress. I did not expect to be joining in training with the ball yet but we are not going to rush anything.'

Coleman, Melville and Symons all have caps for Wales and a Worthington Cup Final appearance at their national stadium would mean a great deal to them. While Coleman believes Fulham's main focus should be a respectable finish in the Premiership, he added: 'I think we have a big enough and good enough squad to go far in one of the cup competitions.' Tigana lined up a session of penalty practice just in case the tie against Spurs was not decided in normal time. Fulham do not have a good record from the spot in recent seasons, with a string of players guilty of misses. With so much at stake, Tigana was leaving nothing to chance. Captain Andy Melville said: 'We'll be practising penalties on Wednesday and every single player in the squad will take one.

We'll see who is most confident, but I would certainly volunteer to take one if needed.'

THURSDAY, 29 NOVEMBER
FULHAM 1 SPURS 2
Glenn Hoddle celebrated what he called a 'romantic night' at Craven Cottage as Tottenham secured a quarter-final place in the Worthington Cup with a late victory. But for Fulham fans there was nothing romantic about it; it was a case of so near yet so far. However, from the teamsheet it was obvious that Tigana did not place the Worthington Cup very high on his list of priorities. He left out Van Der Sar, Brevett, Melville, Malbranque, Legwinski and Saha from the starting line-up and though the next league game was only a matter of days away, Fulham fans would surely have preferred to see a full team on display. For Tottenham, Sergei Rebrov and Simon Davies, with an 86th-minute winner, made the most of rare starting roles by scoring the goals which set up a home draw against Bolton in the last eight, despite Hayles' equaliser on the stroke of half-time.

Tottenham faced an FA inquiry after supporters threw missiles, mostly plastic macs, in the direction of Boa Morte as he attempted to take a corner. Boa Morte was not hit, but he handed a lighter to the officials and Tottenham, already under investigation following Sol Campbell's stormy return to White Hart Lane, came under immediate FA scrutiny after referee Mark Halsey included the incident in his match report. Hoddle nevertheless had fonder memories of the evening as Tottenham gained a measure of revenge for being knocked out of the competition at the same stage two years ago by Fulham. Speaking after the match, Hoddle declared: 'I haven't been here for so long and it's such a quaint stadium, there's something special and endearing about it. It's lucky to come here and get a win. The club were here a couple of years ago in the same competition and got spanked 3–1 so it's nice to reverse that result.'

Tigana made six changes and ultimately paid the price for fielding a half-strength line-up. 'I kept people out because I was looking ahead to our game against Leeds,' explained Tigana. 'For me, that is a bigger game. We have one day less to prepare for a game against Leeds and Sunday's is a very important game.'

DECEMBER

'I think I'll go and put my head in the fridge' ... Tigana after the defeat at Spurs

SATURDAY, 1 DECEMBER

Louis Saha insisted Robbie Fowler had taken the easy option by joining another English club, Leeds, for £11m, rather than moving abroad. Saha said: 'Fowler is such a good striker that he could have chosen any of the top European teams to play for if he had wanted. I'm sure there would have been several Spanish or Italian clubs keen to sign him if he had told them he wanted to leave England. He knows all about Leeds and it is not a big change from Liverpool.' Saha also suggested that the very top world-class players should try to play in different countries, adding: 'I came to England to prove myself. I wanted to show what I could do in one of the best leagues in the world. My style is not too different from Fowler's, but he has been around a lot longer than me and achieved more. Robbie is definitely a much better finisher than me so I have a lot to learn, but I am improving and getting used to the Premiership. Robbie is one of the greatest strikers in England, so he will be difficult to play against. But I will enjoy the experience, watch him closely and learn from what he does. I did the same with Ruud Van Nistelrooy, who is symbolic of all the work you have to do to get to the top.'

Saha said his confidence had been boosted by recent praise from Alan Shearer: 'It was nice for Alan Shearer to say good things about me and of course it was a boost to my confidence. At Newcastle the timing wasn't right for me because there were good players in front of me which limited my chances. But at Fulham there is a good atmosphere and I have the confidence of the manager. It was important for me to get that goal against Newcastle because I wanted to show the manager that I can still score. I needed it for myself, too, and for the team and I hope there will be many more.' He also looked ahead to the game at Leeds: 'It will not be easy at Leeds as they are the strongest team in the Premiership and it is a tougher game than even Arsenal or Manchester United.

They give away a lot of free-kicks and they commit a lot of fouls, so you know it will be a physical game.'

SUNDAY, 2 DECEMBER
LEEDS UNITED 0 FULHAM 0
The problem of scoring goals was still nagging away at Tigana, who said after the game: 'I'm sure the team is progressing, but we need to progress quicker. I need to find a solution in the final forty yards so we can score more goals.' Tigana had mixed feelings about the result: 'We were both disappointed and pleased with the result. It was a disappointment because we worked very hard to win the game, but when you look at Leeds, who are a quality team, then a draw is not such a bad result. We tried to push up on them, because we knew if we did we could create some chances, but their defence played very, very well, and at the end of the game they could have scored themselves, so we were okay with the draw.'

Although all the attention surrounded Fowler's debut, Fulham created a host of chances and had a lot of possession, but could not score. At the other end, Fowler had no service at all and was limited to a couple of half-chances. Fulham out-fought their opponents and the much-vaunted Leeds attack remained largely anonymous, with Van Der Sar untroubled for much of the match. Fulham's miserly defence, which had now conceded only thirteen goals in fourteen games, did not look like being breached, even on the few occasions that the men from Elland Road broke forward in numbers. Legwinski was instrumental in this, performing his defensive responsibilities brilliantly while his dangerous runs forward kept the Leeds midfield busy. The draw stretched Fulham's unbeaten run to six games in the Premiership.

MONDAY, 3 DECEMBER
Portsmouth showed an interest in former player Kit Symons, but their chairman Milan Mandaric hinted that he would not sanction a move for the Fulham defender. The 30-year-old's contract would expire in the summer and Pompey director of football Harry Redknapp wanted to persuade him to return south. However, Mandaric admitted he was reluctant to sign players who may have little sell-on value, saying: 'Every new player must improve the squad, have the potential to be an asset and be an investment for the future. I would want us to think very carefully in the future about signing players over a certain age.' But Pompey manager Graham Rix confirmed he was keen on the Welsh inter-national: 'We are interested in Symons, and Harry Redknapp is trying his best. I think he would be good for us.' Crystal Palace were also reported to have shown an interest in the Fulham defender.

Symons wanted to leave in the summer, but Tigana would not let him go, especially after what happened to Chris Coleman. Symons was happy to stay as long as he was the third central defender after Goma and Melville. But he

Mohamed Al Fayed (front left) and brother Ali (holding the ball), in Alexandria, Egypt, in the early 1950s

Edwin Van Der Sar leads the
team out for the first ever
Premiership game at Craven
Cottage, against Sunderland,
22nd August 2001

Jean Tigana with trademark matchstick, and club tie

Craven Cottage at night (above); fans prior to the Arsenal fixture, 15th September 2001 (below left); Tigana, flanked by fitness coach Roger Propos (left) and assistant manager Christian Damiano (right) (below right)

Players of the season: from left to right,
Steed Malbranque, Steve Finnan and
John Collins

Sean Davis shoots in the FA Cup Semi-Final against Chelsea; Steve Marlet is dumped to the ground in an earlier FA Cup tie at Bootham Crescent

A mixed season for two of the old First Division squad: Barry Hayles (above) is the club's top scorer; Chris Coleman is restricted to a handful of reserve-team fixtures and signing autographs during his year-long battle to regain fitness from a career-threatening injury following a car-accident

Louis Saha (above) and Luis Boa Morte failed to set the Premiership alight, as they had the First Division

Johnny Haynes
(pictured with
Al Fayed) is back
at the Cottage
prior to the
Newcastle game

The chairman takes
a penalty at half-
time, v Everton;
(below) prior to the
Southampton game

Tuesday 19th February, the Riverside Stadium. The start of the dismal ten-game run without a league victory. At the final whistle Tigana keeps Rufus Brevett and Andy Melville off official Dermot Gallagher, following a game in which all the decisions went the home side's way

(Above and right) Scenes from the FA Cup fourth round against York City

(Left) Barry Hayles scores against Wycombe in the FA Cup third-round replay

George Cohen walks on to the pitch as the curtain closes on the Cottage – the final home game, v Leicester City, 27th April 2002

was unhappy after Zat Knight's impact and let Tigana know. Symons suddenly found himself playing in the reserves without any real explanation, but then again Tigana is not a man who worries about being ruthless. Finally Symons was told he could leave. Al Fayed called him up and told him that he could not go unless somebody offered £11m, because that was what he had just paid for Marlet. It was typical eccentric Al Fayed. Symons had joined on a free transfer from Manchester City and was certainly not in Marlet's class.

Tigana showed he was still in the business of recruiting new stars by sending scouts to watch two players in Portugal: Deco, a Brazilian midfielder with FC Porto and Cesar Luis Prates, a right-back with Sporting Lisbon who would be cover for Steve Finnan, the only recognised right-back at the club. Back on the home front, Tigana was heartened by the news that Marlet was making a full recovery.

TUESDAY, 4 DECEMBER
Melville paid tribute to his team's mean defence, which had compensated for their goalscoring problems. Fulham had a better defensive record than second-placed Arsenal, and had kept six clean sheets. While they had only scored fifteen times Melville insisted: 'If you keep enough clean sheets you stay up. Defensively we are pretty happy with things. We were on top against Leeds but didn't punish them. But there is enough quality in the team to get that side of our game right. We have learned from the early part of the season, are a bit more aggressive now and that is good for us.'

WEDNESDAY, 5 DECEMBER
Barry Hayles considered putting club before country after Jamaica's failure to reach the World Cup finals: 'We didn't qualify and the long journeys have caught up with me. I've got to sit down and have a think about whether I should make the journeys if I'm called up again. Travelling over there can lead to me missing games for Fulham and I need to think about that.' Hayles made his international debut with the Reggae Boyz in February 2000 when he first donned the black, green and gold from the subs' bench in the World Cup qualifier against Trinidad and Tobago.

THURSDAY, 6 DECEMBER
Tigana admitted that all the draws Fulham have picked up annoyed him. The normally reserved Fulham boss commented: 'We lost against Arsenal here but then drew against Chelsea. Now we need to beat the big teams.' Meanwhile, Legwinski saw a specialist about a pelvic problem that has been bothering him. 'It's an inflammation,' he said. 'It's been bothering me for a long time, so I want to know if it's serious or not. Normally it's all right and I'm able to play with it.'

FRIDAY, 7 DECEMBER

John Collins, now 33, said he is coping with the physical nature of the Premiership. Fulham fans will be interested in how long Collins, who gives the side much-needed experience, intends to keep playing. He said: 'At this point in time I'll concentrate on playing for two more seasons and then I'll take some time out. I can't see myself playing for another team after Fulham, so at the end of next season I'll stop. I never say never, but that's what's planned at the moment.' Collins refuted claims he had already started coaching at Fulham, but did not rule out a future in management: 'When I finish with Fulham I'll probably take a few years away from the game – and my plan is to go back to France. I'll start to take my coaching badges this season, get working on them and get finished next year. Hopefully I'll have my badges but the plan is to take a few years out first.' With Tigana saying he may leave in 2003, Collins speculated about being put under pressure to take over from him: 'Well, people might say that. I never like to rule anything out, anything's possible, but I don't like to look too far ahead.'

SATURDAY, 8 DECEMBER
FULHAM 2 EVERTON 0

Barry Hayles was the hero, scoring two goals to win this match, but it was a second-half bust-up which grabbed all the headlines. Hayles scored a goal in both halves to put Fulham on their way to a well-deserved victory, but he could also have been sent off for stamping on David Weir. The Everton captain was given a second yellow card after clashing with Boa Morte, who was defending himself on the floor as Weir left a leg trailing in his face. The referee accused Boa Morte of biting Weir's leg and gave him a red card, leading to a twenty-man brawl which saw Saha lose his head and Hayles stamp on Weir. Goalkeeper Steve Simonsen, who wrestled to contain Saha in the fracas, said: 'I thought he was going to go berserk.'

Everton were lacklustre in attack and defended poorly, allowing Hayles to head home Brevett's cross from 6 yards out ten minutes before half-time. The striker was then left unmarked again to knock home another undefended cross five minutes after the break. Skipper Andy Melville acknowledged his teammate's skill: 'Barry's got a lot of tricks up his sleeve. He's a very awkward player to mark and he's deceptively strong. Once he has the ball and is heading towards goal, it takes a lot to shake him off.' However, Hayles must add another string to his bow before he can become a truly feared top-flight hitman: goals away from Craven Cottage. Amazingly, all eight of this season's strikes have come at home.

An unorthodox diversion at half-time saw the chairman, Keith Allen and George Cohen taking part in a penalty shoot-out. Ten fans paid £100 each to participate in the club's fund-raising efforts for the Variety Club of Great Britain.

SUNDAY, 9 DECEMBER

Fulham were drawn against Wycombe Wanderers, last year's giantkillers, in the third round of the FA Cup. Meanwhile, the Fulham players rallied around Boa Morte in the aftermath of yesterday's ugly scenes. Skipper Andy Melville said: 'Luis was very down after the game and we left him alone afterwards. But we were all in on Sunday for a warmdown and the banter started. After looking at the video, I think the club will probably take it further. It is only because so many players were involved that it looks so bad.' Hayles gave his perspective: 'Weir was getting up and he kneed Boa. That's why Louis Saha and I flashed in and said, "What are you doing?" The ref said that he saw Boa bite him [Weir]. That was his reason for sending him off. We've got to wait for the match report to come through, as I think that once the club watch the video they will appeal – as there was no incident of biting.'

Saha was just as sure Boa Morte had been wrongly dismissed. 'It wasn't harsh that the Everton player got sent off. I was very near the situation. I saw that he was still on the ground, he waited for Luis to move and then he left his foot on his head. It was very harsh on Luis. It definitely wasn't him who should have been sent off. We stood up to them very well, although it was a fight sometimes. Maybe teams think we will be easy to intimidate because we have a lot of French players. We have great team spirit and showed we are prepared to stand up to these teams.'

Boa Morte himself could not believe what had happened to him: 'I was just trying to protect my face. I was the player on the ground and I did not move, but then the referee decided to send me off. It was crazy. But this is not the first time this sort of thing has happened.' Boa Morte feels that he has been picked on in the last two seasons by refs who believe he is a diving cheat.

MONDAY, 10 DECEMBER

Everton considered a ban on selling tickets for away matches to their fans to deter racism after a few bigots singled out Brevett for abuse during Saturday's game. Muzzy Izzet and Emile Heskey have also received abuse from Everton fans this season.

TUESDAY, 11 DECEMBER

Four wins and three draws boosted confidence on the road to Anfield. Last season Fulham held the Reds for ninety minutes in a Worthington Cup tie before losing 3–0 in extra-time. Michael Owen broke the deadlock that night and Fulham skipper Andy Melville pledged to make life difficult for the Liverpool star, who is on the verge of a personal landmark. 'Michael is on ninety-nine goals for Liverpool but we will try our hardest to make certain he doesn't get his hundredth goal against us.' On present form Hayles seemed to be Fulham's best bet for a goal, with a goals-to-shots ratio of 30 per cent, second only to Owen among Premiership strikers.

The game will see the renewal of a long friendship between Christian Damiano and Gerard Houllier, who spent eleven years together at the French Football Federation running the national youth team set-up. Houllier had been keen for Damiano to join him at Anfield, but he had remained loyal to Fulham. Damiano said about Houllier: 'It would have been good to work with him again because he gives everything in his job. When you work with someone all the time you share your passion for the game and you become friends. We had a fantastic adventure in France and he asked me to go with him to Liverpool but I had given my word to others. I've called Gerard since his operation and encouraged him to relax, to take his time and sleep because I know what life in management is like.'

Riise could expect boos from the travelling fans after snubbing the club in the pre-season. Damiano said: 'He was an important transfer for us and we were very disappointed that he gave his word to Fulham and the next day changed his decision.'

WEDNESDAY, 12 DECEMBER
LIVERPOOL 0 FULHAM 0

A superb performance by the defence kept the ever-dangerous Owen quiet for most of the game, although the England striker still had chances to get his 100th goal. In a radio interview after the game Tigana conceded that, with the ball hitting the woodwork twice, and the inspired Van Der Sar making some tremendous saves, his team had ridden their luck on occasions. 'I feel we were a little lucky,' he said. 'If Michael Owen had taken his chances in the first half we would have found it very difficult to come back. If Liverpool score first at Anfield, they usually win. It is difficult to win here anyway. We found it hard to play offensively because Liverpool are very good in defence and they have a large squad.'

The stats showed possession was evenly split. Fulham's patient passing game looked potent on occasions, but too often the final ball was missing. While Tigana was clearly dissatisfied that his team had not won, he took several positives from the game and was happy that his team was progressing. 'It's a question of our players getting used to the different level of the Premiership. I'd like them to play a bit quicker offensively, that is the primary thing, and Louis Saha and Barry Hayles need to score more goals. The players are getting more confident on the pitch, and they try all the time to play football, which is important. And we need to relax when we play on the big occasions. We play Tottenham on Saturday and I think it will be a very different game but we need to go there and get a result.' Van Der Sar's display had Collins drooling: 'He is a world-class goalkeeper who makes saves at crucial times and he gives so much confidence to the defence.'

Fulham's performance demonstrated their progress since their last Anfield visit. Then they were tentative and showed little ambition. Now they showed more confidence and passed purposefully, with Saha and Malbranque having chances to steal all three points. Tigana got his tactics right and his players were not sucked in by Liverpool's counter-attacking style, as the home supporters vented their increasingly vocal frustration at their team's lack of forward motion.

Van Der Sar said: 'Everyone is playing for their place and things have been going well. From a defensive point of view I am very happy with the progress we have made.' He had every right to be. Fulham were sitting comfortably in the top half of the table with eight clean sheets, and were unbeaten in their last eight Premiership games. That had been achieved by keeping the same back four who finished as automatic choices in the First Division: Finnan, Brevett and Melville, who have all improved with results this term, and Goma, whose recent top-flight experience with Newcastle has been telling. He is a strong defender like Liverpool's Sami Hyypia, but much quicker, and he is happy to make decisive challenges. He took a while to settle in, and his injuries have been disruptive, but since his return the defence has been brilliant. Rufus Brevett has probably been the most improved player under Tigana. He has managed to keep Jon Harley out of the side despite his £4m arrival in the summer.

THURSDAY, 13 DECEMBER

Fulham's Christmas party was a mild-mannered affair held away from the public eye at the club's Motspur Park training ground. Describing the evening as 'sensible but still enjoyable', Collins insisted that 'you don't need to have twenty pints and be falling about to enjoy yourself'. He pointed out that with a hectic festive period, in which four games are played in a short time, came a responsibility to remain professional and self-disciplined. He revealed that Fulham's players 'have certainly been told we have to watch what we eat and drink over this period, because preparation is vital and can be the difference between winning and losing'. With training scheduled for 9.30 a.m. the next day, it was no surprise that the club's Christmas bash should be a relatively low-key affair. 'It's easy to spot somebody on the training pitch who's been on a good night out,' continued Collins. 'You can spot it a mile away.' In some ways, the club did not need a high-profile Christmas get-together to cement relationships between the players, as these have been in place since the summer. The French players hang out together, as you would expect. Sylvain Legwinski hangs out with John Collins because he had known him from Monaco, and was also friends with Alain Goma, since they are slightly older. Saha and Boa Morte are close friends and their wives socialise together. Boa Morte is one of the nicest men you could ever meet. Saha comes across as aloof on the pitch but off it he is light-hearted, and the pair are the jokers of the squad. Boa Morte is great for the spirit of the team. Lee Clark, Chris Coleman, Andy Melville and Sean Davis hang out together. Edwin Van Der Sar is his own man and crosses over all the groups. Only Steve Finnan keeps himself to himself.

FRIDAY, 14 DECEMBER

Zat Knight has burst into the team and contributed to Tigana's decision to sell Kit Symons to Palace for £350,000. The 6-foot 6-inch defender, bought by Keegan, said: 'It would be great to follow in the footsteps of Tony Adams and have a great reputation like his. I'm a confident guy and in the future I'd love to captain my country.' Knight, who has been compared to Rio Ferdinand, paid tribute to the cultured tuition of Tigana, adding: 'Jean preaches total football and although people might look at me and think "clumsy" because I'm so tall, I actually like the ball on the deck. A lot of that is down to the boss. In training we are told "no long balls" and that suits me down to the ground.'

David Davies, chief executive of the Loftus Road Group, confirmed QPR had been in talks with Fulham over a ground-sharing scheme. Davies said: 'Having Fulham here would be of great financial benefit to us. I am in the business of increasing the revenue from the use of the stadium and such a move would naturally do just that, but at the moment it is all just speculation. I am hopeful of reaching a successful conclusion before Christmas.' However, this did not take into account Tigana's concerns about Wasps, who currently shared the ground with QPR. Wasps' owner Chris Wright was asking the RFU and the Zurich Premiership to waive their own rules and approve a permanent move to Wycombe Wanderers' ground.

Tigana instructed his players to take a leaf out of his book at White Hart Lane by chilling out and playing passing football. The top-flight's least stressed manager had calmly chewed his trademark toothpick as the contest with Everton exploded into a brawl. Tigana continued to extol the virtues of the beautiful game, and urged his men to relax as they attempt to nudge their eight-match unbeaten run towards double figures in north London. Damiano, who had already warned of the problems posed by Sheringham and co. after their Worthington Cup defeat a fortnight ago, knows that Fulham's miserly rearguard, with four successive clean sheets in the league, will have to be on top form again to shut out a Spurs strikeforce that thumped Bolton 6–0 to reach the Worthington Cup semi-finals.

While the defence has performed heroically, in contrast the Cottagers have hit the net only twice in their last 360 minutes of Premiership action. The manager was acutely aware that more goals from Saha and Hayles were essential if the unbeaten run was to be kept intact at White Hart Lane. The pressure on the two strikers increased with the news that Steve Marlet faced another month on the sidelines before he can even think about making a comeback to the first team. Boa Morte in particular was out to impress against Hoddle, his former manager who discarded him at Southampton. So too was Hayles for whom Hoddle was a boyhood hero. Hayles reminisced: 'I remember going to the FA Cup Final replay against Manchester City when Ricky Villa scored that famous winner. The emotion was amazing. I remember the days of Steve Perryman and Graham Roberts and I would always pretend to be Archibald in kickabouts. He was aggressive when he needed to be but he still had a delicate touch. Hoddle was my hero. I'll never forget the chip he scored against Watford; he was a magical player. I was going to try to meet him after our Worthington Cup game a few weeks back, but because we'd just lost in the last minute, I trotted off instead. I want to meet him this time and shake his hand.' Hayles was still waiting for his first goal against Spurs. 'I've never played at White Hart Lane but I've been there many times as a fan. A few of the fans recognised me, which was funny, and they asked if I was coming to play for them. I said I'd love to, but it's one of those things. I used to dream about playing at White Hart Lane and now it's set to come true. But I won't be nervous. I'm just determined to play well.'

SATURDAY, 15 DECEMBER
TOTTENHAM 4 FULHAM 0

Tigana labelled Spurs 'the best team we have played this season' and added: 'They were very efficient, they took their chances and we didn't. I think I'll need some sleeping pills tonight.' Fulham were ripped apart. Having won the Worthington Cup tie, Spurs claimed a win double. Frustrating again were the multitude of chances missed by Hayles, Saha and Malbranque. Les Ferdinand opened the scoring with the Premiership's 10,000th goal and Davies and Anderton both got on the scoresheet before Ferdinand added his second.

Andy Melville described the mood in the Fulham dressing room: 'The lads are very disappointed. Right from the word go we were second-best. It's important now that we bounce back from this defeat.' Fulham played plenty of neat and stylish football but were unable to turn their possession into goals. Melville agreed that the difference between the two teams was Spurs' cutting edge. 'They punished us whenever they got round the box, and they took their goals well. When we were on top in the second half for twenty minutes, we could have sneaked a goal and maybe got back into the game, but it wasn't to be.' Crucially, Hayles missed two excellent chances either side of half-time, and failed to show any composure in front of goal. Melville was quick to emphasise the team needed to gain something from the experience. 'Spurs punished us today, we need to learn how to punish teams in the same way. We'll have to work very hard this week before the Middlesbrough game. Up to now our defensive record has been good, so it's important to bounce back and return to keeping clean sheets.' Fulham have not won at Tottenham since 1948, twenty-three visits ago. With their proud run of eight games unbeaten and four games without conceding a goal coming to an abrupt end, White Hart Lane continued to be an unhappy hunting ground.

Tigana made no bones about his disappointment. 'That is the first time we have lost by such a margin. We had a bad day against an efficient team. It is the first time we have played three matches in a week at this level and my players were very tired. Our problem is that we need to score more. Spurs had two chances in the first half and scored them both. We had two chances and missed them both. That is the difference at this level. I think possibly we need some new blood, but I won't be going out and signing anybody tonight, that is something for the future. Instead I think I will go and put my head in the fridge.'

MONDAY, 17 DECEMBER

Tigana was highly critical of referee Neale Barry, who was in charge of Saturday's defeat at Spurs. Tigana stormed off down the tunnel when Barry booked Boa Morte for 'diving' following a hefty challenge from King. Tigana admitted: 'I won't tolerate my players criticising refs so I had to leave because otherwise they would have seen me showing dissent.' To Tigana's mind, Barry further lost credibility when, following a foul on Freund by Malbranque, he booked Saha instead. Tigana pointed out: 'A white man committed the foul, but a black man was booked. It's a joke.' Barry afterwards realised his inexlicable mistake and contacted the FA.

TUESDAY, 18 DECEMBER

With Tigana still talking about looking for a new striker, the club were linked with Rangers' Tore Andre Flo and Inter Milan's Hakan Sukur. Thirty-year-old Sukur turned down a move to Blackburn but his agent, Hakan Azman, revealed that the Turk was interested in a move to Fulham: 'Hakan is very interested in what Fulham have to say, but they would want to rush any deal through. While there's no concrete offer at the moment, Hakan would have to take time to think things through.'

WEDNESDAY, 19 DECEMBER

An FA video panel scrutinised the controversial events at the Everton game and will issue a statement tomorrow.

THURSDAY, 20 DECEMBER

The club urged referees to stop victimising their players after Boa Morte was cleared of biting Weir and the red card was overturned. An FA statement read: 'Following an appeal hearing held at Soho Square, the FA can confirm the claim of Luis Boa Morte for wrongful dismissal against Everton was upheld by a Disciplinary Commission. Boa Morte will therefore not serve any suspension.' Boa Morte's agent Amadeu Paixco said his client was delighted by the FA decision. 'Luis phoned me when he came out of the hearing and was a very happy man. There's no penalty now and it shows everybody that it was the wrong decision. The referee maybe made the wrong decision, but I don't believe he made that decision purposely.' Boa Morte will now be available for the Premiership trip to Middlesbrough. The club were keen for the verdict to mark the end of a string of decisions which have affected their players, and Boa Morte in particular. 'The video made it clear that Boa Morte was not guilty,' said Damiano. 'For me he was the victim in the Ipswich game, when he was also sent off, and against Everton. Against Tottenham last week he was booked for diving but the defender never played the ball. He played the player. We ask for just one thing: protection for our players. It's not easy for the referee to see everything in the game and, of course, he can make a mistake. We saw the Everton defender get up and touch Luis with his knee – and continue with his foot. Did Luis prefer to have blood on his face or react and protect his face? Sometimes referees miss things and make mistakes. The video made interesting viewing for the referee, and also for us. You can read a game through pictures, and the pictures spoke a lot. I had confidence the FA would come to this decision.' The FA confirmed Malbranque had a yellow card placed on his record after Saha was mistakenly booked in his stead by the referee in the match at Spurs.

Zat Knight was aiming to force his way back into Tigana's plans for the Middlesbrough clash as he was finding life on the bench 'frustrating'. Knight won rave reviews when he played in the centre of defence earlier in the season but has not started a game for the Cottagers since 14 October at Aston Villa. The tall defender, who had to watch from the bench as Fulham conceded four goals against Tottenham, hoped to prove he was ready for a recall and said: 'It's nice to be back in the reckoning and back on the bench for the last two games. But I just want to get back in the side now. It's frustrating not playing and I want to show what I can do. Andy Melville and Alain Goma are both inter-national players and I know it's going to be difficult, but when I came in before I did a good job and the Gaffer knows he can use me if needed. He knows I will do a job for him if he asks and I'll just keep working hard in training and in the reserves and hope I can get back in.' Knight had strengthened his claim for a first-team spot with an impressive display in the reserves' 1–1 draw at South-ampton on Monday night.

FRIDAY, 21 DECEMBER
Tigana's side bid to haul their season back on track at Middlesbrough following the end of their eight-match unbeaten run in the league. Collins was candid about his team-mates' 'embarrassment' at their White Hart Lane drubbing: 'It was a disappointing game and an embarrassing result – the heaviest defeat since I've been at the club. We have to learn from our mistakes. We have watched the video and looking at the mistakes we made speaks louder than words. We have to make sure it never happens again. We want to put it right against Middlesbrough and, as they're just behind us in the league, it's an important game.' Damiano was cautionary: 'Middlesbrough have improved after a difficult start. Their team has a good possibility of scoring through Alen Boksic, who is a good striker. They're at home and it will be a difficult game.'

On a cold and frosty morning at Motspur Park training ground, Damiano took some time off from putting the team through some very complicated training manoeuvres to talk about the side's prospects. His main concern was ensuring that the squad reacted properly to the defeat at Tottenham, but he also spoke at length about the current goal-scoring problem. 'At the moment, we are focusing on one thing. We must score more goals. We have the fourth-best defence in the entire league but unfortunately the fourth-worst attack. We are playing well, we are creating chances in every game, but we just don't score enough. We have two strikers who have scored ten goals and one midfielder who has scored four goals – so out of a total of seventeen goals, fourteen have been scored by only three players. A team needs contributors for goals from a lot more than three players. It's very important, and we are working very hard at this to try to improve, and find a solution to why things aren't going quite the way we would like them to.'

Saha in particular has not been hitting the net with the same regularity. Despite scoring wonder goals against Derby and Newcastle, the young French-man still does not seem to have the same composure in the box as he used to. Damiano conceded that there is work to be done in helping him to make that step up in class. 'At this moment we are working hard with Saha, we are pushing him, trying to get more out of him. He needs to play deeper and he needs to play quicker, and we are spending a lot of time helping him with this. In the Premiership, he is playing against the best defenders in the country, he is being marked tighter so he needs to come deep and move more. There is no doubt that he is finding it a lot more difficult this season. He needs to improve in his movement off the ball. When he has the ball everybody feels that he is able to score, but he needs to work more before he gets the ball. If he works before he gets the ball, deeper and quicker, I think that he will have more chance to score. He has fantastic agility and suppleness. He's a natural athlete. With one movement he can control the ball and take out the defender. Now we need to work more on his head. He needs to get to another level, to become stronger mentally, and also to add muscle to his game. It's the same for Malbranque, but these are young players and it's difficult for them. But they have many fantastic examples to help them here in the Premiership, experienced players like Sher-ingham and Shearer, who can demonstrate exactly what it is they have to do in difficult situations, and what they have to do to improve.'

Acknowledging that Middlesbrough could prove difficult opponents, Damiano looked further ahead: 'On Boxing Day we have Charlton, another team who have improved, and their confidence must be very high at the moment. They have had some good results against big teams recently – Chelsea, Arsenal and Tottenham. They are a very good team and will be very difficult for us. Mentally they are very strong, they never know when they are beaten, and they have some very good players. They have just brought in Costa, which will make them even stronger at the back. Nevertheless, it is a game we should win, and I look forward to it very much.'

Academy player Sean Doherty was called up to attend England's under-18 and under-17 winter-training camp at La Manga. Academy director Steve Kean was pleased. 'It's good for Sean to be involved with the England squad. It's always a good experience for a player to train somewhere else and stay in the international frame. England play a 4–3–3 system with one central striker and two wide strikers. They'll try to bed down quite a bit of the tactical side. We see Sean as a wide midfielder, but in the England system they see him as a wide striker. He's the leading scorer in his age group with the England set-up so it's always good for him to play in a slightly more advanced role.'

SATURDAY, 22 DECEMBER
Disappointment as the game at Middlesbrough was postponed after overnight snow led to safety concerns over approach routes to the stadium. The staff and players flew back to London for training at Motspur Park later in the day.

WEDNESDAY, 26 DECEMBER
FULHAM 0 CHARLTON 0
Tigana's concern about his side's blunt attack was justified after his strikeforce fired Boxing Day blanks against Charlton at an icy Craven Cottage.

While the shut-out established a new post-war club record for Charlton of ten consecutive top-flight London derbies undefeated, the match only remained scoreless thanks to two woeful early misses and a succession of late chances for both sides that also went begging. Firstly, the Addicks' Jason Euell missed a howler when he dispossessed home captain Andy Melville but hit the post with only Van Der Sar to beat. Saha then produced Christmas blooper number two when he advanced into a great shooting position on the stroke of half-time only to make minimal contact with the ball when it seemed easier to score. Damiano's reaction was predictable: 'Our problem is that we need to score more goals. Today was a difficult game for us and we didn't play very well. Charlton played well and that was no surprise because they're a good, organised team with fantastic spirit.' Damiano also leaped to the defence of Boa Morte, who collected a yellow card for diving when he opted to take a tumble over Graham Stuart's 20th-minute half-tackle on the edge of the Charlton penalty area. Damiano said: 'I saw the video. He never dived and the Charlton player never played the ball. I saw it from four or five angles and the pictures speak volumes.'

The first half was a rather disjointed affair, with neither side discovering the fluent passing football of which they are capable. After the break, Van Der Sar almost scored a disastrous own-goal, before making a world-class double save that kept the scoreline blank. A late flurry of chances also failed to break the deadlock. Dean Kiely made a top-drawer save from an impressive 25-yard Saha free-kick in the 76th minute, while Barry Hayles hit the side-netting after a storming run down the left-wing three minutes later. Van Der Sar made two saves – one after a fine Lisbie run, the other following a Robinson drive – while

Cottagers substitute John Collins agonisingly side-footed a yard wide in added time.

THURSDAY, 27 DECEMBER
Marlet made a successful comeback, playing for fifty minutes in the reserves. Despite missing a penalty he looked sharp, setting up a goal for Andrejs Stolcers.

FRIDAY, 28 DECEMBER
Boa Morte insisted he will not change his style in attempting to ditch his 'diver' tag. He has already been booked four times this season for diving, and was sent off against Ipswich. He said: 'I don't care if I have a reputation, I just want to play football. I'll just keep playing in my own way. I like to run at defenders and they'll tackle me. Others can talk and make their minds up and say what they have to say about referees.' Boa Morte talked about his latest booking after a tackle by Stuart in the Charlton game: 'I thought there was contact but it is the referee's decision. Everybody who was watching the game would have seen what happened and if they do have any doubts they should watch the replay on television.'

Boa Morte is definitely victimised by refs. He did not help himself last season, though, when he spat at a Barnsley player and was red-carded. Slowly but surely, however, he has been sorting himself out.

SATURDAY, 29 DECEMBER
Tigana's desire for a new striker was rekindled as Fulham were linked with Tottenham's Sergei Rebrov and Manchester United's Andy Cole. While Cole was keen on a move to London, the financial package was considered too high by the west London club and the unsettled striker decided to move to Blackburn Rovers. Tigana revealed he had been offered Flo by Rangers, but that he only wanted to take him on a loan deal.

Former Fulham striker Karl Heinz Riedle, who retired at 36 when he left in the summer, said he was convinced Saha would fulfil the promise he showed in the opening game of the season at Old Trafford. The German said: 'Louis is one of the best strikers I've played with and has everything you need to be a top striker. Last season he could close his eyes and still score goals. But even really good players have problems. Perhaps things were different at the start of the season because other teams underestimated Fulham. But it's not just down to Louis. He will get out of this patch, I'm sure.' Goma encouraged the crowd to get behind the team for the sake of the players. 'We need the crowd to participate more. It's important for the fans to be involved. I would like to talk about the referees also. On Wednesday Luis Boa Morte was unfairly booked again. He didn't deserve a yellow card. If anything the other player could have had a yellow card and we should have had a free-kick. And later in the game we should have had a penalty. So we would ask the fans to get behind us more and try to influence the game. The supporters can help by putting pressure on him. From the start of the season the decisions haven't been going for us. It'd be good if our fans could help him make the right decision.'

Goma's comments came after the goalless draw with Charlton was played in front of an unusually quiet derby crowd. This is something that Goma is expecting to change with the visit of the champions. 'I'm sure it will be different on Sunday. We need lots of vocal support from now until the end of the season. It can make a big difference.' On the draw with the Addicks Goma added: 'The result was disappointing but, more importantly, the way we played was poor. It was probably our worst performance this season, but of course we have the chance to put that right on Sunday.' Goma was surprised by the amount of goals leaked by United so far this season, but highlighted the threat of van Nistelrooy, who scored twice against the Cottagers on the opening day of the season. United have recovered from a run of consecutive league defeats against Arsenal, Chelsea and West Ham to win their last four Premiership matches, for which they largely have the £19m Dutchman to thank. Goalkeeper Van Der Sar, a friend of Van Nistelrooy from their time in the national squad, joked: 'Ruud has been on fire in the last few games – maybe Ferguson could give him a rest on Sunday. United have got back on their feet in the last couple of weeks. You cannot lose the quality they have with a few bad results. I played for big clubs, Ajax and Juventus, before I came to Fulham and we had poor periods of five or six games but when you have that sort of quality you always bounce back.'

Sean Davis, at 22, is Fulham's longest-serving player. He made his debut at Craven Cottage, aged 17 years and 25 days, against Cambridge United in Division Three. Five years – and five managers – later, he will face the Premiership champions Manchester United in west London. 'I have played under Micky Adams, Ray Wilkins, Kevin Keegan, Paul Bracewell and now Jean Tigana here,' Davis said. 'Micky, with Alan Cork, got us on to a platform but since the chairman arrived he has taken us on to another level, as this game shows. When I came on as a substitute against Cambridge in 1996 there were only a few thousand at the ground. There will be a full house of 21,000 when United visit, so that is the biggest difference I've seen – and heard.

'Everyone wrote off United after they lost a few games but they have since got their heads down and got on with it and now they are favourites for the title again.' While Fulham were struggling to score, United couldn't stop. In recent weeks they had put five past Derby and six past Southampton and while Davis believed they were back in the running for the title, along with Liverpool, Leeds and Arsenal, he was convinced their reign over English football had finished and that we will never see their like again in the Premiership. 'I don't see any team dominating this decade the way United did in the nineties and Liverpool did in the eighties. There are too many good teams. Just look at Leeds buying Robbie Fowler. That was a quality buy.'

SUNDAY, 30 DECEMBER
FULHAM 2 MANCHESTER UNITED 3

Steve Marlet, on as a sub, finally got his chance to impress after his bad luck with injuries in the return fixture of the first match of the season. Unfortunately it was Van Der Sar who grabbed the early headlines, for all the wrong reasons, when he made an uncharacteristic howler to gift United their opener, kicking the ball against Van Nistelrooy while trying to clear, only to see it fall to Giggs, who rolled the ball into an unguarded net from just outside the penalty area. Hayles then hit the bar, while Barthez tipped two efforts by Malbranque over the top and also dived at the Frenchman's feet as he burst through. While Fulham dominated possession, United always threatened on the break and when Giggs' persistence won the ball from Melville on the halfway line, he exchanged passes with Van Nistelrooy and crossed for the Dutchman to volley home. Legwinski pulled a goal back when allowed space to head home Collins' flighted free-kick on the stroke of half-time, but it took Giggs just 80 seconds of the second-half to restore a two-goal cushion. Barthez's floated free-kick was flicked on by Van Nistelrooy and, with Melville short of pace, Giggs superbly beat Van Der Sar at the near post. Marlet finally got his first goal for the club when Brevett forced his way to the byline and crossed for the Frenchman to convert from close range two minutes from the end, but time had run out. Fulham fans went home praying that more goals from Marlet would follow.

Marlet's first goal for Fulham was encouraging but somewhat overshadowed by the defeat. Fulham fans had been waiting with anticipation for the club's record signing to open his account, but when he did his goal proved to be nothing more than a consolation. Marlet could not hide his disappointment but was keen to point out that he was desperate to start repaying his transfer fee. 'I'm very happy to score my first goal but I'm disappointed about the result. I was injured before so it was very difficult for me to play to my full potential, but now that I am fit again, I will prove to everybody that I'm a good player. It's a new start for me.' With their Christmas points haul well below target, Marlet emphasised the need to get back on track. 'It's very important to win the game against Derby. We lost today so we need to get more points to create a gap between us and the teams below. It's very difficult to play against a team that defends and tries to play on the counter-attack. We will just have to be patient and the opportunities will come.'

Sir Alex Ferguson was pleased with his team's performance. 'We played pretty well today. We were scrappy at times but I think that had a lot to do with the pitch. It was a very difficult pitch and it got worse as the game went on and that can make it hard for the players. I'd have been disappointed if we'd thrown a 3–1 lead away. I thought we were in a position of comfort and we could have finished them off. But the state of the pitch and carelessness contributed to giving the ball away at times. Fulham have a lot of quality in their team, and they struggled with the pitch too. If it wasn't for that they could have done a lot better.'

The pitch was young, having been laid in the pre-season. By Christmas it had begun to cut up in the shade of the Riverside stand and the penalty areas. At Tigana's instigation these sections were relaid in January.

Marlet looked quite lively. He scored the type of close-range goal that Fulham have been missing. When these two teams met at the start of the season there was a great deal of optimism around Fulham, but, slowly, a long Premiership season can drag you down and that is the case with Tigana's men now. They are starting to show a few more defensive frailties, particularly because the pressure of not scoring goals affects the whole side. Ryan Giggs was used up front by Sir Alex Ferguson, and Fulham simply could not handle his pace. Many people thought this would prove a tough game for United, and when Saha hit the crossbar it looked like it might be, but United had the edge and extra quality to snuff out Fulham's threat.

JANUARY

The FA Cup journey begins ... with a cold snap ... Tigana is 'like a trump card' says Steed ...

TUESDAY, 1 JANUARY

Jean Tigana refused to be steamrollered into paying over the odds for players even though it meant losing out on signing Andy Cole. 'I think Cole was interested in coming to Fulham but the contract was too expensive,' said assistant manager Christian Damiano. 'Our defence is very good but the attack is a weak point for us and we need more power in the penalty box. The difference with teams like Manchester United is that they have three good chances and they score three goals. We are always looking at bringing in new players but they have to be right for the team and not upset the balance we have. The deal also has to be right but it is not always easy to find.'

While Chelsea were caught up in a drink-culture controversy, the Fulham players were well aware that if any of them stepped out of line they would face the sack under the Tigana regime. Sean Davis said: 'On the very first day the manager came to the club he told us, "I don't agree with drinking." It's still that way now. The Boro game was cancelled and we had a few days off but there was no drinking. The Gaffer is really strict on that.' Club doctor Charlotte Cowie said: 'We could test people who had been out three days before and nothing would show. It is not something you can do routinely unless you do it every day. We screen new players for drugs and alcohol and carry out routine tests once a year. Otherwise, the FA randomly tests players after matches and that includes a breathalyser test. It also carries out random testing out of competition and the players know they could have to go through that at any time. But if there were any suspicions of a problem here the manager would probably come to me and discuss it and we might then take a blood test. The manager and coaches are keen to promote healthy lifestyles and it is clear they do not take risks with their health. Tigana and his staff lead by example. There are long-term risks of binge drinking such as cirrhosis of the liver and in the short term anyone who has had a hangover will know that they do not function as they would like. In players it can also affect the energy in the muscles and dehydrate the body, which affects performance. But generally at Fulham, there is an emphasis from a number of players which makes the culture health orientated. The club is not like others I have worked at, where there was a drink culture.' John Collins, Tigana's eyes and ears inside the dressing room, observed: 'We're professional footballers and we have to look after our bodies. All the boys understand that.'

Goals have been at a premium for Tigana's side but Steve Marlet was convinced his Premiership career would take off after he finally broke his scoring duck against Manchester United on Boxing Day, ending a run of seven games without a goal. Rufus Brevett, whose surging run created the tap-in for Marlet, wants a more ruthless streak in front of goal: 'Louis Saha and Barry Hayles both hit the crossbar and we had other good chances to put the game beyond United. We didn't take them and we were punished. At this level, you have to put your chances away. We know all about United's quality and if you cannot take the chances when they come your way, you know what to expect.' That was echoed by club skipper Andy Melville: 'We gave away three sloppy goals against United, mistakes which we cannot afford to make, but we're still learning in the Premiership.'

Edwin Van Der Sar reckoned Colin Todd's men would go on all-out attack after their 1–0 win over Blackburn, but hoped that Steve Marlet's first goal for the club would be the boost Fulham needed in front of goal. Van Der Sar said: 'Earlier in the season Derby came to Craven Cottage and spent most of the game defending. But they will go for it this time because draws do not get you high enough up the table from the position they are in. I hope the goals we got against United will give us confidence.' Van Der Sar was eagerly looking forward to his first game in the FA Cup in a tricky tie against Wycombe Wanderers. 'The FA Cup is a big chance for us. I wasn't convinced about the team's qualities at first but now Europe must be our goal.'

Chris Coleman was still battling to make a comeback. 'It's almost a year to the day that I had my car accident and in many ways it feels like longer, just because it feels so long since I played a proper game. Given the state of my leg last January, it's a miracle I've made this much of a recovery so far. If someone had said to me back then that in twelve months' time I'd be playing a bit of five-a-side and joining in training, I'd have bitten their hand off.'

The Cottagers will face Derby without Lee Clark, Sylvain Legwinski and Luis Boa Morte in midfield because of injuries.

WEDNESDAY, 2 JANUARY
DERBY COUNTY 0 FULHAM 1

Marlet managed to force only one good save from Poom despite four decent scoring chances. But Damiano said: 'I know what people's expectations are but he has been injured and I think he will prove some people wrong. He is expensive now because he has not played but when he is scoring and playing well things will be different. He is a creative player, who likes to shoot and has a good eye for goal. He jumps very well for headers and he is not afraid of big or aggressive defenders. He will be a very important player for us in the future but he will not be properly fit for another four or five games. After that he will be in very good form.'

Fulham's goal came from a quick break down the right in the 73rd minute. Carbonari put the ball into his own net as he tried to cut out a low Steve Finnan cross at the near post with substitute Louis Saha lurking behind him. Van Der Sar was a little lucky that referee Barry Knight did not give a penalty for his last-minute challenge on Malcolm Christie. John Collins commented: 'It was not pretty but it was getting a bit tight behind us in the league and now we can start looking at the teams above us instead. The squad may be stretched a little bit but that means other players get the chance to come in and try to prove themselves.' In a change of tactics, Zat Knight played in front of the back four, with Collins and Davis either side of midfield and Malbranque in front of them. Damiano explained: 'We played a different system and the idea was to give us a solid foundation. It also keeps the team fresh to play in a different way.' Steve Finnan was delighted after his side picked up their second away win of the season at Pride Park, saying: 'It was unfortunate for them to score an own-goal, but to be fair we had other chances to win the game even though they managed to scare us once or twice themselves. I crossed the ball in and if the Derby player had left it Louis Saha was always going to score from that distance. He was under pressure and the only thing he could do was to try to clear it. Luckily for us it ended up going in. It was nice to get a win away from home where we've kept a lot of clean sheets. Tonight's performance was typical really. We didn't give them many chances and it was important that we got all three points. With the game against Middlesbrough called off, a draw against Charlton and a loss to Man United we suddenly found ourselves dropping down the league a little bit and looking down, especially with teams below us doing well. This win will have put that right and now we can start to look up again.'

The middle part of the season had become a battle for Sean Davis, who took a while to adapt to life in the top flight, but a starting place against Derby had given him renewed confidence. 'It was very nice to get the game against Derby and it was nice to play in a position I haven't played in for a long time – on the right side of midfield, and I thoroughly enjoyed it. It was hard work, but we got the goal that gave us the three points that we desperately needed. I think Boa Morte came down with a slight hamstring injury, so Zat Knight played in my position and I moved over to the right. They didn't really want to risk the injury so he had a run-out in the warm-up but it wasn't up to it. We never take risks at this club. So the change was forced on us a bit, but the players dealt with it well and we worked very hard as a team. We've been good defensively all season, we've kept a lot of clean sheets and again the back four and Edwin did well, and I thought we created quite lot of chances in the second half. We could have won by two or three in the last ten minutes.'

The previous season, Sean made the holding midfield role his own. Now he is vying with Sylvain Legwinski for that position, a comforting sign for Fulham fans that there is such strong competition for places. The Derby game also showed that Tigana has more options. Davis admitted he relished the challenge: 'I enjoyed it a lot,' he said. 'The first half was a real battle, but in the second half it opened up a bit and I was getting a lot of the ball and able to get forward more with it. I was just glad to be playing really, and my confidence is high now so hopefully I can get a few more games and try to repeat the form of last season. My favourite position is in front of the back four but I'm happy to play anywhere. I enjoyed it at Derby because it allowed me to get forward a lot and in theory it gives me the chance to score some goals. It's hard to do that from my normal position, I'm not really allowed to get forward all that much otherwise I get a telling-off from the Gaffer. So it was nice to get in the box and try to score some goals. It's great when you do score because that gives you confidence in itself.'

Desperate to play against Wycombe, and on a high after the win at Derby, Sean remained very focused. In sharp contrast to most games this season, the Wanderers are somewhat of an unknown quantity. Did Sean know much about them? 'A little. I played in a reserve game against them a few years ago, and won, I think 7–1, and I made my first home-team start against them back under Kevin Keegan. We won that one 2–0. So I've come up against them a few times. They're a nice side with a nice stadium and a good bunch of fans. There's no doubt that it'll be a hard game, though. They'll be looking to have another good cup run again this year, so when we go there we'll have to show them respect, but not too much. When we were in the Third Division we had a League Cup tie at Ipswich which was a huge game for us, but now we go to Wycombe and they're massive underdogs. It's just an indication of how dramatically the club has changed since I joined. We're the big boys now and we have to go there and show them what we can do. We need to get that win and get a good cup run going for the fans. With the players we've got in the squad, we've got a lot of ability and if we play to our potential then we should definitely come away with the victory.'

THURSDAY, 3 JANUARY
Valencia's imposing Norwegian striker John Carew flew into London for talks over personal terms relating to a £7.5m deal. Tigana wanted the 6-foot 5-inch, 22-year-old Carew to bolster his goal-shy attack. Carew said: 'I'm here to see what Fulham's ambitions are and what they think my part in their future might be. I have always been keen on football in England and London is very attractive. But it is the prospect of working with Jean Tigana which is most exciting.'

Though out of favour with Valencia since manager Hector Cuper moved to Inter Milan, Carew was an irresistible force the previous season, scoring eleven goals as he helped the Spanish club to the Champions League Final. While he has yet to score in seven league appearances this term, Tigana was confident he could regain the form he showed under Cuper. Valencia's current coach, Rafael Benitez, is not a fan of Carew's and club president Jaime Orti confirmed: 'The player is going to London to sign for Fulham.'

FRIDAY, 4 JANUARY

While Tigana may be French, and the FA Cup not as important to him as the Premiership, it was a way into Europe and he did not like Wycombe Wanderers boss Lawrie Sanchez ridiculing his interest in it. Sanchez, who reached the semi-finals the previous season, said: 'I don't think this third-round tie means as much to Fulham as it does to us. Jean Tigana has come here to make them a Premiership side, which he has done. Now he wants to make them a title-challenging side. The Cup does not hold as much allure to him as the league. Cups in foreign countries don't mean a lot.' Meanwhile, John Collins hoped the tie would survive the cold snap: 'If the weather stays cold like it has been then I suppose there must be a bit of doubt it will go ahead, but I would rather we played it than had a rest. After a victory everyone is always looking forward to the next game and it helps get rid of any tired legs. Wycombe is an important game for us. They proved last year that they are not a team who can be taken lightly. It is always the same against a small team. You have to treat them with respect, but if our attitude is right then the result should not be a problem.' Wycombe's Division Two game against Huddersfield on Tuesday was called off because of a frozen pitch. Adams Park does not have undersoil heating, and the pitch was frozen on New Year's Day despite being covered. The signs were ominous for the 10,000 sell-out crowd even though Wycombe brought in extra heating equipment. Rufus Brevett was looking forward to the game: 'I played at Wycombe a couple of times when I was at Queen's Park Rangers and the atmosphere there will be good. It will be a battle because of how they did last season. I am sure that they will be up for it. Their manager will get them going, but it is how we prepare for the game that counts, because if we do it properly we should not have too many problems. We have to make sure we are not one of the ones who go out to a lower team. It's different to last season when we were beaten by Manchester United in the third round because we were not expected to win. This time there will be a bit of pressure on us, but we should be able to cope with it. The FA Cup has a great tradition, so we want to win it.'

No Fulham player had scored in the previous four away games.

SATURDAY, 5 JANUARY

Game off. An unexpected rest for the lads just when they were looking to get on a roll. Brevett revealed: 'It was a bit of a let-down. We were told on Friday that the game had a good chance of going ahead if the weather improved, and when I woke up in the morning and looked out I thought it was definitely going to be on, so I was very surprised that it was called off. All the lads are disappointed, as we were really looking forward to the game. There was a pitch inspection at ten-thirty, I believe. The players were due to assemble at Motspur Park at eleven-fifteen, so when we got there we discovered we were in for a training session instead. But it is a bit of a downer, as you get yourself prepared for the actual game, and it goes a bit flat when it's just more training instead.' Rufus remained quite sanguine about the disruption to the schedule. 'It's not really that difficult getting yourself psyched up for the game again. You want to go out and win all the time and you want to play well. It doesn't matter whether you're playing Wycombe or Manchester United, your preparation has got to be the same. I've not really seen much of Wycombe. I know that the manager will have got them all geed up after their terrific cup run last year, and it would have been a very difficult game for us, but if we had approached the game in the right way then I'm sure we would have had too much for them.'

MONDAY, 7 JANUARY

Carew's transfer collapsed as a result of his medical on Saturday. A brief statement revealed Fulham's doctors did not consider the striker was fit enough to be signed. Carew jetted back to Spain, but Valencia's representatives tried to save the deal in last-minute talks with Fulham officials at Al Fayed's Harrods store. Valencia's representative Manuel Llorente actually claimed the transfer had been agreed on Saturday, saying: 'There was interest from other clubs in England, but Fulham pushed hardest.'

Carew was expected to make the unusual move of holding a news conference in Valencia – rather than in west London – on Monday. However, a statement from the Spanish club was issued instead, revealing the deal was off. It read: 'Valencia Football Club have refused to renegotiate the transfer of John Carew to Fulham FC after the English club wanted to modify the agreement, alleging that the player had not passed his medical. Valencia refuse to accept any modification to the agreement. Therefore Carew will train with the club tomorrow. Valencia's medical director Jorge Candel wants to assure that the striker is in perfect condition to play football, and more so because he is a player who has a lot of physical strength and who has never missed training. He has not suffered an injury that may have damaged his fitness.'

Carew told a Norwegian newspaper: 'I am leaving without having signed a contract, but I am not worried. What is happening now is beyond my control and I don't know what the outcome will be. With Jean Tigana I can perform at a better level than at Valencia. I want to resolve my future and these medical exams show that I'm in perfect physical condition. In Spain I'm not happy because I want to play. I'm not a player who was made to sit on the subs' bench. I got a very good impression of Fulham. Some things are very good and some not so good. What I am most interested in is the plans Fulham have for the future and how I figure in them.' Unfortunately that future will not include Carew, whose wage demands complicated negotiations. Fulham called an end to the deal unless Valencia agreed to drop their price to £5m.

Tigana looked at Venezia's £5m-rated striker Filippo Maniero as a possible alternative. The 29-year-old has scored nine times in fifteen games for Serie A's bottom club.

Confusion surrounding the future of Lee Clark eased after his agent reassured Fulham fans that the midfielder was not tying up a shock move to Glasgow Rangers. The news will come as a relief to Cottagers supporters after a day of uncertainty, in which Clark was quoted in a Scottish newspaper apparently revealing he was in talks with the Ibrox giants. Clark's representative Paul Stretford added: 'There has been no contact between the clubs – and Lee only signed a new long-term contract at Fulham in the summer. I would like to state unequivocally that Lee has not spoken to anyone in the media nor given any quotes with reference to Rangers, his future at Fulham or any topic regarding his career.' Clark was reported as saying: 'The first I heard about Rangers' interest was at the end of last week. Talks are continuing at the moment and I hope everything will be sorted out by the end of the week. I have a problem with my Achilles just now and probably wouldn't pass a medical at the moment – but it should be sorted out by Friday. They are a big club, they have a great set up and they are also pretty much guaranteed European football every year.'

However, Stretford angrily denied Clark had spoken about his future, adding: 'During the course of today, I've been trying to get to the bottom of quotes attributed to my client. It is deeply upsetting to keep reading, seeing and hearing quotes of no validity attributed to someone. Lee has given no quotes to any media with regards to his footballing future. It is incidents like this that serve only to create further animosity between football clubs, players and the media.' Clark was concentrating on his daily swimming regime at Motspur Park after a calf injury on Boxing Day, but his resumption of training had been put back.

Rebrov's name continued to crop up in the papers on a weekly basis because of his inability to secure a first-team spot under Hoddle. 'Fulham could be a good decision for Sergie,' said his agent Sandor Vargas. 'He doesn't want more salary, he just wants to play.'

TUESDAY, 8 JANUARY
WYCOMBE WANDERERS 2 FULHAM 2
Tigana can't wait for the new Wembley to be built so the fairy tale of the FA Cup can continue. The normally dispassionate Tigana said: 'The FA Cup is very important, especially for me. When I played, my dream was to play in a final at Wembley. It was always a very exciting place and in France we always saw the finals and everyone talked about them. I watched many finals at Wembley and I hope it becomes a big, new stadium because all the stories associated with

it are very important. We have big teams against little teams in cup competitions in France all the time as well. It is very difficult because sometimes the team plays at their best and sometimes they arrive and think it is easy, but it is not. But the Cup is just as important to me and my foreign players as anybody else. The Premiership is still the most important to us because we want to move higher and make sure we stay in the league, but we have come a long way in five years and we have to do it step-by-step. It was only three years ago we were playing Wycombe in the league.'

Tigana's dream of his team playing in an FA Cup Final is still alive after an eventful game which Fulham might easily have lost. Legwinski had a powerful shot blocked on the line but struck home the rebound, but when Goma brought down McSporran, the penalty was converted by Brown past Maik Taylor. Nine minutes later Wycombe were in front, when McSporran drove in from Taylor's weak punch. But Marlet headed in Hayles' lob two minutes from time, leaving Tigana to sum up: 'It was a very good cup tie. We showed our spirit in coming back in the end but I was worried. We played a good team, and will have to be at our best in the replay.'

Fulham nearly snatched it right at the end but Martin Taylor pulled off a fine save from substitute Davis' fierce drive. Laurie Sanchez was philosophical after-wards: 'When you are leading a Premiership side 2–1 with two minutes to go it's disappointing when you only manage to draw. You usually only have one bite at the cherry. But I'm really pleased with the way we played. We'll go to the Cottage and give it a go. Fulham had a bit of a shock tonight but they got out of trouble in the end. Martin Taylor had to pull off a save which kept us in it but Fulham had just scored a goal which had given them an unexpected shot in the arm.'

Although Marlet got Fulham out of jail to earn a replay, Tigana still needed a new striker as well as a bigger squad as he saw his move for Carew collapse with the disclosure that the striker has tendinitis in his knees. Tigana will keep looking – although it will not be Spurs' Sergei Rebrov who bolsters the squad. Tigana said: 'It was a shame about the collapse of the Jon Carew deal but that was just a medical decision, there is nothing I could do about it. We need to add another striker to the squad. Barry Hayles is suspended soon because he speaks too much and gets booked. If we have an injury to anybody else then we are in trouble. I need a bigger squad. But there are lots of teams looking for a new striker and it is not that easy, as we have proved. He has to be the right man for the correct direction of the club. He also has to be the right age and fit into the pay structure we have because I do not intend upsetting any of the players we already have. It can be dangerous to team spirit and then difficult to manage.' He added: 'Marlet is not fully ready yet so you have not seen the best of Steve. He stopped for two months because of injury, but I think it will be at least another month until he is completely match fit. Then he will play at a different level. But the goal was very good for him and the team's confidence. I'm glad for Steve,it was only his second goal for the club.'

THURSDAY, 10 JANUARY

Fulham were charged with failing to control their players after last month's mêlée in the game against Everton, with Hayles singled out for an individual charge of violent conduct. Fulham said in a statement: 'The club are obviously disappointed by this decision and intend to mount a vigorous defence.' While Tigana has generally been disappointed by the standard of refereeing, and has even held meetings with the FA about it, he was also upset by the number of Fulham players who lose their heads in games.

FRIDAY, 11 JANUARY

Hayles is in line for a lengthy ban, as the FA handed him a second misconduct charge for violent behaviour in the space of twenty-four hours. The FA notified him he was to be charged once more after clashing with West Ham's Hayden Foxe during the Premiership game between the two sides at Upton Park. If found guilty of both charges it could mean a six-match ban for Hayles, as well as a heavy fine. Foxe was charged with the same offence, which carries a recommended punishment of a three-match ban and a fine.

SATURDAY, 12 JANUARY
FULHAM 2 MIDDLESBROUGH 1

Tigana's vision of Marlet and Saha as a dream scoring partnership was rekindled when, for the first time, they both scored in the same game. Saha started on the bench but was given his chance after Legwinski was injured. Finally he took it, scoring his first league goal since his stunner against Newcastle back in November with a great header from a Malbranque free-kick which equalised Cooper's opening goal for the visitors. Then Saha set up Marlet for the winner after carving the Boro defence wide open. However, Hayles picked up his sixth booking to make his disciplinary problems even worse and looked disappointed as he admitted: 'I'd already decided that I was not going to tackle as much, just in case. But I still got booked anyway. Everything seems to be against me. You could say I get picked on a bit by referees, that's the way I feel at the moment. I only got booked once up to November, and now suddenly I have got six. But I haven't changed anything. I've always played the same way. I came on against Wycombe last Tuesday, made one challenge and was immediately brought up for it. I asked the referee what he was giving a free-kick for and he booked me, saying I was using abusive language, which I know I didn't. It's frustrating.'

The debate both before and after this contest centred on strikers who got away. As Damiano put it, the search for 'one big player' continued.

MONDAY, 14 JANUARY

Van Der Sar wanted the club to apply for the InterToto Cup. 'We are in sight of seventh position in the table,' he argued, 'that's very important. It's the highest we can aim for and there are seventeen games to go, so it should be our goal.

Seventh could be enough to get us into Europe if things go well but realistically we need to aim for the InterToto Cup. That's a big thing for us and I think the club should enter. I've got a long holiday ahead because of missing the World Cup and I would be happy to do it. We all want to play in Europe and the InterToto may be the best way to get there.'

TUESDAY, 15 JANUARY
FULHAM 1 WYCOMBE 0

Tigana was accused of lacking class as an amazing slanging match erupted after the Fulham manager criticised the rough-house tactics of the visitors. Wycombe's assistant manager Terry Gibson was incensed Tigana refused to shake his hand at the end of the tie, saying: 'Jean was a wonderful player in his time who I've always respected for his talents, but to avoid shaking hands with us was disappointing after a cup tie which had so much that is good about English football.' Fulham didn't see it that way, especially after Saha was forced off early on with a broken nose after being kicked in the face. Assistant manager Christian Damiano was horrified that referee Graham Barber didn't send off Chris Vinnicombe and felt Wycombe were fortunate to escape with only six yellow cards, the last of which added up to a red for Jason Cousins. It was a close encounter, but Hayles finally broke the deadlock with a low shot after twisting and turning the Wycombe defence. Fulham's reward was a fourth-round tie against York City. It was only four years ago that these two teams were playing each other in the league. Now they are poles apart.

Rufus Brevett said: 'We have a good chance of going further this year because we are playing lower-league opposition. If we approach every match like we do league games then I think we could go quite far in the Cup. York will be a difficult game. They are fighting for their lives at the foot of the Third Division and it is a good money-spinner for them. I am sure they will be looking forward to it, but we will not be feeling sorry for them.' Wycombe approached this game with a physical and defensive attitude which shocked Fulham. Brevett commented: 'They got what they deserved, absolutely nothing. We knew what to expect and stood up and tried to play our football. They tried to upset our rhythm but it did not work. We knew if we had reacted we would have had a man sent off and let the team down.' However, Cousins, who was eventually sent off for a tackle from behind, responded: 'The Premier League must be a non-contact league. Every time we went in on them, they were going down like flies. I've looked at the video of my sending-off and the first booking was a disgrace. There was hardly any contact between myself and Hayles. I also think Brevett has to realise where he's come from before shooting his mouth off. He was playing in the Second Division himself not so long ago.' Brevett sparked a mêlée when he went down in the area. He defended himself: 'As for the incident involving me, I went down because their player caught my ankle. But for some reason, another one of their lads started giving it the big one. I couldn't understand it.' Gibson added: 'Lower-division footballers have the right to battle within reason for the chance to beat Premiership teams. I resent their accusation we were too physical. They obviously haven't seen too much lower-league football in England if they think we were out of order. I could see they were getting irate, jumping up off the bench at tackles you see all the time in the Nationwide League. Fulham have spent £34m on new players this season alone and £11.5m on one striker. Of course they expected to beat us but if we irritated them, then good. Getting under opponents' skin is all part and parcel of English football.'

WEDNESDAY, 16 JANUARY

Football's crowd-control measures came under further scrutiny when Saha revealed he was hit by a barrage of coins as he walked past Wycombe's fans nursing a broken nose. Saha told club officials that missiles were aimed at him as he was led around the perimeter of the pitch.

THURSDAY, 17 JANUARY

There was much celebration at the club with the go-ahead announced for the £70m development of Craven Cottage, reinforcing the chairman's vision of turning Fulham into the Manchester United of the south. Fulham issued a statement when a High Court judge ruled against the Fulham Alliance, the body formed by eleven residents to represent those opposed to the redevelopment of the Cottage. The alliance had taken the Department for Transport, Local Government and the Regions to court alleging contravention of Article 6 of the European Convention of Human Rights. The club statement read: 'The challenge brought by local residents against the Secretary of State's decision not to call in the club's planning application for his own determination was dismissed by Mr Justice Collins. The club has been a party in these legal proceedings. The club's planning application was approved by the London Borough of Hammersmith and Fulham (subject to the completion of a legal agreement) in February 2001. The Secretary of State declined to call in the club's application for determination by way of a public inquiry in March 2001 as it is his policy to do so only in exceptional cases, and as the application did not raise planning issues which were of more than local importance. Fulham Football Club is extremely pleased by the High Court's decision to dismiss the challenge particularly as the judgment clearly dismisses every issue raised by the complainants. The decision is vital to the club's redevelopment aspirations for its ground at the end of this season and the proposals include many benefits to the local community, for example: the riverside walk, improvements to Bishop's Park and the Conservation Areas, the continuance of the club's extensive Community programme, and additional security provisions in the locality. Prior to and since submission of the club's initial application in 1999, an enormous amount of time has been spent in consultation with the requisite bodies to ensure the development will be of the highest standards and will meet, as far as possible, the criteria required for a stadium in this urban area. The club believes that the new development will provide a landmark building in harmony with both environment and the club's brand values. In tandem with the Motspur Park training ground, this new stadium will provide facilities that allow the chairman's vision to be fully realised into the new millennium.'

Al Fayed himself said: 'Today's judgment is a significant milestone in the judicial process to grant the club planning permission and I am naturally delighted. The case put forward by those who continue to oppose our plans has once again been shown to have no substance. An enormous amount of time has been spent to ensure the development will be of the highest standards. Throughout this process we have given a priority to the needs and concerns of local residents and the proposals include many benefits to this community. It is my vision that Fulham Football Club should continue to maintain its family values and I believe that the new stadium will epitomise this philosophy. I have always been determined that the club should remain on the same site in Fulham and continue to entertain local people at the heart of the community where it has been for more than 120 years.'

Wasps still have to find a new home before the temporary ground-sharing deal with QPR can be completed. A QPR spokesman said: 'We are still in negotiations with Fulham and think they would rather stay in west London than go elsewhere.' QPR chief executive David Davies added: 'In terms of Fulham's use of the ground, a deal could be done in a matter of hours, not weeks. It's the logistics of Wasps moving out that is the problem and that is some way off. That's something between Wasps and Wycombe and until we know they're happy we won't sign.' Fulham would pay £1m for Loftus Road, about five times the amount Wasps pay.

SATURDAY, 19 JANUARY
SUNDERLAND 1 FULHAM 1

Tigana had spoken of a 'voyage of discovery', but so far his armada of strikers had sunk without much trace. Fulham were unlucky not to get their third away win of the season, and Tigana was still an unhappy man. His side took the lead through a Malbranque belter, but Phillips equalised in the second half. Van Der Sar was again outstanding – unlike Fulham's strikers. Tigana said: 'I am very disappointed because I thought we were going to win. The players are very disappointed because they consider it two points dropped, and that pleases me because it shows the standards they have set themselves. We had many chances, and I know it is a problem we are not taking them. We have to score more goals. Steed's making progress step-by-step. He is only twenty and is becoming a formidable player, although he has got to learn to take the kicks in the Premiership. He scored a terrific goal.'

Knight protected the back four, while Collins was a source of invention.

Sunderland manager Peter Reid also had a problem with his forwards. Sunderland, with nineteen, had scored even fewer goals than Fulham this season. Reid said: 'It does not take an Einstein to work out what our problems are.'

Tigana was still searching for a tall centre-forward in the mould of Kanu or Flo and revealed he would love an out-and-out scorer, like Phillips: 'Phillips is a fantastic player. He's quick, clever and moves well in the box.' Even Niall Quinn, or, as Tigana called him, 'Queen' would do.

Boa Morte was stretchered off in the 90th minute with an ankle injury and Tigana was also worried about Saha's fitness for the Cup. 'I don't know if Saha will be available and it might mean I have a problem up front. It's possible I will have to make a comeback,' joked Tigana.

SUNDAY, 20 JANUARY
Half-term report. David O'Leary praised Tigana's team: 'Fulham are my outside tip for a top-six finish and a place in the UEFA Cup. If they get a better cutting edge it will make them even stronger. Well organised, hard to beat at home and with a chairman prepared to spend money, they could surprise everybody.'

MONDAY, 21 JANUARY
Jon Harley was growing increasingly disillusioned on the sidelines, kept out of the side by the form and consistency of Brevett. He complained: 'So far it's been quite frustrating because I would have liked to have played more.'

TUESDAY, 22 JANUARY
Morocco defender Abdeslam Ouaddou was sent home from the African Nations Cup for 'personal reasons' after rumours of an incident at the squad's training camp in Mali. The Moroccan management refused to explain their decision. Meanwhile, the club were linked with a move for French left-sided midfield player John Micoud who'd just been offered out on loan by Parma.

WEDNESDAY, 23 JANUARY
Davis suffered a broken nose in the reserves against Ipswich at Woking after he was struck by an elbow in the 17th minute, ruling him out of the FA Cup tie. Boa Morte feared he had suffered ligament damage but the indications were that it was not so serious, although the club awaited a full report from physio Jason Palmer. The club made no comment on reports linking them to Ipswich defender Fabian Wilnis.

THURSDAY, 24 JANUARY
Al Fayed could have his dearest wish realised by renaming the Riverside stand. A spokesman for the Harrods owner said: 'There is a strong possibility the stand will be renamed in honour of Princess Diana and Dodi Al Fayed, which is something very close to the chairman's heart.' It was also revealed that Craven

Cottage is to be renamed. Thamesbank or Riverside Stadium are likely candidates, possibly with a sponsor's name involved. The 100-year-old Cottage will either be demolished or moved to another site as a museum. The spokesman added: 'There are commercial sponsorship possibilities to consider as well, although it's hoped fans' wishes will also be sought before a final decision is taken on the new ground's name.' The fans were asked via a questionnaire for the most appropriate farewell to the old Craven Cottage. A showpiece friendly was not possible as the bulldozers are due to move in two days after the final home game against Leicester on 27 April.

FRIDAY, 25 JANUARY

Saha had an outside chance of a return as Fulham geared themselves up for their trip to York City in the fifth round of the FA Cup. Brevett, who knows what it is like to play in Yorkshire at a lower-league club as he started his career at Doncaster, warned the Premiership side to expect a physical welcome at Bootham Crescent. He said: 'They'll be sat in the dressing room saying, "Let's go and show them". They'll want to get stuck into us. They'll fight for every ball. I know what it's like to be at a smaller club for a game like this. I was at Doncaster when we played Arsenal and there was a real buzz. When you're in that position, drawn against a big club, you want to show what you can do. I've played at York and I know what it's all about. The lads know it's going to be a battle out there and have got to stand up and be counted.'

Fulham added to their reputation as a caring club by offering to donate their share of the gate receipts to struggling York, who are more than £1m in debt. City chairman Douglas Craig rejected the idea, despite the fact that the club can't even afford to pay for pre-match meals for the players, because he did not think it was appropriate. Al Fayed decided to give the proceeds, around £50,000, to the recently formed York City Supporters' Trust. 'Football is the people's game,' Al Fayed said. 'It is the supporters who are the life-blood of the game in this country. York is a historic club with fine traditions and it would be a tragedy for the fans if the club were to die.' The FA take 10 per cent of gate receipts, the clubs 45 per cent each. Sophie McGill, a spokeswoman for the Save City campaign, commented: 'This generous pledge will help empower the Supporters' Trust in our efforts to ensure the survival of York City FC and to secure representation for supporters in the future of the club. This heart-warming response to our plight underlines Mr Al Fayed's awareness of the importance of a football club to a local community. It is good to see there are individuals who still have the supporters' and the game's best interests at heart.' McGill was surprised the club turned down the money: 'It seems a bit odd to us. We don't know his [Craig's] reasons or whether they are political, but we're glad. It means the money will end up in the hands of fans who have the club's future at heart. It is a massive boost to our campaign to save York, not just in financial terms but also in the amount of publicity it will bring.' Fulham had to get permission from the FA before pledging the money, partly due to fears the gesture could be viewed in the wrong way in light of the cup tie between the two teams. FA spokesman Adrian Bevington said: 'Fulham did everything in the right way and approached us first. We were delighted to say yes. We think it's a great gesture to help a club who are having financial problems.' York City manager Terry Dolan chipped in: 'It is a generous gesture from Fulham, but I don't think they'll be so generous on the pitch tomorrow.'

Dolan was sent the lowdown on their Premiership opponents by Martin Ferguson, brother of Manchester United manager Sir Alex. The Third Division's second-bottom club had already knocked Colchester, Reading and Grimsby out of the competition but Dolan knew he needed all the help he could get. The York boss, who also received a bulging dossier from his own scout, Arthur Perry, following Fulham's draw at Sunderland last week, said: 'I have had plenty to read and four videos to watch in the build-up, so we certainly know plenty about Fulham, as you would expect. We have only lost one FA Cup tie in ten in the past two seasons and of all the teams we have met, only Radcliffe Borough were below us in league positions. If we can get our sell-out crowd behind us and get into Fulham from the start, we have nothing to fear.' Dolan has fond memories of Fulham since eight years ago he took his former club Hull to Craven Cottage and pulled off a 1–0 win, thanks to a Dean Windass goal. Dolan still remembers that triumphant day in west London and said: 'Before the game, I went to the boardroom and the commissionaire wouldn't let me in because he didn't know who I was. When I told him I was the Hull manager, he reluctantly let me through the doors. After we'd won 1–0, I went back to the boardroom and the commissionaire was still there, so I said, "You won't forget me now."'

The tie highlighted the gulf in today's game, with Fulham's Third Division opponents having spent just £51,000 on 21 players in the last two years.

SATURDAY, 26 JANUARY
YORK CITY 0 FULHAM 2

Fulham fans were deliriously happy when Malbranque opened the scoring again with another cracking goal. Van Der Sar played an equally significant role in finishing off York with an enormous punt to Marlet, who overpowered Basham with his run and Fettis with his shot. Collins said: 'We knew it was going to be difficult and the pitch was not easy to play on. York deserve credit for giving us a few frights but on the whole I think we deserved to win. Edwin Van Der Sar showed he is a world-class 'keeper. He didn't have much to do in the game but he pulled off a great save from Brass to keep us in it.'

SUNDAY, 27 JANUARY

Despite eye-catching performances, Malbranque was still a virtual unknown among French football fans. France Under-21 head coach Raymond Domenech said: 'I don't think people here know that Malbranque exists. He is only playing for my team and in France they are not well known. A lot of people thought he was talented at Lyon but he did not stay long enough to establish himself as a good player.' Malbranque, 22 earlier this month, joined the French club as an 18-year-old and made more than 50 appearances before leaving for London. Tigana was manager of Lyon when Malbranque was in that club's youth ranks and the midfielder's decision to link up with him again has paid off. Malbranque's skilful displays and tally of six goals have seen him hold on to his place even when Clark has been fit and Domenech believes recognition at home cannot be too far away. He said: 'Every time he plays for the Under-21s he is one of the best players on the pitch. We have qualified for this year's European Championships and he will be one of the most important members of the squad. The other French national coaches know about him as a result of this although I don't think he has much of a chance of going to the World Cup finals this year because there are a lot of other good players. If he continues to play as well, then he could get into the senior squad for the next European Championships. At Lyon it was just that he was not in a good position because the coach did not play him all the time, but I think Fulham got a good deal.' Damiano believes Malbranque has thrived in the responsibility as a first-team regular: 'The move has helped Steed because he has been playing all the time and that is what he wanted. It has given him the confidence to show the things he knew he could do. I spent perhaps eight years with the national team and he was always the best player in his age group. When I selected him for the France Under-17s he was my captain and for two years he was fantastic – the best.'

Although Belgian-born he moved to France at the age of four, twice won the French Championship with Lyon at under-15 level and the Cup at under-17 level. He has found himself very much at home with the French contingent at the Cottage. 'It certainly helped my decision to know there were French players and French coaching staff here. I knew that would make settling down easier,' he said. However, a place in the world champions' squad was still remote, with such luminaries as Zidane, Pires and Djorkaeff ahead of him. He said: 'At the moment I am in the under-21 side and I have to concentrate on the European Championships in May. That is all that is in my mind at the moment. After that, who knows what might happen? It will be difficult to break into the national team but it starts here with some good performances with Fulham and the Under-21s. I am surprised how fast I have settled into the Premiership as I have had to get used to a different style of play and the rhythm is much faster. It is noticeable in England that players always give a hundred per cent for the whole ninety minutes. Physically, it is so much tougher than in France.' Not noted for his goals at Lyon, he has emerged as second-top scorer to Hayles. English lessons were progressing well and he now fully understood that the crowd's chant of 'Steeeeeed' is endearing not deriding. 'It is nice that they encourage me. I now know that is what they are doing,' he said. He also revealed that Tigana has been a big influence. 'I haven't had that many managers in my career but Tigana knows how to motivate and how to encourage. He gives advice when he needs to. He is like a trump card.'

MONDAY, 28 JANUARY

Next Walsall in the fifth round of the FA Cup. Goma looked ahead, saying: 'It will be a difficult game for us because it is such a prestigious competition and Walsall will want to win badly. They have already beaten Charlton and we have to respect them.' Goma warned the Cottagers not to get carried away with reports that they are one of the favourites to lift the trophy, with Manchester United, Liverpool and Leeds out. If Fulham were already dreaming of a repeat of the glory days of 1975, Goma insisted it was foolish even to think about reaching the final just yet. 'The best way to win a cup is not to look forward. You have to take it step by step. Our next match is Walsall and we have to be focused on that game and that round, there's no point in talking about being favourites or it will never happen.'

Goma also urged his team-mates to concentrate on the league. With an unbeaten run of six league and cup games, the influential defender urged all-out effort at Ipswich. 'It will be difficult, but if we want to achieve what we hope to then we must be ambitious and try to win this kind of game. If we could play in Europe next season it would be fantastic. Playing in the UEFA Cup just a year after winning promotion would be something very special and we need to aim high.' Collins agreed that games away to Ipswich and at home to Villa within the week promised much: 'If we can take six points out of them then we're pushing for a European place.'

TUESDAY, 29 JANUARY

Van Der Sar should be looking forward to a different type of cup – the World Cup – but unbelievably the Dutch failed to qualify for this summer's tournament in Japan and South Korea. All van der Sar has to think about is club football, so winning the FA Cup would help make up for any disappointment. He said: 'I usually have games with the national team throughout the season but we did not qualify for the World Cup this time and the FA Cup is a nice replacement for those games. It is the sort of thing which makes it good to be a footballer. A lot of the big teams have already gone out so it is very open and maybe there is a chance for a smaller club. I think we have a decent team and I want to win the Cup. I think having to face a smaller team probably gives us a better chance of going through, but it does not really matter whether we have to play Premiership teams or sides from divisions below. The English guys tell you how physical it can be and you have to prepare yourself for it. In the Premiership you play on good pitches and you can play the ball and show your abilities but against lower-league sides something else is needed and I think we have shown against Wycombe and York that we can respond to that. The FA Cup is something special, with different stadiums in different divisions and teams that fight until they can't go any more. It is not always good football but there is always good spirit. I think that is the charm of the competition.'

It was revealed that Lee Clark would be out for at least another fortnight.

WEDNESDAY, 30 JANUARY
IPSWICH 1 FULHAM 0

Tigana was not a happy man after Fulham surrendered to revival kings Ipswich and let rip in the dressing room after this defeat. A first-half strike from Bent, his seventh in eight games, saw George Burley's rejuvenated side leapfrog three teams to fifteenth position in the Premiership.

It was a poor performance from Fulham, who stumbled to their first loss in seven games. They were unlucky to concede a fluky goal, but still could not get back on level terms.

Saha revealed after the match that Tigana has a tough side, despite his laid-back nature, saying: 'The manager was angry. He said we did not show enough guts and that we have to work harder. That was a bad game for us. We did not create much going forward and did not play as well as we have done lately. Our confidence was low and nothing was happening out there. We were not in a good way. I certainly did not get many chances.' Club captain Andy Melville added: 'We had lot of possession but that is not enough. But you have to give Ipswich credit, as they proved why they are moving away from the bottom. We are disappointed, but now have to pick ourselves up for Saturday's game with Aston Villa. We have to learn to grind out results when we're not playing well. The Villa game is a perfect opportunity to show how well we can play. But their boys will certainly be up for it as they'll be looking to impress any potential manager.' John Gregory had walked out of the Birmingham club and was on his way to Derby.

THURSDAY, 31 JANUARY

Speaking after training Hayles summed up the players' frustrations. 'We didn't play well, to be honest,' he said. 'We kept the ball like we usually do, but we didn't seem to have any cutting edge. Everybody's very upset with the performance, the manager especially, because it was a game that we could have won. For some reason we didn't approach it properly, so now the manager's trying to sort that out and get us back to winning ways.' Tigana was clearly unhappy throughout the game, his touchline gesticulations getting more and more agitated as the match went on. The players would not have been looking forward to the next day's training and being on the receiving end of the Frenchman's exasperation. 'We were all in for a meeting this morning to go through what went wrong,' said Hayles. 'The players know what they have got to do, we didn't really need to be told. We want to be pushing for Europe and we all want that badly. The manager doesn't shout, but he made it very clear that he thought we should have done better. He said we should have been more clinical and approached it in a more positive frame of mind. He's not someone you want to be on the wrong side of, and really we came off knowing that we should have done more. We didn't penetrate enough and that's what the manager was saying. He wasn't just picking on the forwards. The team as a whole has got to start taking some more risks, and push people forward more, and that's what he said we've got to concentrate on. The only time we did take a few risks was in the last five or ten minutes when we pushed bodies forward, but really it was a case of too little too late.'

Tigana had changed the shape in the second half, with Hayles coming on to play up front with Marlet and Saha pushing wide, and Collins brought on to try to provide the creativity missing in the middle. 'The Gaffer changed it round at half-time,' Hayles said, 'because we really weren't penetrating and weren't doing anything in the last third or getting balls into the box enough. Their goal was a bit dubious, but we could have bounced back from that.' There was also a strong feeling in the camp that the fans had been let down and Hayles spoke about the players' resolve to get it right. 'We've got two home games up next, and we're looking to get all six points and climb up that table. The team are very determined to put on a good show against Villa for the fans. There were a lot of supporters that went down to Ipswich and we sent them home disappointed.'

FEBRUARY

Still few goals in the Premiership, but FA Cup glory in abundance

FRIDAY, 1 FEBRUARY

Jean Tigana's first season in English football's top flight had not lived up to his high standards but it convinced him he could not return to management in his native France: 'The atmosphere in England is incredible. In France it is different. Arsène Wenger said to me, "If you come here to work it is not possible to go back to work in France". I agree with that. England is very exciting. In France, nobody understands why I signed here. I've had so many proposals from big clubs in Europe. When I arrived here at Craven Cottage I don't know why but I said, "Yes, this is my new club." ' While not keen on returning home to work, if it went off the rails with Fulham Tigana revealed he would not remain in England, either. 'I work with my feelings all the time. If I am not happy, I leave,' the Frenchman said. 'The priority now is the respect around me. I want the players and the people to progress – then I am very happy. I think business is very important in English football but for me, my heart comes first. If another club offers me double my salary I still won't want to leave. I lost my father last year, but he had said to me: "If you can eat breakfast in the morning, then lunch and dinner you don't need more, more, more." That is my philosophy. I don't understand leaving somewhere to get more money. Money is not my motivation.'

Tigana's father died the previous summer when pre-season training was in full swing and the manager made frequent trips to France during this time. Such is the commitment to his 'vision' that he made sure it caused no disruption to the team's preparations. His tough, hard-working approach to the game probably stems from his upbringing. Tigana hinted at great struggles in his early life: 'I am from a bad area in Marseille. Very bad. No money, nothing. I am one of ten children and my mother and father had a very small flat.'

Tigana's ambitions for a European place look beyond Fulham via the Premiership. They are now tenth, as close to relegation as they are to European qualification.

SATURDAY, 2 FEBRUARY
FULHAM 0 ASTON VILLA 0

This has not exactly been a great season for Bjarne Goldbaek, who has hardly featured at all. He made a few sporadic appearances early in the season but was given a rare start against Villa, in what turned out to be a bore draw. The Danish international said: 'We didn't play our best. On the one hand it was quite good to get a point, but on the other hand we had some chances to win, so we've mixed feelings really. Even though in the second half we put them under more pressure and created chances, they still had opportunities and Edwin had to pull off some good saves, so all in all I suppose we should be quite pleased with the point. I thought that Villa looked technically very good today.'

It was a bold move playing with three forwards from the start, but the more familiar line-up in the second half, with Sylvain Legwinski moving back to a holding role, saw the team start to dominate the game and create a number of clear-cut chances. Goldbaek insisted that tactical considerations should not hide what were some basic shortcomings of the team. 'We did change formations today, but I don't really think that's what it's about. I think we lost the ball too early a lot of times – as soon as we got it we lost it again and that always kept us under pressure. If we don't keep possession we are always going to make life difficult for ourselves.'

Injuries had a significant impact on team selection. John Collins, Sean Davis, Luis Boa Morte and Lee Clark were all missing from the midfield against Villa. Did Goldbaek feel that has had an effect on the past couple of performances? 'I think it would be sad if we turned round and said this squad wasn't good enough,' he said. 'I don't think that's the problem – we have the players to do very well in this league. At the moment I suppose it could be a combination of things: confidence is always a big issue in every player's head, and some of the players have played in every game and perhaps they could be feeling that a bit. But I don't really know, it's very hard to put your finger on why a team goes through a spell when they don't play as well as you know they are able to. We didn't really get hold of the game like we know we can, but we had the most and the best chances by the finish, so it left us feeling disappointed in the end.'

Tigana was still desperate to add quality to the team, but knew it was difficult given that Fulham was not a household name on the continent. He said: 'It's difficult to buy a good striker because they want to play in the Champions League. At the start of the season many of the players I looked at had never heard of Fulham and they wanted to play in Europe. That is why I lost John Arne Riise to Liverpool. He is playing in the Champions League. I knew this would be the case before I came to the job. It is not an easy job but it is still a good job. It is a fact and I have to aim to keep us at the top level and build a structure for the future. I train with the first-team and academy players because that is important to me and the club's future.' Tigana's eagerness to capture big-name signings is summed up by the fact that he was so delighted when Edwin Van Der Sar joined Fulham that he took Dutch newspapers into training every day to make him feel at home.

Talking about the Villa game, Tigana added: 'We had many problems in the first half, both tactically and in getting the ball. It was better in the second half but we had problems trying to score. The finishing was disappointing, but not only today. The forwards need more determination and confidence in the box. We had problems, but it's not only the strikers. It's all through the team. It can only improve by working on them. I have injuries and the squad is not big. It's difficult. We will have to get into Europe next season to help us attract players to the club.'

MONDAY, 4 FEBRUARY

Confirmation of a new home for next season. During the £70m revamp to transform the Cottage into a 30,000-capacity all-seater stadium, the team will play at the 19,148-capacity Loftus Road. West Ham had been an option because Tigana preferred the pitch at Upton Park. But Mohamed Al Fayed is used to getting his own way, and he made sure Fulham stayed in the borough by completing a deal to play at QPR's ground next season. It is understandable that a lot of fans would much prefer that the Cottage remained as it is, but the Taylor Report does not allow it. Al Fayed was buoyant about the outcome: 'I am delighted that we have now secured a temporary home within the borough and we will be working hard with our supporters and other parties during the coming months to ensure a smooth transition. Both Fulham and QPR will be arranging a series of forums to meet members of the local community to discuss the new arrangements. I am personally very pleased that we are able to offer help to QPR through what is a very difficult time in the club's history because the survival of local clubs steeped in tradition is of paramount importance to me.'

The club will pay QPR £700,000 for the season, which helps with their £11m debt. The agreement could extend for a further year if building work is not completed on time. London Wasps were to be paid £300,000 to move out to Wycombe's Adams Park. Fulham's first game at Loftus Road could be as early as 22 June in the InterToto Cup. QPR revealed that the Whites had already spoken to the Loftus Road chief executive David Davies about the ground hosting Fulham's back-door attempt of getting into Europe. Davies said: 'If Fulham qualify for the InterToto Cup they will be able to play their matches at Loftus Road. Last year the pitch was completely relaid so only the top layer needs removing after the final game at the end of April, and there will be plenty of time to do this before the end of June.' Tigana has kept his decision close to his chest about whether to enter the much-maligned competition or not. He said:

'I haven't decided yet. It will depend on how many players we have who are fit and ready to play. If everything is okay, with a big enough squad, we have a fitness programme which can be adapted to take in the needs of this competition.'

Fulham were selling naming rights for their new all-seater stadium for around £10m to recoup some of the outlay of their project in a ten-year deal. Leading sports marketing company IMG was brought in to talk to companies. Bolton sold their naming rights and club sponsorship to Reebok in a deal worth around £1m a year in 1997 when they moved to a new stadium, while Middlesbrough secured a £3.5m ten-year package from BT Cellnet for their new ground in 1994.

TUESDAY, 5 FEBRUARY

Goldbaek had talks with Tigana about his position and said: 'It's been difficult but I decided to perform in training and make myself available.'

WEDNESDAY, 6 FEBRUARY

Fulham were linked with out-of-favour Bayern Munich centre-forward Carsten Jancker again but Christian Damiano said: 'While it's true we are looking for a target man, Jancker is not for us.' Tigana was also linked yet again with Sergei Rebrov, with the Spurs misfit suggesting he would move to Fulham, but as usual Damiano denied this.

THURSDAY, 7 FEBRUARY

Lack of goals is proving to be a nightmare. It has become a habit and after every game the forwards are rueing their luck. The lack of firepower up front has also put pressure on the midfielders and the defence; however, Tigana has been working to rebuild players' confidence. Legwinski and Goma talked about how much emphasis was placed on sorting out this problem; they both stressed that it was a team issue, not just a concern for the strikers. 'We've spent a lot of time discussing this together as a team and with the manager,' said Legwinski. 'It's our biggest problem and we know that we have to work very hard to sort it out. It's something that concerns the whole team of course, so we've been working on what we do across the whole of our play. When a team doesn't score enough goals it doesn't mean that there is something wrong with the attack, it means that the whole team is not performing properly. One of the things we have focused on is that we haven't been scoring from set-pieces as much as we should have done. I don't know why this is, but again, it's something that we've been working very hard on. We are very disappointed not to have scored the goals that we should have, and there is no doubt that does have an effect on confidence. If you haven't scored for a while then you get into the frame of mind where you think you will never score again. When you are out on the pitch you have a collective responsibility. There are eleven of you out there, some are more attacking and some more defensive, obviously, but it is up to you all to make sure that the team scores. The first stage of an attack comes from the defence, so if we don't score it is not right to say we have a problem only with the attack. We are all disappointed, all of us, and we're all angry when we don't score. The thing is, we've lost a lot of points. For our first season in the Premiership, our position isn't too bad, but when you look at the potential of the team it's very disappointing just to be mid-table. I think that if we had won the games that we have dominated without winning, then we could have had another ten points, and that would have meant we could have been challenging for a Champions League place, even if we are not yet a Champions League team.'

Goma agreed that any failings within the team were a collective responsibility. 'We have had a couple of games where we have let in a lot of goals, Tottenham and Manchester United for example. But for a promoted team I think we have done quite well defensively. We don't really look at statistics. Whether we have the best defensive record is not important, we just concentrate on the football and focus on making sure that we play to the best of our ability. We have had a problem with scoring goals, but this is not just a problem for the strikers, it's a team problem. We are eleven on the pitch, and if we have done well defensively it's because the whole team has defended well. Our situation is that the team has done well defensively but the team has not scored enough goals.' Goma was looking forward to setting the record straight against Andy Cole: 'He scored against me last time we played and I must admit he won our little battle.' Goma was convinced that his team's defensive strength came through settled personnel. 'When you have such consistency it is possible to build up a good understanding and a good sense of trust in each other. We are all on the same wavelength now and maybe we cover for each other without even thinking about it. We have had good support in defence from the rest of the team and we are proud of the fact we do not concede many goals. When we start to score a few more, I think Fulham will be close to challenging for a place in Europe – if not this year, then certainly next season.'

FRIDAY, 8 FEBRUARY
Tomorrow will see the first meeting with Blackburn since that historic night at Ewood Park when ten-man Fulham made manager Graeme Souness choke on his proud boast that his team were the best in the division. The moment when Sean Davis scored his last-gasp winner is one that Fulham fans will remember for ever. Collins said: 'That victory was one of the highlights of last season. Down to ten men, losing 1–0, away from home against our main rivals – to get a win out of that was incredible. Blackburn were a very good team: to get back to 1–1 and then get the late winning goal like we did effectively won us the title and made it a special day. We played ever so well with ten men. It was a big, big game; it was really like the Cup Final of our season. We took a lot of

support up there, they were on a good run and we'd had a little bit of a dip in form, so the pressure was on us to go out and try to get a result. As everybody knows we went down to ten men early doors and conceded an early goal as well. But we showed a lot of character that day. That one performance epitomised our season for us. It wasn't just the football we played; it was also the team spirit, the determination to come back when things were going against us. I'm sure that they will think they will owe us one for that game. It was a hard defeat for them to take.'

Any doubts Collins had about stepping down a division to join Fulham were quickly eradicated as the Whites romped to the First Division title. In his mind it ranks up there with everything else he has done in football. Winning a League Championship is always a special occasion. I've only won one before – the French title with Monaco – although I came second on numerous occasions in Scotland. To win a championship is the ultimate goal: at the start of every season that's the big prize that everyone wants to win. People say that it was only the First Division, that it wasn't the Premiership, but it was still a great achievement and a terrific feeling, and I felt very proud. To get the club back into the big time after being out of it for so long, and not just winning the title, but winning it with style and by playing entertaining football, was fantastic. Wherever we went we scored goals and we entertained; we played football the way it should be played. We've proved that we can do it in the Premiership; perhaps not as consistently as I hoped we would, but we've shown against some of the big boys that we can compete and that we can play well and on our day we can play them off the park. Our weakness is that we haven't been able to score enough goals this season, but as a collective we know that we've all got to work hard and put that right. We're not a million miles away from it.'

Steve Finnan observed: 'We are confident we can improve our position. Getting into Europe would mean a lot to the club.' Bjarne Goldbaek pointed out: 'Last year they [Blackburn] were telling people they were better than us and I hope we finish them off. I hope we give them problems because if we beat them and win another couple of games we are away from the relegation area.'

SATURDAY, 9 FEBRUARY
FULHAM 2 BLACKBURN ROVERS 0

Hayles was still out to prove his critics wrong after he scored yet another Premiership goal. He netted Fulham's opener to take his tally to ten, easily the club's top scorer. 'Things are going very well for me now,' he said. 'At the start of the season everybody thought I'd be the make weight, the man who was kicked out. Don't forget I was only a Conference player a few years ago and a chippy before that. Fulham signed all these players and people looked at the team and said, "Barry's on his way out." But all I had to do was put my head down and say, "You've had a hard life, fight it out." That's what I did. I fought back and now I'm in the side and it's up to the others to try to get me out.'

Malbranque weighed in with Fulham's second as they gained a much-needed victory.

With Souness in charge it was always going to be a grudge match. Davis said: 'They were really up for it. They started off very quickly, but the first goal just killed them, and after that we were able to stamp our authority on the game. I wouldn't say that we dominated everything, but we created a lot of chances. We were the home team and we took advantage of that. They've actually got a lot of quality in their squad and a very experienced manager, so even though they are right down there at the moment, they were a very difficult side to play against. I'm positive that they'll win their relegation battle and stay up. With the quality they've got in their side, and with the determination and aggression that they showed today, I'm sure they'll be all right. Everyone really wanted to win today. We are not going to be happy just sitting in mid-table, we really want to push for a European place so that we've got that to look forward to next season.'

In a thoroughly entertaining game, the only mystery was what really happened in the sending-off of Rovers defender Craig Short. He rightly received the red card for his unprovoked assault on Marlet, but study of the video failed to show why the Frenchman received his yellow card, or why Blackburn were awarded the foul. Could Marlet throw any light on the matter? 'I don't really understand what happened. All I know is that I received an elbow and he was shown the card. But then I read in the paper that he said that I cheated. Perhaps it was because he was disappointed that he is now going to miss the Worthington Cup Final. I am very sorry for him, but I didn't ask him to elbow me, and I didn't give him the card! The referee said he gave me a yellow card because I had kicked the player first. I couldn't understand that because it is not true. And then the free-kick was against us, so it was not a very logical situation. I am very disappointed that he is calling me a cheat. I don't dive and fall over for nothing. If I was a cheat I would have fallen down just before I passed the ball to Barry for his goal, because someone was trying to pull me over, but I don't do that kind of thing.'

SUNDAY, 10 FEBRUARY

Zat Knight has proved to be one of the biggest successes of the season. Although he has not come through the full youth set-up, he has benefited from Tigana's policy of trusting in youth and developing a young English base to the club. Knight says Tigana deserves credit for helping him to break into the England Under-21 squad, after he was called-up for the first time for Tuesday's friendly against Slovenia when Tottenham's Ledley King was promoted to the senior squad. Knight insisted he owes much to Tigana, saying: 'I did not think I would be representing England at this stage. Tigana has always said he thinks highly of me and he gave me a chance in the first team last season. That was my break and I really praise him for giving me the opportunity.'

MONDAY, 11 FEBRUARY

With a short break from league action, cup glory beckoned once again. Facing a potentially dangerous but winnable tie away at Walsall, a lot of fans had the feeling that this could be Fulham's year. Did the players share the optimism? Sean Davis was upbeat: 'Last time we played at Walsall we won 3–1,' he said. 'So I'm looking forward to going back. There is definitely a feeling here that we could go all the way in this competition. We're determined and focused. If we can get that bit of luck that everybody needs, then who knows?'

With Fulham's academy side through to the FA Youth Cup quarter-finals after an enthralling victory over Ipswich Town, three of the players involved in last week's action at Kingfield were awarded professional contracts. Sean Doherty, Zesh Rehman and David Shevel all signed their first professional contracts on the Craven Cottage pitch during half-time on Saturday. For the three academy players, it was just reward for their hard work and progress over the last season. Academy director Steve Kean gave an insight into the Whites' latest professionals. Probably the most recognisable name of the three is Doherty, who has put in a series of impressive displays. 'We would class Sean as a winger. He's a natural left-footed player who likes to go past people and put crosses in. Probably his biggest attribute is the fact that his delivery on the cross is very, very good. Not only that but he can also score on a regular basis and he's proven at international level. Zesh Rehman is a central defender who's very composed on the ball. We've done a lot of work with him and he's a very good technical player. He's improved dramatically and the next step is to make sure that he's aggressive enough as a defender. Because he's so good technically, he'll sometimes let a player come at him then take the ball off him, as opposed to asserting himself. But he has a lot of potential. David is a central-midfield player who can also play on the right. He's a small, Dennis Wise-type player, with a very good knowledge of the game and you can see that he's a thinking player. Sometimes younger players can play passes either too firmly or too softly, but David's got a very good weight of pass.' Praise for Shevel also came from reserve-team captain Paul Trollope who, according to Kean, commented after one of the reserve games that for a young player Shevel is as good as he's ever seen. 'David has done really well and has already played a lot of reserve games, which is a good sign.'

WEDNESDAY, 13 FEBRUARY

Tigana reaffirmed his commitment to the club and his intention to see out his contract until 2003, despite the fact that he had previously declared he would 'pick up his bag and go' if he was unhappy at Fulham: 'After each club at which I have been coach I have taken two years off before starting again. It was the same at Lyon and Monaco, but I'm happy to stay at Fulham. I want to build an academy set-up as well as a first team.'

With the Cup dominating the week's agenda, Melville was wary of a potential banana-skin tie: 'They may not be in a great position in the First Division but they outplayed Charlton in the last round and were worthy winners. We've probably picked a bad time to play them too because I'm sure they'll be looking to bounce back after their 3–0 defeat by Sheffield Wednesday on Saturday. The key to victory for us will be to go into the match fully focused and motivated and then, hopefully, our class will tell. We did that against York in the last round so we know what is required. On paper, we have a fantastic chance of making the quarter-finals.' Collins, himself a victim of giant-killing in the Celtic side humbled by tiny Raith Rovers in the '95 Scottish League Cup Final, suggested: 'If we approach the game in a proper manner and work hard we should win, but if we go out with an eighty per cent attitude then upsets can occur. I remember Celtic were overwhelming favourites against Raith Rovers. We dominated the game and had loads of chances but just couldn't put the ball in the net. They raised their game like smaller clubs do against the big boys and we must expect Walsall to do that. If our attitude is not right then we could be in trouble. But I am sure it will be. Whenever you play a smaller team, the first thing their manager will tell them is to stop the opposition playing. As professional footballers we've got to be able to deal with that tackling, contact and aggression, as they're part of the game. Walsall have a new manager and knocked out Charlton in the last round, so we'll treat them with respect. We always try to play flowing football, but first you've got to earn the right to play. We'll have to work hard and win possession in the early stages of the game.' With Manchester United, Liverpool and Leeds already out, there couldn't be a better chance of cup glory. Collins added: 'It's a big chance for anyone now as we are just three games from the FA Cup Final. Europe is open to all now that many of the big guns are gone.'

THURSDAY, 14 FEBRUARY

When Marlet arrived he was a French international. However, as France gathered for a friendly against Rumania in Paris, Marlet was left behind at Fulham's training ground, trying to ensure his goal-scoring form would give him a chance of making the World Cup squad. Although, due largely to injury, his form has stuttered, Fulham fans were just starting to see what a strong player he is. His run and shot in the last minute against York, and his powerful surge for the first goal on Saturday, when he shrugged off three challenges before exchanging passes with Hayles, showed a power and physical presence admirably suited to the English game. 'It's something I work on in my game. I try to keep going if I have an opponent on top of me. I am getting stronger. Day by day I am closer to getting back to my top physical level. I think the run that ended with Barry's goal shows that. It's not just in England that the game is physical, it is the same in France and other leagues. But it's true that the pace of the game is quicker in England – it never drops. I think that all the players who come to play here for the first time have to learn to keep focused for the whole game, and to play at their best level for all the ninety minutes. The more games that I play, the fitter I will be and the more used to the speed of the game I will get. I've worked very hard with Roger Propos, I'm a lot stronger now and I'm able to withstand a lot of the tackles. I'm also able to stand up to the situation where an opponent tries to use his strength to get you off the ball.' Coming back from a serious injury is never easy, and it is easy to forget that as recently as December Marlet was still recovering from a fractured leg. 'I still need some more games to get to my top level of fitness, and I need to score some more goals to boost my confidence, but I feel very good. Jean Tigana and Roger Propos thought it would take me about a month to get back properly and it's been a little bit more than that now, so I'm very close to getting there. I'm still very ambitious to go to the World Cup with France. I looked at the squad this week, and saw that the manager hasn't made too many changes. He has taken only three strikers, so perhaps for the next game he will make some changes, and maybe I'll get a chance then. I really hope so. All I can do is play well and do my best for Fulham. And if I can score some goals I must hope that that is good enough for me to be selected.'

Saha, too, was overlooked by France, with his lack of goals in the Premiership the main reason. Saha reflected: 'Next season I will make getting into the national team a big target. I need to beef up my game to get in but it will be tough because this generation has produced so many good strikers.' Saha, who was a dormitory friend of Henry and Anelka at Clairefontaine in the early nineties, was then the brightest prospect of the trio. 'We were all at the same level, but Thierry was very, very strong mentally as well as being quick and technically strong,' he remembered. 'Now I think he has made himself the best in the world and the way he can take one touch and score is amazing. I go to Highbury to watch him as often as I can and we still talk a lot. He is always telling me to keep working on my game.'

Cup glory beckoned again with the trip to Walsall. Marlet, a big fan of the competition, felt there was an outstanding chance of the club doing well: 'In France, we watch the final on TV, so I know what a good atmosphere there is and what an important competition it is. I've been very excited to play in the Cup and we have a very good chance to reach the next round. We are very focused on the Cup. We want to play European football next season, so it's very, very important for us. It would be a tremendous achievement for a club in its first season in the Premiership to win a competition like that. Although Fulham prepared for the high-noon tie comfortably placed in the top half of the Premiership, Damiano warned: 'It's a hard competition and perhaps more physical than tactical, but we expect a good result as we're in the Premier League and are playing against a team from the First Division. But to win the Cup you not only need a strong team but also luck, as any team can beat another team in one game. A fantastic shot, a mistake by us or the referee could mean losing the tie. That's the beauty of knock-out competitions.' Damiano, who was one of Gerard Houllier's assistants when France conceded a shock last-minute goal against Bulgaria that cost them a place in the 1994 World Cup finals, went on: 'It just goes to show that absolutely anything can happen if you slacken.'

FRIDAY, 15 FEBRUARY

Tigana's dream has always been to create his very own Clairefontaine, the French academy which produced most of the World Cup-winning team, in SW6. Damiano was a central figure in the development of Clairefontaine, so Tigana was extra keen to bring him to Craven Cottage in the hope of recreating a successful production line of young players. Damiano, who wrote many of the coaching manuals for Clairefontaine, has brought many of them to Motspur Park and believes that they helped Fulham's Under-18 team reach the quarter-finals of the FA Youth Cup for the first time in seventeen years. Tigana's radical ideas would see academy players living and being schooled privately on site, although the local education authority in Merton would have to make an exception to their rules to allow dormitories at the club's training ground in New Malden. This ambitious five-year plan will cost £5m. The French boss, who has already overhauled the medical and dental treatment at the club, said: 'England are behind France with their youth set-ups, but it is not only the case here. In Italy they are possibly further behind than England. In France, you build the school around the football club. Here you have the school and the football after. Here you have five training sessions a week, in France we have twelve sessions as a young player – that is the difference. In the school you have one teacher for four players and afterwards the players eat and sleep at the stadium.'

Fulham's plan is mainly based around the training ground and the development of an indoor facility at the North-east Surrey College of Technology in Epsom. A planning application has been lodged for the indoor centre. Tigana and Damiano intend to give guidance, as well as helping to train football coaches in the community. In return they hope Fulham will get the pick of the best local players at 14-years old who would already be used to Fulham's methods because the coaches would have utilised the club's routines. Academy director Steve Kean said: 'This would be revolutionary. In France it was agreed at government level, but the closest we have come to it here was the national school at Lilleshall and then the boys left the centre to go to a local school.' Damiano backed this up: 'We want to develop English talent. If your academy is well organised and working well it protects the first team and the club. If the club has financial problems you know it can survive because you have lots of good young players that you can use. We want to use the French model because we know it, not because we think it is better than the English one. It is just that we have had success with it, we know it works and what can be achieved at each level of a boy's development.'

Steve Finnan has been a Fulham favourite since the moment he signed from

Notts County when Keegan was boss. Leicester City have tried to buy him, while Arsenal have had him watched. Manchester United were the last side to be linked with the Republic of Ireland international after Sir Alex Ferguson said he was a great admirer of the 25-year-old. But Steve, who has recently signed a new four-year deal with the Whites, insisted he has no interest in moving to Old Trafford: 'This was news to me but just in case anyone wants to read too much into it, let me put the record straight. I signed a four-year deal with Fulham last summer and I couldn't be happier here. I'm at a club that is going places and I've no desire to play at Old Trafford or anywhere else. I think the same applies to all the Fulham players, especially the younger ones. The manager has been looking to tie us all up on long-term deals and he's got no intention of letting me or anyone else go. I heard about this earlier in the week, but it's just media talk. I haven't spoken to anyone. The chairman isn't exactly short of cash either, so there's really no need for the boss to think about selling anyone.'

Walsall manager Colin Lee was puzzling over the way to crack a mean defence with a dozen clean sheets. He said: 'People have always talked about the way Fulham have played football and how attractive Jean Tigana has got them looking when they go forward. But nobody seems to have noticed that they are resilient at the back as well. We feel there are certain areas we can exploit and we have been working on that this week. But, let's face it, there's no escaping the fact that Fulham are a very good side and one that you would pay good money to go and watch. We are there to try to stop all that. We are well aware that they have the ability to hurt us and we accept that they will probably have more of the ball than us. But it's up to us to adapt our game to that and try to hurt them whenever we get the chance.' Fulham are the only Premiership side to travel to lower-league opposition in the fifth round, and while Tigana's team are anything but prolific they have only lost once in nine games since the turn of the year.

Walsall goalkeeper James Walker was philosophical about keeping out Fulham's attack. He observed: 'I watched Van Der Sar on Wednesday against England and he had a great game. It will be nice to play against him and get the chance to meet him. But realistically, we've not got much chance.'

Clark was ruled out for a further three weeks, but Saha was back after a hamstring injury and with only six goals in twenty-eight games, including three within four days of the start of the season, he had enough problems in the Premiership not to have given Walker a sleepless night. Saha confessed: 'The defenders here are better tactically and are also stronger, so you have to be mentally strong and right with your movement if you are going to score because you will only get two, maybe three chances a game. When I am in the right position I need to do a little more but I am happy with my all-round game. The manager wants me to play differently to last season, to be more of a normal striker, but that is hard for me because I always like to be involved. I am not a Jimmy Floyd Hasselbaink – my game is not just about scoring goals but making crosses and passes that bring goals for my partner. If I were missing too many passes or things like that, I would be more worried but my overall game is not bad.' Saha, who sat on the Wembley bench as a non-playing squad member when Newcastle lost to Manchester United in the 1999 final during his short spell on loan from Metz, continued: 'It was good to play with men like Alan Shearer. It would be fantastic to reach the final this year and play against them.'

In a cup tie of contrasts the First Division club's finances are aided by a Sunday market in the ground's car park that will attract more people than will attend the match. Even Al Fayed remarked: 'I have heard of the Walsall market. I am told it is the biggest outdoor market in the country and is very impressive. I am a shopkeeper myself and I might make a trip back to Walsall to see the market. There might be some tips I can pass on to help their profits and maybe an idea or two I can use. I know how very difficult it is for football clubs to continue to survive in the lower divisions. My hat goes off to clubs like Walsall, who find every way they can to survive and prosper. The Sunday market is an excellent idea.' Walsall chairman Mike Lloyd remarked: 'When Al Fayed bought Fulham it was because he couldn't find a Premiership club. He bought a lower-division one and then bought a team to get into the Premiership. We finished second to Fulham when we were promoted to the First Division in 1999, but there the similarity ended. I remember Fulham's old chairman Bill Muddiman saying how difficult it was for them financially, but now they have no worries thanks to Mr Al Fayed. Once we were on level terms with Fulham, but now they are out of sight. We tried to consolidate in the First Division but got relegated and have fought our way back. We can only dream of the millions Mr Al Fayed has invested. Walsall is the perfect example of how a small club should be run and we get other clubs coming to see how it's done. Without our outside income we could not survive, even at this level. But if the next television deal brings in less money, as is expected, then Fulham, with Mr Al Fayed's millions, will be one of the few who won't be affected.' Walsall knocked out a Premiership club in the last round and their manager Colin Lee joked: 'If we can do it again then perhaps we'll get a day out shopping at Harrods.'

SATURDAY, 16 FEBRUARY
WALSALL 1 FULHAM 2
Tigana, eagerly awaiting the draw as the team headed back down the M1, reflected after the game: 'My priority is to stay in the Premiership, but if you ask me whether we can win the FA Cup, I would say, "Why not?" My main concern is to stay in the top flight because our fans want to see us playing against Manchester United and Chelsea next season. But the FA Cup is not a distraction and that is why I put out my strongest team today. It was a difficult game and when they came back to 1–1 I was very worried. But the FA Cup is always difficult because there is so much passion involved.' A quirky cup tie at the 9,000-capacity Bescot Stadium saw Fulham eventually convert their superior

possession into a victory when Hayles scored a magnificent winner. But who cared in the Fulham camp that this was such a narrow victory? Fulham had made the quarter-finals of the FA Cup for the first time in twenty-seven years. The last time, Booby Moore was playing for Fulham, for God's sake! In 1975 Fulham went all the way to the final, but lost. This time Tigana's men were hoping to go one step further.

Fulham took the lead after a Malbranque free-kick forced the Saddlers into a terrible own-goal blunder. However, Van Der Sar's equally erroneous contribution allowed Walsall back into the game and it was left to Hayles to score the only 'proper' goal of the tie. Despite his team's territorial advantage, Tigana was by no means sitting comfortably in the dug-out. 'When they came back to equalise I was a little bit worried. FA Cup ties are always difficult to win as there is so much passion in the games. It was a poor goal from our point of view, but Barry Hayles scored a great winner. We are now only two games from the final and we have as good a chance as anyone of winning the competition.'

Colin Lee thought his side deserved a replay and was disappointed that Hayles grabbed his winner while Wrack was off the field receiving four stitches. The Walsall manager said: 'Full credit to Fulham because they played good football. But we are disappointed because we felt we deserved a draw. Fulham scored their second twenty-five seconds before Darren Wrack returned to the field and that is tough to swallow. I wouldn't criticise the team for conceding the goal from a set-piece today -it was just unlucky. I thought we were worth the draw because Fulham did not create that many chances despite their possession.' Hayles, whose goal was his first away from home for over a year, enthused: 'Whatever people might have thought, our overseas players are now beginning to grasp how important this competition is.' Moroccan Abdeslam Ouaddou made a rare appearance and produced an assured performance at the back, while Van Der Sar made a crucial stop at the end from Byfield, who said: 'I thought it was definitely in, it's only because he's so big that he got there and managed to get his fingertips to it.'

The only previous time in their 123-year history Fulham made the quarter-finals was 1975. Hayles, who had previously been only as far as the first round with Stevenage, said: 'Everyone keeps telling me the last time we came this far we went all the way to the final and that can happen again. Anything can happen at this stage. I definitely think we can win it with the squad we have at the club. It is a realistic aim for us to have and if we can do that then that could be the boost this club has been looking for to take us into the top level in the Premiership. That first trophy is always the hardest one to get, but once you get your hands on it, it can really be lift-off for a club.'

SUNDAY, 17 FEBRUARY

A great quarter-final draw. Whilst playing at home would have been the ideal tie, with the likes of Tottenham, Arsenal, Newcastle and Chelsea still in the competition, drawing West Bromwich Albion away was a godsend. The Baggies are flying high at the top of the First Division, but facing Jason Roberts and Danny Dichio was far preferable than having to line up against Jimmy Floyd Hasselbaink, Alan Shearer or Thierry Henry. However, Tigana found himself in the same position as so many managers in the past, wanting his players to put thoughts of cup glory on one side in order to concentrate on the league. Damiano described the rearranged match with Boro as 'a very important game for us' and went on: 'The team is doing well and we have confidence. The group is very together and we have improved our position in the table, but we have to beat teams below us because the first priority has always been to stay in the Premier League. I think you need between 35 and 41 points. The Cup and talk about getting into Europe are exciting but staying up is the most important thing.' There was a possibility of moving up to seventh place with a win at Boro. Fulham were ninth, just eight points off sixth place, and Hayles revealed that behind the scenes Tigana was looking up, not down: 'He is thinking about a top-six position, and not about being dragged down into mid-table. If the players we have now don't believe that is possible, Jean will get in those who do.' Hayles, who also knew that Tigana was seeking yet another striker, was upbeat: 'If I think about that, my concentration will go. At the moment, I'm relaxed and scoring goals. We do create a lot of chances and luckily I am the one putting them away. Once Louis Saha is fully fit, he'll give us another option.'

MONDAY, 18 FEBRUARY

Goma has won two caps for France, but it could have been many more for the 29-year-old defender whose career has been blighted by injuries. His last international appearance was four years ago, but Damiano felt the former Newcastle United player stood a chance of going to South Korea and Japan. He said: 'Alain's played for France before and now he is back to his best. He has had some great performances for us this season and has the quality to play for his country. He has a big reputation and is a very important player for us. I don't know who France will take to the World Cup, but he must be close to getting into the national team. There is still time for him. Fulham have the best defensive record in the Premiership this season, which is a remarkable achievement, and Alain has been important in that. He has played many consecutive games, which has helped, and he is much stronger than when he first came here. Touch wood his injury problems are behind him.'

TUESDAY, 19 FEBRUARY
MIDDLESBROUGH 2 FULHAM 1
Tigana could not believe that Boro still had eleven men left on the pitch at the end of this match, and nor could his players. The normally super-cool Fulham boss was involved in trying to keep a clearly angry Brevett away from referee

Dermot Gallagher at the final whistle. Boksic had scored what looked like an offside opener, before Marlet equalised. Szilard Nemeth then scored the winner for Boro. Tigana was angered after a 74th-minute incident which he felt cost his side at least a point. Boro defender Franck Queudrue, who had earlier been booked for a foul on Collins, clashed with Hayles, who got to his feet and looked likely to score, only for Gallagher to stop the game and, after talking to the Frenchman, award a free-kick. 'I don't understand why, at the end, when we had a chance to score he stopped the game and didn't give the defender a yellow card,' Tigana said. 'I never discuss the referee when it's a penalty or an offside, but this action is difficult to explain to my players because we could have scored. We did not play too badly. We tried all the time to come back into the game, but that's football. The referee, the same as a player, can make a mistake. That's life, that's football. But I have to disagree with that last action because I don't understand why he stopped the game when we had an advantage. We had the chance to score, and normally if you stop the game, you give a yellow card. That, for me, is a big mistake.' Tigana explained his actions at the end of the match: 'I had to pull my players away from the ref because they could have got themselves sent off after the final whistle.' Tigana had the sympathy of Middlesbrough boss Steve McClaren, who admitted he would have been annoyed in similar circumstances: 'Franck just went for the ball and it seemed to be a fifty–fifty challenge. I'd like to see the incident again, but we'll take that little slice of luck.'

WEDNESDAY, 20 FEBRUARY

With Saha and Davis breaking their noses this season, and Marlet taking a blow in the neck, Damiano insisted steps must be taken to stamp out 'intentional violence'. Damiano said: 'If a player hits someone in the face he can break their nose, but if struck in the neck they can be dead immediately. It's terrible, but perhaps there needs to be one very bad incident and then everyone will understand. If I hit someone in the neck I could cut their breath, so for the offender in these incidents on the pitch they must receive a very hard sanction. I saw one incident in France, at Marseille, when Jurgen Klinsmann received an intentional hit and his tongue went down his throat. It was a terrible situation, but he was very lucky because the physio immediately ran on to the pitch and took his tongue out. You accept bad accidents – but when it's intentional it's very, very dangerous. I hope the situation with intent is stopped quickly. Football in England is fantastic, but sometimes there is a bad hit, and that destroys the game. It's impossible to accept, and we don't need it.'

Damiano was still fuming over Short's elbow on Marlet in the victory against Blackburn, which earned the Rovers centre-back a red card. 'I have looked at the tape, and the pictures speak for themselves. These fouls are not within the rules of the international board of referees. If they accepted hitting that would mean it was okay. If you accept it you can kick each other in training and matches because the door will be open for everybody to do it.' Asked if he expected a rash of bookings and sendings-offs in Japan and South Korea this summer, Damiano replied: 'Yes, I'm sure the referees will be very strict in order to set an example. FIFA and referees will see to the situation and protect the game and the players. They won't wait an hour for a yellow card if they need to give one after five seconds. In the 1994 World Cup in the United States FIFA decided on a hard line to deal with tackles from behind. Each player tackling from behind got a red card.'

THURSDAY, 21 FEBRUARY

Steve Finnan insisted that not only were Fulham determined to bounce back from the Middlesbrough defeat, but they also felt they had a point to prove against the Gunners. 'Arsenal away is going to be a very, very difficult game. When they beat us at home they showed that they are a quality team, so we are really going to have to be at the top of our game to get a result on Saturday. And then we've got Liverpool and Chelsea after that, so it's three massive games, but it's why we're in the Premiership and it's great to be involved against these sorts of teams. Most of the lads would say that over the first half of the season, after we'd played most of the teams, that Arsenal were the best that we'd come up against. I think that Manchester United are probably going to win the Championship, but they and Arsenal are the top two teams in the division, so to go away to them is obviously very difficult, but we're confident. The lads are really up for this one, and we are determined to get something positive out of the game.'

It will be a slightly unusual Arsenal line-up – definitely out are Keown, Upson, Cole and Ljungberg, all suffering long-term injuries, but Finnan dispelled any thoughts that this might make the game easier. 'I suppose there's a chance that we can capitalise on that, but to be honest they've got a very big squad and they've got some real quality, there are internationals who can come in, so it's still going to be an extremely difficult match. Really, we've just got to concentrate on our own game. We played some decent football at times against Middlesbrough without really creating enough in the final third. It was disappointing that we didn't get certain decisions going our way, but that's football. That's behind us now, and we've just got to get on with it. If we can continue to play our good football and get our final ball a bit better in the last third, then hopefully we can create chances against Arsenal and put them away. This sequence of games won't make or break our season, but it will show us how far we've come. We haven't had great results against the top sides so far; we've lost to Man Utd twice and Arsenal once, we've drawn against Chelsea, Leeds and Liverpool, so we're really determined to get a win now. You have to say, though, away from home, a point is a good result.'

Good cup runs can be the making of breaking of a side. There have been plenty of teams whose league form has started to slide the further on they've got, while others have used it as a springboard to improve their overall form and confidence. How did Finnan feel the Fulham players were coping? 'It can be used as an excuse if you're not doing so well in the league,' he said. 'If you're doing okay, then you would say it's not interfering at all. If the squad's big enough then it's not a problem, but if you've only got a small number of players to choose from then perhaps the number of games you're involved in might start to tell a bit. Really it's just fantastic to be involved in a cup run and when you get to this stage, you're just looking forward to all the games. We're in the last eight, some great teams are already out, although there are plenty of quality teams still involved, but we're confident that we can do well, as we are against Arsenal on Saturday. We need to be at our best because we're playing the best, but that's where we want to be, up there with them, and we're determined to do it.'

FRIDAY, 22 FEBRUARY

Steve Marlet was meant to be the saviour. Although he was beginning to find the net, he had a difficult introduction to the Premiership after his serious injury, and then found himself dropped from the French national squad. However, he insisted: 'My goal is to play in the World Cup, and if Roger Lemerre had said joining Fulham was a bad idea then I might not have signed.' Marlet wanted Lemerre to watch him play against the Gunners, who boast four of the national squad and particularly striker rivals Henry and Wiltord. Marlet said: 'I don't feel that I am in direct opposition with the Arsenal players for a World Cup place. Robert Pires, for example, is a player of the highest quality, someone of whom France have a real need. My concern is not to compare myself with anybody in the same position as myself, but to give everything that I have for Fulham, to score goals and to see whether that's enough. But every match from here on is important, especially those in which there are other French players playing well, like at Arsenal and Chelsea. I need to play well in every match, not score a hat-trick in one and then be rubbish in the next. Physically I feel well, not far off where I was last season, although technically and tactically in England I still have things to add. It was difficult for me at Fulham in the beginning because I was injured. Everyone was talking about the transfer price and I was not able to prove that I was a good player. The big difference in England is the pace of the game. My position has not really changed, rather my role. I have been asked here to score goals, whereas before I always had a goalscorer alongside me. It's a bit like Thierry Henry. When he went to Arsenal, he played wide, but then he transformed himself into a goalscorer. I hope I can succeed as well as he has. I've always had confidence, never doubted myself. I've got a fighter's way of thinking. I've never regretted for a minute coming here and the injury I had could have happened at Lyon. It's a question of bad luck, nothing more.'

Marlet, who was groomed by Wenger at Monaco, pointed out: 'It's true that

I was never considered as the number-one striker in Lyon. Sonny Anderson had that role. I really came here for that – to score goals. I know it's not enough just to play well. I can play on the flank or can come back and defend because that's my way from my days at Auxerre. But at Fulham I must only think about scoring. It's the first time I've had so much pressure on me. I'm supposed to be the major striker.'

SATURDAY, 23 FEBRUARY
ARSENAL 4 FULHAM 1
Tigana was distraught. Former pupil Henry netted twice but Tigana could not help but praise the young Frenchman. Looking back on their time together at Monaco, Tigana admitted that Henry is now a far better player: 'He was very young at that stage and was often a substitute as we also had Sonny Anderson and David Trezeguet. However, he has progressed very well since then. He has more experience and confidence. He works hard every day in training and scores more goals now. Henry is a great player, but they have too many great players for my liking. Arsenal have all the top-quality French internationals and we have the French players who are the next level down. There is a big difference in class between the teams. I knew that before but I know it even better now. We gave the ball away and had bad organisation. We have to learn from this. We started very badly and I don't know why. For thirty minutes there was nothing from us. We kept giving the ball away, lacked concentration and in the end we got what we deserved from the game. At 1–1 I thought it was possible to get a good result but there were far too many mistakes by the team overall. Arsenal are on a different level to us, playing in the Champions League. They have so many good players and so much cover in different positions. They have a very strong squad.'

Fulham were given a harsh lesson, especially as they contributed to their own downfall, with Brevett making the worst mistake, which led to Vieira's goal. Marlet was responsible for the only bright spot of the day for Fulham, scoring with a header, but the Gunners then ran away with the game. Recalling how Vieira had run the show at the Cottage, the manager delegated Knight to mark him, but the youngster was out of his depth. Hayles and Knight, both substituted, were spotted outside Highbury ten minutes before the end trying to organise a lift. The club insisted they had received permission from Tigana to make their own way home.

MONDAY, 25 FEBRUARY
Damiano analysed a defeat that was a tough footballing masterclass for Fulham. 'I think we took two lessons today,' he said. 'We took a lesson in football and a lesson in humility. When you look at their big players, they work very hard for each other and they are very focused on doing well for the team. It was a very big lesson for us. The defeat at Middlesbrough was more disappointing. You are

never happy when you lose, but the defeat there was abnormal because of two big mistakes by the referee and this is always very hard. But the Arsenal game has taught us a lot. At the end I think that we know our level and we know that we have a long way to go before we can match Arsenal.' He felt two more wins were needed to guarantee survival. 'The first objective was to stay in the Premier League. I think we need 41 or 44 points to do that. We have had a couple of disappointing results, but the important thing is to get back to winning games. After that we can think about higher things.'

TUESDAY, 26 FEBRUARY

The club planned to repeat an operation carried out at the home match with Manchester United designed to stop ticket touts, when five arrests were made by extra police officers paid for by the club. Fulham wanted to protect the interests of their loyal fans from illegal ticket operators because of such high demand for the remaining matches. Lee Hoos, deputy MD, said: 'No other club has ever sponsored an operation like this and we hope it sends a message to any touts not to bother coming to Fulham.' Hoos visited Loftus Road for QPR's match with Wigan to observe the corporate and press facilities.

WEDNESDAY, 27 FEBRUARY

Barry Hayles withdrew from an FA disciplinary hearing relating to the misconduct charge from the incident at West Ham in November, the first of two charges he faced. Having reviewed the incident, Hayles 'subsequently decided to change his original plea to that of guilty with mitigating circumstances'. Squad member Stolcer was called up by Latvia for a friendly in Luxembourg at the end of next month.

THURSDAY, 28 FEBRUARY

Tigana confessed he will need a far bigger squad for next season to avoid, as he did against Arsenal, playing Knight out of position because of the absence through injury of Davis. The manager said: 'This year we haven't played in Europe but if we are to play in Europe we will need a bigger squad. I have always said that we need two players for each position and I still do not think that we have this.' His chairman was backing him totally: 'I have great faith in Jean Tigana and his proven talent as a manager and coach. Whatever we need to spend is governed by him. I have made it clear I will back him all the way. I am not in football for the money – it is my passion.'

MARCH

FA Cup march cannot disguise Tigana's black mood ... Crisis meetings in boardroom and dressing room ... Marlet: 'It would be wrong for us to go down with all the talent we have, but sometimes talent is not enough ...'

FRIDAY, 1 MARCH

Jean Tigana's future was the subject of increasing debate, but he said: 'I am happy here, but if one day I'm not happy I'll go back to my country. It's my philosophy.' Yet he can also leave when he is happy! Just as he did when he was living with his wife and three children in Cassis in the south of France, tending his vineyard and working as an agent, as he was until Fulham came calling. And the boardroom was growing concerned that he would not put up with the failures at Fulham and defect maybe to Anfield to replace the stricken Gerard Houllier, or would be next in line to coach France.

But John Collins was not convinced. 'The impression I get is that this will be his last job. He sees it as a big job and one he wants to see through. He does not just want to build a team. He wants to build a club. His aim is to be able to look back and say he has built a club which can go on competing at the top, and the foundations have already been laid. People see the surface, the quality we seek to play, but they don't see all the facilities which have been built at our training ground to bring on the young kids, or the scouting network we have now got across Europe. The next stage is for a new stadium to be built next season. Jean doesn't just see it in terms of what trophies could be attached to him. He has a bigger picture than that. Some clubs do it back to front. They spend all their money at the top trying to build a team, but forget about what's below. We are fortunate to have a benefactor in Mohamed Al Fayed. But there have been a lot of clubs in Europe which have had benefactors with plenty of money, but that hasn't guaranteed them sustained success. It was easier to buy instant success a few years back, such as when Jack Walker took over at Blackburn, because there weren't many teams around with money. Now there are more which can attract the top players. If he feels there is a player who can improve the team, he will put it to the chairman that it will help the business plan. Jean has already brought a professionalism here that few clubs have got. The boys have responded and changed their lifestyles a bit from the days when we would go for a pub lunch after training, play pool or pop to the bookies.'

Tigana is driven by the will to win, even in a kickabout with the staff at Motspur Park. 'He's always the same, he plays to win,' observed Steve Marlet. 'He likes to win and he's unhappy when he loses. I played football tennis with him earlier and we won. He was delighted. It's just natural for him to be competitive. When he is among us he talks to us and plays football with us. At every other club I have been with the manager stayed in his office. His ambition, even in a practice match, is a tremendous example. It leaves us with a desire to be successful too.'

More often than not, therefore, Tigana was not a happy man chewing on his toothpick. He stressed: 'We have arrived and we play well, but we need to learn quicker. That is the problem for me as manager. We need to bring the squad to the top level. Arsenal, Manchester United and Liverpool play all the time in Europe. They are used to it.' The team's mid-table position did not sit comfortably with Tigana. 'I don't like this position because all the time in my career I was in the top three. When we were third, I wasn't happy. Now that is not too bad for the players. But if we can finish around sixth position, it is good for the first year. Between sixth and tenth is a good position.' Clearly Tigana was taking stock, but was not want to sell and buy. Look at the progress of Rufus Brevett and Andy Melville. Many players progress. That is my idea.'

Optimism was still running high as Steve Finnan prepared to face Dietmar Hamann in the Liverpool match, knowing he would do so again in the World Cup having overtaken the injured Stephen Carr and Leeds' Gary Kelly in the reckoning for the Ireland team. He said: 'While there's still a lot to play for this season at club level, the World Cup's in my mind as it gets closer and closer. Hamann's a top-class player, there's been talk of him going to loads of clubs so he must be playing well. It would be nice to win the match against Liverpool, hopefully with Hamann having a bad game, and then the Republic will try to beat Germany in the summer as well.'

These were lofty thoughts. More realistic was the prospect of the dreaded InterToto Cup! The FA Cup seemed to be the last hope for a route into Europe without having to endure a shortened summer holiday. Boa Morte revealed: 'The players haven't really talked about the InterToto so far. When we get closer to the time we'll start to think about it and we'll see how the players feel. At the moment, though, I would say that the FA Cup is our best chance. We are in the quarter-finals and I think we can go far in this competition. An FA Cup Final would be something special, everybody would be proud of getting there.'

Tigana planned to give Abdeslam Ouaddou his first start in the league after two appearances in the Cup. The youngster said: 'It is my job to work hard and to be prepared for when the manager needs me to play. I would be ready to play tomorrow. You have to give respect to players such as Owen and Heskey but I would be confident against them. It has been difficult this season because I have not had many chances to play and we've sometimes had three players in the same position. When you play in the reserves it is not the same level and you need three or four games in the first team to get up to speed. But I am still working hard and have no regrets about joining Fulham. I know my time will come.' Ouaddou turned down Monaco, Bordeaux, Kaiserslauten and Borussia Dortmund on the advice of his pals in the national team, Mustapha Hadji and Hassan Kachloul. 'They told me it would be good to come to England because it is one of the best leagues in the world and I wanted to experience it. I also knew Tigana had been a great player and had given youngsters a chance when he was manager of Lyon and Monaco.'

On Liverpool's title hopes, Saha observed: 'We have played all the big teams this season but Arsenal's self-expression is very, very good. Robet Pires is the best counter-attacker because when Patrick Vieira wins the ball and gives it to him he feeds players like Thierry Henry straight away, and that three-man forward line is better than anything else in the Premiership. Breathtaking. You can do nothing against that. It should be like that when you watch Liverpool. When you have a player like Steven Gerrard, who is similar to Patrick Vieira, you should use him much further up the field.' John Arne Riise could expect a stormy reception after his blatant snub of Fulham but Steve Finnan said: 'I don't know the circumstances of how it happened. All I remember is he had a choice between us and Liverpool. You have to say it has been a very good signing for Liverpool. It would have been nice if he'd come here because he's a very good player. But he turned us down and you can't blame him, not when Liverpool are in the Champions League. It's true you have to be in Europe for the majority of top players to come here.'

SATURDAY, 2 MARCH
FULHAM 0 LIVERPOOL 2
Thrashed 4–1 by Arsenal last week, and now victims of Liverpool who eased into their tenthth away win of the season even with Owen left on the bench. Anelka struck early in Liverpool's first real raid, but Fulham could have hit back through Hayles and Boa Morte. It was the same old sorry story, as the Whites failed to convert their chances. Comically, with Van Der Sar out of position as he was trying to get the equaliser, Litmanen scored Liverpool's second. Fulham have struggled against all the big sides in the Premiership and Tigana was again upset: 'This is the type of game you need to prove yourself in. We need to show the mental strength to win these games. But we did not have enough. We need to work on it.' It was a view echoed by Damiano: 'I think we were unlucky and Liverpool were lucky. We played well, the players gave their maximum and we deserved to get at least a point. But this game was typical of our season. When

we should win we only draw, and then when we should draw, we lose. We have the capacity to play well and I think we have the third or fourth best defence in the Premiership. We have got to get more firepower if we want to make a big impression on this league. We had three or four good chances and missed them. It's hard to find fault with the players because they gave all they had but we are always falling a little bit short and know we have to do something about our lack of goals.' In fact, although only Liverpool, Leeds and Chelsea have better defensive records than Fulham's 31 goals conceded, only Sunderland, Derby and Leicester have scored fewer than Fulham's 27. Little wonder then that Fulham were always being linked with the striker who opened the scoring, Anelka. Damiano observed: 'Nicolas is ideal for Liverpool's style. When you play long balls forward you need a striker who can play alone and hold it up. Nicolas has the ability to do that. Liverpool play everything on the counter-attack. They are very condensed and have a great defensive spirit. But Arsenal are more spectacular and have a greater capacity to score.'

Goma highlighted the fact that the management and the players were fully aware of the team's defects. He said: 'We've got to be more ruthless in attack and I just hope we learn from these lessons and emerge as a stronger team next season. Liverpool are a very frustrating side to play against but it's so disappointing to lose a game when we've had so much of the ball. Last week was the first time I have ever faced Arsenal and I was very impressed. They have a great understanding between the players and pass the ball so quickly. They're the best team I've played this season and I think they will win the league.' In Fulham's six league meetings against the big three they have managed just one point, from a goalless draw at Anfield back in September.

MONDAY, 3 MARCH

Steed Malbranque reiterated that a place in the World Cup squad looked out of his reach: 'Apart from my club duties, I have the Under-21 European Championships in May to look forward to.' And the World Cup? 'There are just too many players ahead of me in the pecking order.' Zidane, Pires, Djorkaeff and Dugarry spring to mind. 'However well I play, there is no way I will be picked at the expense of these guys who have been part of the group for years. This is an established set and I don't think any youngster will be given their chance until the summer. But that's normal to a certain extent. These players have remained very close and have been very successful. You can't suddenly ask them to pack their bags.' Damiano was full of praise for the youngster. 'I have known Steed since he was a young teenager and I can tell you that he is destined to do great things. For a 22-year-old he is incredibly complete: he works hard, he's willing to progress and he can pass and score from central midfield. He is Fulham's Gianfranco Zola, and one day he will be France's new Zidane. But for now, he has no choice but to wait his turn with the national team.'

TUESDAY, 5 MARCH

The club considered an appeal against a £30,000 fine for their part in the brawl with Everton at the Cottage back at the beginning of December. The club was also warned as to its future conduct while Everton were fined £25,000 after a charge of failing to control their players was reduced to the lesser offence of disorderly conduct. 'The club is extremely disappointed by the decision and is in the process of consulting our experts regarding a possible appeal,' Mark Collins, acting MD, said. Everton were similarly aggrieved, with chief executive Mike Dunford commenting: 'We are disappointed with the outcome but we have to accept it.'

Sean Davis was hoping to play in the derby with Chelsea despite a thigh injury.

WEDNESDAY, 6 MARCH

CHELSEA 3 FULHAM 2

This was the one Fulham wanted to win more than anything. At the promotion party at Fulham Town Hall Tigana stood on the stage and said: 'I want to beat Chelsea, that is my main priority.' It did not happen, despite two goals from Saha, his first away from home since the opening day of the season. Tigana reflected: 'I think we deserved a minimum of a point, but we are learning. We had so many chances but this is not the first time this has happened to us. I'm used to it now. It's difficult for the players to accept because they have played well and got nothing. All the time we create chances away from home but we need to score from them.'

Forssell ensured a late-season bid for the top four by Chelsea on a newly laid Stamford Bridge surface, as he scored a late winner. Fulham could have taken the lead when Marlet rose highest from a corner to head powerfully against the bar, but it was Chelsea who scored first when Melchiot ran unchallenged before cutting in to shoot past a static Van Der Sar with his left foot, via a deflection off Brevett. Within 60 seconds Fulham were given the chance to level in controversial circumstances. A burst into the area by Saha was halted by a well-timed tackle by Gallas, but referee Peter Jones pointed to the spot as Saha hit the turf. Last season's top scorer in English football took the kick himself, tucking the ball inside Cudicini's right-hand post with the 'keeper diving to the left. But just short of the half-hour, Chelsea regained the lead. Le Saux exploited holes in a Fulham defence that had conceded eight goals in three consecutive defeats by inviting Gudjohnsen to run deep into the visitors' territory. The Icelandic striker picked his spot, sidefooting past Van Der Sar for his 12th league goal and 19th in all competitions. After Malbranque watched a volley deflect behind off Gallas, Fulham were denied a second, this time seemingly legitimate, penalty as Marlet was tripped by Lampard's trailing leg. Ouaddou then inexplicably directed his free header from a Malbranque corner wide, and Saha, seizing on an inventive ball from strike-partner Marlet, galloped clear before dragging his shot wide on the stroke of half-time. Coaxed forward by Collins, Fulham hauled themselves level again with seventeen minutes left. Collins sought out Marlet's pace down the left and the France international checked his run and picked out Saha, who beat a bizarre bicycle kick from Gallas to head in his second of the night. Ranieri responded immediately by employing his third substitute, Forssell, in place of Gudjohnsen, and he continued his phenomenal record when coming off the bench with his seventh goal from such a position in twelve games.

Harley, who has had few chances to impress, made a rare appearance. He's been kept out of the team by the exceptional form of Rufus Brevett, but playing against his old club at Stamford Bridge was a real boost. The defender said: 'It was an exciting game, good for everyone to watch, but the important thing was the result and it didn't go our way. We were all gutted to be honest. It's vital now that we put things right in the next league game. We did have a lot of chances and we should have put some more of those away really. Louis Saha did well to get the two he scored and there was another penalty that we might have got, but really it's another of those days when we've let it get away from us again. All we can do is keep creating chances. Eventually they have to start going in – last season they were flying in from everywhere, and if we keep playing the way we have done we'll start sticking them away and start getting the results again. We just need a little bit of luck maybe. If we could get a win against one of the bigger teams then that would boost our confidence enormously, and really set us up to push on for next season.'

Claudio Ranieri gave his view of the opposition: 'Everybody at Fulham plays good football. Maybe they need one striker who doesn't play well but who scores goals. They created a lot of chances.'

THURSDAY, 7 MARCH

Eddie Lewis urgently needed a loan move to cement his US World Cup place. He moaned: 'From what I understand another player went out on loan [Kevin Betsy to Barnsley] not long after they told me they weren't loaning any more out. Unfortunately the manager will always have the final say, but hopefully I can find a club. Any club that's competitive in the First Division would be a good option.' US manager Bruce Arena had faith in him: 'He deserves to stay in this squad.' Betsy, a 24-year-old forward, eventually joined Barnsley permanently. He featured in some of Tigana's earlier selections but only once in the Premiership, in the club's opening game at Old Trafford. He said: 'I am thrilled to have signed a permanent contract with Barnsley as I enjoyed my loan spell with them. I have fond memories of my time at Fulham as it is a great club with fantastic support, but playing first-team football is vital for me to progress as a player and I am looking forward to being given that opportunity with Barnsley.'

It was against Barnsley that Eddie Lewis had made his debut in March 2000, a month after he became Paul Bracewell's final signing for Fulham. A speedy left-winger and a good crosser of the ball, Lewis came from Major League outfit San Jose Earthquakes for £1.3m. Despite scoring a possible goal of the season against Derby in a Worthington Cup tie his opportunities have been limited at Craven Cottage as he has been a victim of Tigana's diamond formation in midfield, which has no place for an out-and-out winger. (At the time of going to press, Craig Brown, impressed with his performances for the USA in the World Cup – and particularly the cross which set up the USA's second against Mexico – was rumoured to be interested in taking him to Preston.)

FRIDAY, 8 MARCH

Tigana was linked to Anelka, on loan at Anfield from Paris St Germain, with the Damiano connection being a key factor. Meeting Anelka's and his multitude of agents' financial terms would more likely be the decisive factor, however. Damiano, though, was supportive of Anelka's return to English football, saying: 'As a striker he has everything, he can shoot well with either foot and also has the capacity to hold up the ball and adapt to any formation. I remember him well from the French training camp because he had a big talent. He has fantastic ability and could play up front alone as well as with others.' Despite such a commendation and Anelka's preference for a move back to London, the personal terms were incredibly high.

Stefan Effenberg caused great interest in the dressing room when he announced on his website that he will be signing for Fulham this summer. Sean Davis said: 'Stefan has played in World Cups and for Bayern Munich for years. So if the Gaffer wants to bring in someone like that, I'd be more than happy. Staying at the top level is what the manager wants and that's what we've got to achieve.' But while the ageing German's comments on his website firmly suggested that he was Fulham bound – 'Things are looking that way' – in reality he wasn't. Unfortunately the German star obviously hadn't spoken to Jean Tigana lately, since the Fulham boss considered him to be past his sell-by-date! The club was again linked with Kanoute but there was a buzz going around the Cottage that the chairman was not entirely happy about the profusion of Frenchmen arriving at the club. There was a record six fielded against Liverpool. Meanwhile, Manchester City boss Kevin Keegan was on the trail of £2m-rated Maik Taylor, with his first choice Nicky Weaver injured.

SATURDAY, 9 MARCH

Rufus Brevett took over the captaincy in the last round of the FA Cup when skipper Andy Melville was dropped. Brevett recalled: 'Tigana didn't give me a clue. He just pinned the teamsheet up on the wall and there was a "C" next to my name. I suppose seeing me lead the team out must have surprised a few people. I was being written off when Fulham signed Jon Harley from Chelsea in the summer, but I did the only thing you can do in those circumstances – I worked my socks off.' Despite four successive defeats Brevett remained upbeat: 'It's a sign of how far we've progressed that people outside the club are actually calling it a crisis because we've lost four in a row. We don't like losing one game, never mind four. It's the first time it's happened since I've been at Fulham and we're determined to stop the slide.'

Sean Davis, the team's longest-serving player, having starred in every division for the Cottagers, knew more than anybody what an FA Cup Final would mean to the fans who only six years ago saw their side in 91st place in the league. He said: 'We think we have had the best draw. We have avoided many of the big teams and it is a great chance to get some silverware this season. I think we have proved that if we play well and take our chances we can beat anybody. The problem is, though, we have not been scoring and a lot of teams have been punishing us recently. West Brom don't concede many goals and always seem to win 1–0 so it will be a hard test for us. But if we did win then that is us in the semis. One more win and we are in the final and if we get one of the big guns like Arsenal at Cardiff, then we could get into Europe without winning the trophy.' Ouaddou's enthusiasm emphasised that the foreign imports knew the significance of the Cup: 'It has always been one of the highlights, one of the occasions you had to watch. It was wonderful, so exciting to watch Manchester United in the days when Cantona was the icon. Even on TV you could sense the excitement of the Cup.'

Fulham's opponents were fired up by Barry Hayles' remarks when the draw came through that Albion were the team they wanted, in other words an easy touch. Hayles said: 'We have to fancy our chances of making the semi-finals.' Collins agreed that the door was opening: 'When you see the other teams left in, we have to look upon it as a good draw. We can go there and win. It's a great opportunity for the club. We are just three matches away from winning a trophy, and this is my best chance of winning something really big. I don't care what some say, the FA Cup is still huge. Even as a boy growing up in Scotland, it had allure. The sun shining in May on a perfect pitch . . . all the pomp. Some of the younger players may not get this close again. They may not realise it, so I will be going around the dressing room reminding them to make sure they are focused and prepared to give the last drop of their energy. Their attitude must be that this could be their last chance, too.'

Only Liverpool and Plymouth have conceded fewer goals than Albion this season. West Brom 'keeper Russell Hoult observed: 'Fulham are a star team from London with a lot of big-money names, but West Brom? No one knows who we are. But we've done well this season and every team has found it hard against us.' Midfielder Andy Johnson, who scored the winner at the Stadium of Light, said: 'Fulham are a good side, well organised and it will be a hard tie but it's one that we can certainly win. They don't have the firepower to pose a threat.' Over to Marlet to prove them wrong. With six goals from twelve starts he was optimistic: 'It's frustrating when you arrive at a new club and you are on the sidelines. But I've started scoring since the turn of the year and it's getting better all the time.'

SUNDAY, 10 MARCH
WEST BROMWICH ALBION 0 FULHAM 1

Tigana had received a letter in November from an unknown source threatening the players. Fulham's security staff believed it was a hoax, but called in the police nevertheless. An extract from the letter read: 'Seven million pounds must be paid in US dollars and sent to the given address. If you do not comply your players will be infected with the HIV virus. This is a real threat and SHOULD be taken seriously ... I will be placing an advert in the *Chicago Herald* to which you should reply immediately. Further instructions will follow.' A similar threat was made to Manchester United a year before. A second letter was sent two months later to Tigana and Al Fayed, which said the squad had already been attacked. Steve Finnan confessed: 'I don't mind admitting a shiver went down my spine when I heard about it.' The police were no nearer finding the black-mailer than they had been in November.

Tigana was buzzing about his side's prospects after this win. 'The FA Cup is a special competition. I've known that for years even before I came to England. I used to watch it on TV in France and it was always my dream to play at Wembley. To lead out a team at Wembley would be another dream and to do it at Cardiff this year would be fantastic.' Still in line to become the first Fulham manager to win a major trophy, Tigana emphasised the Cup's dual significance: 'It'd bring European football,' he said.

This was not the greatest performance against First Division opponents, but on this occasion it was only the result which mattered. Damiano's post-match comments revealed as much: 'It was a very professional performance against a side who fought very hard and we deserved to win. Louis Saha missed a very good chance just after the goal to clinch victory. If that had gone in, it would almost undoubtedly have been it. It would be really fantastic to make history but there are still two matches to go and we know we are a long way from winning anything.' For the first time in twenty-seven years the club which had never won a major trophy in its 144-year history had reached the semi-finals of the FA Cup. Though the league was not going too well, an FA Cup final would offer considerable compensation.

Marlet scored the goal, with a header at the start of the second half. Collins admitted that West Brom pushed Fulham all the way: 'It was a hard-fought second half. We could have got a second goal but all credit to them, they kept pushing us back and we couldn't retain possession. They kept coming back but we are delighted to be there. We knew they were a dangerous side but we were patient and got our rewards. It was a great cross and a terrific header by Steve. But one goal is never enough and we should have got a second but this is a great opportunity. We may never get a better opportunity to get to a Cup Final.'

To intensify the atmosphere, radio commentary of the late Jeff Astle's Wembley winner in 1968 was broadcast over the tannoy before kick-off. The club were dedicating their cup run to Astle's memory after his death the previous month. Albion boss Gary Megson was frustrated in seeing his side lose the game from a set-piece, but wished Fulham well for the rest of their involvement in the competition. 'I'm bitterly disappointed to lose in that manner. We didn't defend a set-piece properly and they defended theirs well. We've had problems all season dealing with set-pieces and once again it has proved costly. It has cost us the opportunity to go forward in this competition. We must take our disappointment on board and make sure it doesn't happen again between now and the end of the season. When games are tight, it usually comes down to a mistake, a little bit of individual skill or a set-piece. We've got to learn from this. They've got exceptional players and I hope they go on to do well as there's some solace in losing to the eventual winners.'

MONDAY, 11 MARCH
The chat at the training ground was inevitably all about the FA Cup semi-final against Chelsea, who had demolished Tottenham 4–0 to make their way to the last four. For all the players and staff at Motspur Park the enormity of it all had not really sunk in. Damiano said: 'West Brom showed fantastic character. It was difficult to move them. It was the sort of game where just one goal was going to decide it. West Brom have the best defence in their division but, in the end, we deserved to get there. They were a hard team when we played them in Division One and are a lot stronger this year. We try to play good football in every game and obviously we're delighted to be in the semi-finals.' On facing Chelsea, he added: 'This would give us a marvellous chance of revenge because we lost last week when we should have won or drawn. The Cup is very important to all of us and it would be fantastic to win a trophy for the team, the staff and everybody.'

Even Al Fayed had caught the Cup bug. He said on the club's website: 'In Tigana we have a great manager and I am fully committed to him. Whatever it takes now in terms of effort, determination, commitment and finance, I am there. I think it's a magical achievement to reach the Premier League in such a short space of time and to get to the semi-final. I can hardly believe it. It is very exciting.' Andy Melville could be forgiven for thinking he might be lifting the Cup at Cardiff. The Welsh international said: 'It would be brilliant for me to hold up the Cup at the Millennium Stadium and I feel we have a strong chance. We've shown we can go to big stadiums and play against the big clubs without being outclassed. But now it's not just time to play well – it's time to claim a big scalp.'

TUESDAY, 12 MARCH
It was decreed that the two clubs from the Fulham Road were to make a 100-mile trek north for the semi-final. FA chief executive Adam Crozier endorsed

the decision: 'The best solution is Villa Park. It has been done before and you get more fans in to see the game.' Immediately the repercussions started...

WEDNESDAY, 13 MARCH
Ken Bates was furious that the FA Cup Challenge Cup committee were ignored in the contentious decision to force fans from Chelsea and Fulham to travel to Villa Park for a 7 p.m. Sunday kick-off. Bates, chairman of the Challenge Cup committee which normally decides FA Cup semi-final venues, said: 'I want to emphasise that the FA Challenge Cup committee had no part in that decision.' He advised his fans to read his programme notes for Saturday's Premiership match with Sunderland, which promised to be highly explosive in its condemnation of the decision. The Chelsea chairman couldn't fathom the reason for choosing Villa Park as the venue for the tie, only suggesting: 'Ask the FA.'

An FA spokesman said: 'It was the wish of Fulham to go to Villa Park because they felt it would mean a better and fairer distribution of tickets for their fans. The FA has an obligation to ensure as many fans as possible can go to see the semi-final.' It was also suggested that the police objected because of the London Marathon on the Sunday. Bates countered: 'Not at all. The police had no problem with a 4 p.m. kick-off on the Sunday.'

However, the BBC, who have first choice of the FA Cup fixtures for their prime-time 7 p.m. slot, chose the London derby. Villa Park is clearly a bigger money-spinner because of its vastly superior crowd capacity to Highbury and Bates felt the additional room for corporate hospitality was behind the FA's decision. Bates continued on the attack: 'The M6–M1 on Sunday afternoon and evening becomes a car park. This means that fans from both clubs will be lucky if they get home before 1 a.m.–2 a.m. on the Monday. So much for putting the fans first!' The Fulham fans were allocated the Holte End, the traditional home end and the largest seated stand behind the goal in Europe, as well as most of the Doug Ellis stand on Witton Lane. Each club was allocated 19,000 seats but again that didn't please Bates: 'We have an average gate of 38,000, with over 22,000 season-ticket holders. Fulham have an average gate of 19,000. Yet again the FA have given the clubs 19,112 tickets each for the semi-final. So Fulham get one per fan and we get one for every two fans.'

THURSDAY, 14 MARCH
Tigana, who was personally in favour of Villa Park because more fans could go, was contacted by *fourteen* players from all over Europe who would like to play in the FA Cup semi-final. Fulham were inundated by faxes and calls from agents representing players who wished to sign because of their cup exploits. The club's PR spokesman Chester Stern said: 'It was remarkable how many players wanted to play for the club just days after reaching the semi-final. Jean is sifting through all the names to see if there are any players who he might be interested in.' The club was linked to Flo and to Batistuta as Tigana continued his search for a

goalscorer. Veteran Kaiserslautern defender Hany Ramzy, recently prosecuted and sacked for sexually harassing a woman in a restaurant, for which the Egyptian received an eight-month suspended jail sentence, was also linked with the London club. 'Yes, we are interested,' said Tigana. 'We have an imminent need for a rock at the heart of our defence.'

Having refused to meet Andy Cole's inflated wage demands, speculation started again that he would still end up at Craven Cottage, even though he had only recently signed for Blackburn. Stern commented: 'He was struck off Jean's list last time round even though we were given first refusal. We turned him down because of his wage demands and also because Jean is insistent he predominantly signs players below the age of 25 so he can develop them, and in some cases increase their value if he chooses to sell them on.' Agents know Fulham are one of the few clubs in a financial position to make significant signings before the transfer deadline later this month.

Perhaps an early psychological blow was delivered as the reserves beat Chelsea 1–0 at Motspur Park. The goal came when a Harley cross was converted by Elvis Hammond.

FRIDAY, 15 MARCH

Tigana still needed to consolidate the club's position in the Premiership but after five straight defeats they are closer to the bottom than they are to a European place via the Premiership table. Plenty of plaudits, but not enough points. Andy Melville stressed: 'We lost our last four league games on the trot before we beat West Brom in the Cup. Maybe we didn't deserve to lose all of them and there was a bit of naïvety there. Although we did not play that well against West Brom, we ground out a result. We need more of the same, some good, professional wins. I am a bit fed up with people saying we played well and did not get what we deserved. Everton is a massive game for us and people don't realise that because they think we're comfortable in mid-table. But games are running out and we need to get to around the 42-point mark to be safe, hopefully, before the FA Cup semi-final against Chelsea next month. We are not being negative, that is the reality.'

The sacking of one manager and the appointment of a new one always inspires the players. As David Moyes replaced Walter Smith at Everton, Melville stressed: 'The feeling will probably be that they've let themselves down a bit and want to do something about it. They are fighting for their lives so we will have to be ready for it.' He promised there would be no settling of old scores. 'It's been taken care of, it was a big fine, we have taken it on the chin. The chairman would have something to say if we got involved in something like that again. Most of their lads will have forgotten about it, like we have. Most of the lads went in to try to break it up, but when you see twenty bodies it looks worse than it is. It was a one-off. We try not to get involved in that sort of thing. The manager tells us to keep calm before every game anyway, and tomorrow is just another Premiership game.' Clearly the FA Cup was a distraction for the players. Van Der Sar put it into perspective: 'The FA Cup is the biggest cup competition in the world and it's a big achievement for Fulham to get to the semi-finals. But we aren't talking about that yet. If we now relax and just prepare for the semi-final, it's not going to help us. We have to be ready for the game against Everton and not put the league to one side.'

With a high Premiership finish seemingly out of reach, Fulham's main chance of playing in Europe in 2002–03 was through either the FA Cup or the dreaded InterToto if they didn't make it to Cardiff. But there was a third way: Fulham were vying for a UEFA Cup place because of their emphasis on fair play. England were in line to have an additional representative in Europe via UEFA's Fair Play League. With Manchester United and Liverpool unlikely to need to qualify for Europe by this route, the spotlight fell on the two teams just behind them in the Fair Play table, Fulham and Ipswich. If they continued to impress in the Fair Play League for the rest of the season then a place in Europe was a possibility.

The club denied reports earlier in the week that Clark's persistent Achilles injury ruled him out for the rest of the season. Damiano said: 'He has chronic tendinitis but we are still awaiting advice from the doctors treating him.'

SATURDAY, 16 MARCH
EVERTON 2 FULHAM 1
Tigana lost his cool after this fifth successive defeat – the worst run for the club in eleven years – left his team just five points from the drop zone. He was threatened with a red card from referee Graham Barber and, through an interpreter, explained: 'I never usually shout at referees because I have great respect for them. I thought Steed Malbranque had been elbowed. The referee came at me and I thought he was going to send me off for something I said. It's the first time I have been involved in something like this.' With David Moyes in charge for his first game after replacing Walter Smith, the Toffees were always going to be favourites to win this game. Unsworth scored in the first minute, and Ferguson took advantage of a ridiculous miskick by Van Der Sar. Malbranque got a goal back after Gravesen was sent-off, but despite an onslaught from Fulham, Tigana left Goodison Park knowing that, as another defeat compounded his relegation fears, it was going from bad to worse. The Frenchman still came out fighting, though, insisting that he would not change his style of football even if it meant relegation: 'We started ten minutes late. This is the problem. When you go two goals down it will always be difficult. I am disappointed, but it is a problem that I need to accept. I could change the way we play, but I won't. I have a philosophy and I will not abandon it. I want my players to keep going this way. We are in trouble but I do not believe in changing our way. The other way for me is not a good way. Yes you can win games, you can stay up, but for football at the highest level that is not a good way to play,

and I said that when I started here. It is not a good way to play with the elbow, it is not the way I think and I will not ask my players to play like that, to kick people, that is not acceptable for me because I respect people. There is only one way to play. It is good for me, for the supporters and the players; it is good to keep this philosophy. It is possible that we could be relegated trying to play football and sticking to this philosophy, but if you want to play in the top flight you need to be able to play, not just kick and rush.'

However, Damiano was realistic: 'We have lost five Premiership games in a row now and we need some power and aggression. Staying up is all-important.' Everton were far from short in this area. When you get clattered by Duncan Ferguson you know about it: Goma had to leave the pitch groggy and with blurred vision after tangling with the Everton forward. He said: 'I was involved in a clash of heads with Duncan Ferguson, and then this lump came up straight away, and I found I couldn't see properly. I think I burst a blood vessel and then I ended up with a lump like an egg! I suspect that the referee wouldn't have allowed me to play on, but it was serious enough to stop the game. Ferguson was okay, he has a very strong head, I think! But I'm fully recovered now, with no after-effects, so I'm ready for Sunday.' Goma was full of praise for Ferguson, who was returning after an injury lay-off as captain of the side: 'He's very strong, and he's very good in the air. He knows how to use his body to make things difficult for you. When a striker plays the way he plays, it is always difficult for a defender to get the upper hand, especially with high balls. Trying to stop him in the air is very difficult.'

SUNDAY, 17 MARCH

The *News of the World* reported that Barry Hayles was involved in a nightclub brawl the previous Wednesday, and was interviewed by the police. According to the paper Hayles was part of a group of revellers at Eve's in Regent Street when a waitress was mauled, while later a fight broke out. 'Fulham Ace Quizzed Over Bar Brawl – trouble flared as waitress was grabbed' was the lurid headline. Hayles responded: 'I am very unhappy about this newspaper story linking me with trouble in a nightclub. The incident had nothing to do with me and you can rest assured I'm going to be taking legal advice.'

MONDAY, 18 MARCH

With the team going into freefall in the Premiership, Tigana's present attitude of mind was top of the agenda at an emergency session of the board. The FA Cup glory trail was all very well, but his team were slipping precariously close to the bottom rather than moving towards the target of European qualification via the league. The stakes had risen in a season when so much depended on maintaining Premiership status and all the finance that goes with it. Fulham, increasingly in a delicate financial position, simply couldn't afford relegation. On the issue of finances the chairman was beginning to question the value of record-signing Marlet. A club source revealed: 'What would we do if Jean walked out? That was the topic under review. It was going badly in the league and the subject of Jean's temperament was an issue. He had never suffered any sort of failure in his career as player or manager and we were concerned that it might be a volatile situation for someone of his temperament. Did we have a Plan B? If Jean walked out who would we appoint? The board concluded that there was no readymade replacement, not even when the season was over, and that they had faith Tigana would keep his nerve, avoid relegation and stay on.' The board also decided not to discuss this issue with Tigana as it would only undermine his position.

While such fundamental matters were under discussion at boardroom level, back in the dressing room the players were still coming to terms with the team's problems. Tottenham were next up. With the last meeting resulting in a thrashing, the team needed little in the way of motivation. Goma explained: 'We've played them twice and lost twice. We played quite well at home in the Worthington Cup without getting what we deserved, but in the second game they beat us 4–0 and that was very hard to take. Recently they haven't been doing so well, like us, but it would be very dangerous to take them for granted. In our last match you could see how well Everton, a team who were having a bad run, responded to their difficulties and were very positive. So the important thing is that we concentrate on our own performance and make sure that we are positive. When you get beaten 4–0 by a team, you remember. I wouldn't say it's exactly revenge that you feel, but you remember. You are a professional and you have pride, and you want very much to turn that result round on them. It doesn't matter who plays for them, we just have to be ready for a big game. We have had a bad run, but you have to say that four of those games were away, and the home game was against Liverpool who aren't a bad side. That isn't making excuses, but now we are at home, we have to put this bad run behind us. But we can definitely win on Sunday.'

TUESDAY, 19 MARCH

Tigana has been impressed with the development of the England team under Sven Goran Eriksson in the World Cup year. Tigana discussed the merits of the England team without betraying any worry about his own team's present predicament: 'Eriksson is very clever with the players. It's possible for your country to arrive at the top. In France, to arrive at the top level we needed twenty-five years. In England, you need only five years because you are very strong mentally. You have good discipline. We had bad discipline. I'm sure you can win the World Cup. Yes, I say that not for pleasure, it is my feeling.' Owen has impressed Tigana. 'For me, he is a good player and deserves to be European Player of the Year on merit. It's good for English football that he won. He's a good example for young players. He's a fantastic player and a good man. He wants to progress. If my son has the same attitude, I'll be happy.' The game itself in this country has impressed him: 'The atmosphere at the stadiums is incredible. In France it is different.'

John Collins rejected an approach from the Scottish FA to come out of retirement to play for new coach Berti Vogts. After trouble with his hamstrings, Collins, who retired from the international scene in 1999, was not keen to add to his 58 international appearances, admitting: 'My heart said yes, but my head no. I had a phone call from the SFA and Berti's number two asked me if I was at all interested in coming back. If I was he said Berti would come down and speak to me. But I think it would be the wrong move for me. It's time for some of the younger players to have a chance now and I'd hate to take that away from them. I was very flattered to be asked, but I just felt it was the wrong decision at this stage of my career. I'm 34 and I want to concentrate all my efforts with Fulham at club level. Don't get me wrong, I thought about it, visualising myself in a Scotland shirt again, but I had to stick by my original decision.' Vogts' appointment had tempted Paul Lambert out of retirement but not Collins or, indeed, Gary McAllister. 'Like myself,' continued Collins, 'Gary's wise head would defiantly say no. We had our time, and now is a good opportunity for others to shine.'

WEDNESDAY, 20 MARCH

Roger Lemerre called up Marlet to face Scotland in a World Cup warm-up match, exactly the boost Steve needed in the face of competition from Liverpool's Nicolas Anelka for his place. 'My wife called and told me I'd been picked for the national team so naturally I'm very happy. The World Cup is only two months away so a it's a good sign to be in the national team now.' Lemerre had watched Marlet against Liverpool, Arsenal and Chelsea and was impressed. Marlet admitted: 'I'm happy now, but I heard the comments about me and I was hurt. But I kept my focus on my work and had support from my family and friends. When you have difficulties like I had, you become tougher. I know I can go forward now and be much stronger mentally. I don't know if I'll make the World Cup squad, because there are many good strikers competing for places, but I can also play on the wing and maybe that's an advantage for me. I'm 28, which is the right age to go to the tournament; maybe next time I'll be a little too old and there are so many good young French players coming up behind me. If I don't get to the World Cup, I'll have to go far away on holiday and try to forget about it.'

Marlet also revealed that while he had taken a liking to London, he also enjoyed the best of both worlds: 'It's a nice place to live. There are four airports and a railway station where you can get a train to Paris.' Also, if he is in need of a chat he can always dial a friend. 'Sometimes I telephone Thierry Henry or Bernard [Diomede] but there's never much time to go and see people or explore London. Even when I am free I just like relaxing at home with my girlfriend and our son. He is one year old on the day after we play Scotland, you know, and I'd like to score a goal for him.' Marlet emerged from the rough suburbs of Paris with an inner will to succeed, which he has brought with him to his new club. He explained: 'As a child we didn't have much money. My parents separated when I was a kid and myself, my two brothers and sister moved to Paris. We lived in the suburb of St Denis, where the Stade de France is. It was a tough place to live and still is. Everyone has problems with money there. It was a very difficult time for me. But football helped me avoid any trouble and brushes with the law.'

Having been compared to Ronaldo by Auxerre coach Guy Roux, Fulham fans were beginning to wonder whether he was a class act. 'When I first came here and played number-one striker, I'd stand and look around, but I'm trying to alter my game and be in the box more. I used to think for the other players. Now I have to be more individualistic.' The feeling among Fulham fans is that while Marlet is good in the air, committed and strong, he probably won't be a big hit until next season. As for Steve McQueen, after whom he was named, Marlet says: 'I like him, but he's not my favourite actor. My mother used to watch him in a television series where he played a sheriff and, because of him, Steve was quite a fashionable name in France for a time.'

THURSDAY, 21 MARCH

Al Fayed invited Ken Bates to lunch at the Georgian Restaurant at Harrods to patch up any differences they had had in the past. Top of the agenda was their shared grievances over the FA's choice of semi-final venue. 'He is a very generous host,' Bates said. 'There were also lots of laughs as we discussed all sorts of things. We discussed how best to forge a better cooperation between the Premier League clubs and how best we can work together.' Other Premier League chairmen had been regular guests at the grand Harrods eaterie, as well as Adam Crozier and FA company secretary Nick Coward.

Chris Coleman was ready for his long-awaited comeback. 'I've just started full-time training. The last three weeks has been almost like a mini pre-season for me, as I've been working hard on fitness and there is a reserve-team game against Charlton next Wednesday which I'm pencilled down to play in. If all goes well I could maybe play half an hour in that. It will be superb. I'm not going to play ninety minutes, but it will be a platform for me, because although you can do as much work as you like, it's games that you need.'

Midfielder Paul Trollope joined First Division Coventry City on a free transfer. The former Welsh international's first-team chances have been limited, although Trollope has often captained the Whites' reserve side, always showing a great attitude. Paul was one of the first big signings of the Al Fayed era when he joined the club from Derby County for £650,000 in November 1997 and made a distinguished contribution to the 1998–99 season, scoring some vital goals that helped secure the Division Two Championship. He is another member of the Keegan and Bracewell era to fall by the wayside.

FRIDAY, 22 MARCH

Tigana summoned his entire squad to the gym at Motspur Park for a crisis meeting. The boss was showing signs of growing more nervous as his team slipped close to relegation. He was feeling the pressure and could not understand why such talented players were not performing to their potential. Tigana was desperate to get to the bottom of it. He also knew that his chairman was beginning to get twitchy and had questioned the wisdom of big-money signings, particularly Marlet. Barry Hayles revealed what had been said: 'The manager said we must close down teams more and that players are switching off at crucial times. He wants the errors stamped out.' Alain Goma added that the meeting was important in order to get a reaction from the players: 'We need to show more determination in the way we play. We have conceded a lot of goals recently. We haven't been creating chances and we have not been defending properly. At the meeting the manager pointed out the mistakes we have been making and how we can improve. I think the meeting did us some good. It is important we react positively. We simply talked about how we can improve, how we can produce better results. We must be stronger at the back and score more goals. We were shown our mistakes and told how to avoid them. All the time it was clear we have to keep playing football a certain way, but we must be stronger. After tasting life in the Premiership nobody wants to go back to the First Division. I didn't join this club to play in the First Division again. None of us did. We signed because we had ambition and that ambition is to ensure we do not play in the Nationwide League.'

Tigana was anxious to avoid a sixth successive defeat against Tottenham. Goma stressed: 'At the moment we are prepared for Tottenham, and despite what has happened in recent league matches, our confidence is not bad, the spirit is good and there is solidarity among the players. We have had a difficult run of matches and we have not been in the best form, not hundred per cent ready for them. There are periods when you are not in top form. It is unfortunate it should have happened to us at this point, but the season is not finished.' Setting the scene for this important derby, describing it as a 'massive match for both sides', Goma continued: 'We both need maximum points to bring a halt to disappointing runs which have put our campaigns on temporary hold. We also know victory over Spurs will put us on the same points total as them and that's a major incentive.' Hayles, meanwhile, insisted minds have not wandered to the Cup. 'The manager wouldn't allow that to happen anyway, but we honestly haven't talked about it.' He added: 'We owe Tottenham because they knocked us out of the Worthington Cup in November and then beat us 4–0 at White Hart Lane just before Christmas. It's important to get something from the game because the clubs at the bottom are edging worryingly closer to us, although we prefer to look up rather than down the table.'

In training, Tigana has been shaking up his strikers. With a recent record of 15 goals in the last 18 league games behind them, Damiano said about the strikers: 'In training I told the players every time they missed the target they had to pay with some physical work. For each shot wide of the goal they had to give me five sit-ups and five press-ups. I wanted to put pressure on them and make it like a match situation. It showed them how much they must concentrate. It was amazing, they scored twice as many goals and I told them that even if they miss they will have beautiful muscles in the summer!'

SATURDAY, 23 MARCH

Spurs were facing their own crisis – four straight defeats with a 13–0 aggregate – but this was nothing compared to Marlet's problems. His fee was more than Fulham's entire turnover in the previous season, and people continued to question whether Tigana's decision to sign him had been wise. After early-season optimism that Europe would be a serious target, reality had set in. 'It's difficult to say what is wrong,' said Marlet. 'We've lost five games in a row yet in the first four of them we played well. Only in the last game against Everton did we play badly and that was a special occasion because they had a new manager and were very charged. But it's amazing how things have changed. Between the bottom and middle of the league there are so few points that if you lose a few games you're in trouble. We're fighting relegation now.'

SUNDAY, 24 MARCH
FULHAM 0 TOTTENHAM 2

Tigana was chewing his toothpicks to pieces; he had never before suffered six defeats in a row. He offered up two solutions: 'You can sack the manager – which is not going to happen – or the players can change inside. Fulham have come a long way in five years and we've had to learn quickly in the Premiership to keep working and stay calm. It is looking very dangerous now at this stage of the season and it is a worry that we are so close to the bottom three, but the key is the reaction from the players in our next two games. We will see whether it is possible or not. We always knew it would be a very difficult league after coming up from the First Division. It's not only today; we've not taken our chances all season and need to work harder. People say to me "you are unlucky". We are not unlucky; we need to work more. For us the game only started in the second half, so we need to change our attitude. I believe we can still win three of our remaining games and hopefully that will be enough to keep us up. My target at the start of the season was to stay in the Premiership and then build and that's still my ambition.' Fewer than 16,000 attended the match, by far Fulham's smallest crowd for a game back in the Premiership. While emphasising the team's slide, this was also due to the problems of ticket touting and Spurs fans' reputation for trouble. Although 4,000 extra people wanted to go and could have been accommodated, missile-throwing incidents and problems caused by Spurs fans buying tickets for Fulham areas earlier in the season meant entry was restricted on police advice. Spurs were given an allocation of only 750 seats and their supporters were kept out of the standing area next to the pitch from where a lighter was thrown at Boa Morte in the Worthington Cup tie. Home areas were also only available to Fulham members and season-ticket holders. A club spokesman said: 'An agreement was reached about the ticketing for the game between Fulham, Tottenham, the Football Licensing Authority, the Premier League, local authority and the police.'

Sheringham enjoyed a huge slice of luck scoring his first goal in the Premiership since 3 December to damage Fulham's league position even further. Fulham were still stunned by the Spurs captain's 28-minute opener – a fluke as it struck Sheringham in the eye – when Poyet grabbed the second goal just three minutes later. Tottenham's victory, their third over the west Londoners this season, eased their fears of being dragged into the relegation dog fight but increased the pressure on Tigana.

Sean Davis was pleasantly surprised to start after his absence with a torn leg muscle, but was naturally disappointed with the result. 'They had the little touch of luck that they've been missing and we didn't. When you are near the bottom of the league, you don't get the luck, but we still have a good spirit and I know that we can fight our way back. Hopefully we can start the next game with a bit more passion and we can go on from there. We came out a different side in the second half so we know we can do it. But really we can have no excuses.'

In spite of the loss, there was still no budging Tigana from his preferred way of playing: 'This is football, not rugby and I will never tell my players to kick the opponent,' he insisted.

MONDAY, 25 MARCH
Barry Hayles revealed the gloomy atmosphere that had descended within the dressing room: 'The rallying call has been sounded and it's time for us to roll up our sleeves and dig our way out of trouble,' he said. 'Our defeat against Spurs was unfortunate but there's no hiding the fact we have lost our last six matches and been sucked into a relegation fight. We will settle for any type of win right now. It doesn't matter if it comes from an own-goal. We want to play exciting football but results are what count at this stage. People have said we are too good to go down but we can't relax until we are mathematically safe. The gulf in class between Division One and the Premiership is rather bigger than we expected but the experience is invaluable and if we can upset Chelsea in the semi-final and remain in the top flight then it will have been a marvellous season.'

TUESDAY, 26 MARCH
Chris Coleman was on the verge of a landmark after months of agony and ten operations as he looked forward to a thirty-minute run-out in the reserves against Charlton tomorrow. He said: 'Once I get on the pitch I will feel that I

have won. I will have overcome it. A lot of people thought I would never play football again but I will be doing that even if I am well off the pace. It will probably be nine or ten games before I can say, "That is it, I am back," but tomorrow I will be in a reserve game and feel like I have beaten it. If I'm lucky enough to get back into the first team, the first game will probably be the most important of my career, but if that does not happen this will be the next best thing. I don't think playing in this reserve game will compare to anything else I have experienced. I think it will be my biggest achievement in football because of the severity of the accident and the injuries I had. Just to get back on the pitch for about half an hour will be the best. I have played international football for Wales against some of the best players in the world, I won the First Division Championship with Fulham and had good times at Crystal Palace and Blackburn. But without a doubt this will be my biggest achievement. What happened to me has made me appreciate what I have got. It makes me look back and realise how lucky I have been. For about fifteen years I lived a charmed life and I know that now.' Finding out the ligaments in his knee were not ruptured helped his recovery rate by about eight months, but the mental trauma he suffered after his car crash have been difficult to measure. He added: 'I wouldn't have reached this stage without my wife Belinda. She has had to deal with me every day and she never knew what mood I would be in when I came home. Without the medical staff and the fitness coaches at Fulham I would probably be limping for the rest of my life and I will be forever grateful to them. But it is my wife who has pulled me through as a person. I have thought loads of times that I would not do it and I have gone home loads of times and told her we should forget about it so that we can get on with our lives. She said that I had to try. No one would blame me if I did retire, but I would spend the rest of my life wondering if I could have got back and that has stuck with me.'

Melville was named Wales skipper for his fiftieth cap against the Czech Republic just days after being on the subs' bench against Spurs. He had a message for Tigana: 'Maybe he thinks I'm to blame. We've not been too clever of late, but Tigana knows what I can do and it's a good chance to prove a point.' Melville had been dropped for three of the last five games. 'I can go from being on the bench to leading my country,' he said.

WEDNESDAY, 27 MARCH

He did it; he passed his crucial test. Not only that, he came through with flying colours. Coleman played for 45 minutes, not the planned 30. It was his first game for fourteen months, but those at Woking's Kingfield Stadium will never forget it. The delighted 31-year-old said: 'I'm getting pats on the back but I've been like a guinea pig. The medical team and fitness coaches have guided me through. I owe them an awful lot. That was the most important 45 minutes of my life. I was a bit tentative at first and didn't know how it was going to turn out but then the adrenalin kicked in and I didn't really think about it. This is a massive step on my road to recovery, but I've still got a long way to go. It's wishful thinking to think I could get back and help the team this season. I need another ten or twelve reserve games to get match fit. I've been training for the last two weeks but it's different in a match. I was the most nervous I've been in my career.' By the way, the result was a 1–1 draw.

THURSDAY, 28 MARCH

'Cookie' was in bright and early at Motspur Park training ground. 'He's on a fantastic high,' observed Rufus Brevett, who revealed that a 'let's do it for Chris' campaign was under way. Brevett explained: 'We want to be in the Premier League next season for Chris. He has been in the changing rooms and it's been brilliant to have him around. He's always laughing and joking. He brightens up the atmosphere. He's been a real captain while he's been sidelined. He's had a very, very bad time with his injury but he's come through it. He's battled back, he's been working extremely hard from eight in the morning to eight at night so he deserves to get back. He didn't know, even quite recently, if he'd ever actually make it back. We're all behind him. That's why most of the first-team lads were at Woking to cheer him on. It was such an important game for him and for the club.'

However, at the moment it was this season that mattered most. Brevett added: 'The mood is very good. It's not critical yet but it could be after the Bank Holiday weekend if we don't end this losing run.'

FRIDAY, 29 MARCH

Time for Tigana to get tough. He gave an ultimatum to the squad: 'You are staring relegation in the face so start earning your massive pay packets' was the message Tigana delivered to his under-performing side at Motspur Park. After seeing the team lose six Premiership games in a row Tigana had lost his patience. And rest assured there was no toothpick in his mouth when he was giving his warning. He said: 'We have given everything to our players, and now it is time they gave something back. I am looking for a reaction from them in the next game. If we do not get a reaction from them soon we will go out of the Premiership. It is as simple as that. I want us to win three more matches. I think we need at least six or seven more points to stay at this top level.'

Sacked Derby boss Colin Todd was in no doubt that Fulham would be relegated. Under the headline 'Tig's Gonna Get Dumped', he suggested in the *Sun*: 'The Easter weekend is always important and some teams could be six points better off by Monday. The team that I have noticed are Fulham and their six defeats in a row. They remind me of Wimbledon a couple of years ago. They dropped like a stone and everybody said they wouldn't go down – then they did. Fulham need to pull a couple of results out of the bag and quickly. I also think that the fact they are in the FA Cup semi-final could be a bit of a burden to them. I saw their manager Jean Tigana on television the other day when

Fulham lost to Spurs and he looked as if he was feeling it badly. He has spent a lot of money and this is new to him. Once again it's been a lack of goals, especially from Louis Saha. When a team gets into that losing habit it needs something special to stop the rot.' Southampton boss Gordon Strachan was surprised by Fulham's slide: 'It's a mystery what is happening to Fulham. I watched them recently and they are doing a lot of things right and making chances. But the game is all about putting the ball in the back of the net.' Simple, but true.

SATURDAY, 30 MARCH
SOUTHAMPTON 1 FULHAM 1
Fulham really needed to win this game, but in the end it was another Jones blunder which cost Southampton victory. The south-coast club's Welsh international goalkeeper, whose gaffe in the previous Premiership fixture allowed Deane to convert and Leicester to leave with a point, gifted Fulham an early lead. With little apparent danger, Jones spilled a through ball, allowing Marlet to sidefoot into an empty net. Delap equalised for Strachan's side, leaving both teams still involved in the relegation equation. But at least Fulham's dismal run of six consecutive defeats had come to an end.

APRIL

Rumours of the sack ... Relegation becomes a possibility ... Defeat in the semi-final ... Debts of £61.7m ...

MONDAY, 1 APRIL
FULHAM 0 WEST HAM 1

Jean Tigana's assistant Christian Damiano observed in the programme: 'We seem to have acquired a fragile attitude.' And he was proved right. It turned into a disastrous Easter weekend for the Whites, with a haul of one point from a possible six. Gone was the pre-Christmas optimism that followed the thrashing of West Ham at Upton Park, Fulham's best performance of the season, replaced by relegation fears. 'Pass and move, it ain't rocket science,' someone shouted from the crowd, betraying the fans' displeasure. Tigana made one change, relegating Marlet to the bench in favour of playing Saha in tandem with Hayles but it made little difference.

Damiano pointed out the desperate need for points: 'We are perhaps in the worst period of the season. We have five games left and we need five points. If you look at the last six seasons, 41 points has been enough.' He added: 'It is possible for us to remain in the Premier League, but we have players who are less experienced than their opponents. Perhaps only Steve Marlet has enough experience for the Premiership. It's the first time Louis Saha has played regularly at this level. Luis Boa Morte has great ability in the First Division, but is allowed less space in the Premiership, where he plays better in midfield. We are not scoring enough goals but up until a month ago we had one of the best defences in the league. Now we are conceding goals and not scoring them either. We have arrived in the top level of football, perhaps in the world, and every week there are big, big matches for our players.' One-time Tigana transfer target Kanoute broke Fulham's hearts and at the final whistle there was booing from a section of the crowd as some fans' patience finally ran out. Yet West Ham manager Glenn Roeder was convinced Fulham would survive: 'Looking at their fixtures I am as sure as you can be in this game that we will be playing them next season. I hope so, because I like teams who get the ball down and play.'

Damiano insisted the Cup was not playing on his players' minds. 'The semi-final is not a problem, it's just another objective. We prepare only for the next game,' he insisted. However, Sean Davis gave a warning to the big-money stars: 'We're not too good to go down. If we took our chances people would say we are a great team, but we have not been doing that. Everyone wants to play at the top level and we wanted to come into the Premiership and do ourselves justice, but I don't think we have done that. Time and time again we have dominated teams and got absolutely nothing. We played well against West Ham but we let them off the hook and got punished. It is frustrating when you play well and lose but we have all got to stick together, us and the fans, and try to get the two wins we desperately need. Some people are saying we should play a long-ball game, but we are never going to do that while Jean Tigana is in charge. We have got to keep plugging away and show everyone how much character we have got collectively and individually. We've got a lot of big games to play and have got Bolton and Leicester still to come at home and it is important we win those two.' What the fans did not realise, however, was that the night before Davis was arrested for drink-driving, not something Tigana was particularly pleased about, especially given his attitude to alcohol. What was worse was that Davis was caught out in the middle of a busy Easter weekend which was so important to the future of the club. However, what angered some of the senior players most was that Tigana did absolutely nothing about it. Rather than give Davis a carpeting and make an example of him, not a word was said, even when the full facts of the incident emerged. Perhaps the threat of relegation had become more important to Tigana than principles at this crucial stage of the season.

WEDNESDAY, 3 APRIL

Louis Saha tried to explain where it had all gone wrong: 'The expectations have been too high on us from the start of the season. It's very hard to live up to that. For the first two or three games we played well, but we had just arrived. Maybe if we'd lost heavily at Manchester United it would have been easier for us. We could have surprised more teams. It could be very difficult dropping into the relegation area so late in the season because you don't have time to react.' As for resolving the lack of goals being scored, he argued: 'We need to be more direct. The manager has asked us to shoot more. Sometimes we have to surprise teams. If we play the same way all the time, it's easy for the opposition to get their tactics right against us. Maybe it's time to change our mentality. We've been playing good football, but beautiful football alone is not enough. You can't just say it's not working, but it's not working enough. We show our ability every week but it's not always been enough to get the three points.'

Saha maintained he had nothing to prove in the upcoming fixture with

Newcastle United, where he spent five months on loan during Ruud Gullit's time in charge, scoring two goals in eleven appearances. Although Saha's spell was blighted by injury, he revealed he had enjoyed his time on Tyneside: 'It was my first taste of the Premiership. I do not think I have anything to prove against them because I was young in those days and I have improved. And I liked the club very much because the fans there were very passionate.' Saha was hoping he could keep them quiet.

Coleman made his second successive start for the reserves, playing 65 minutes in a 3–1 win over Coventry. Academy director Steve Kean reported: 'Chris's positioning was excellent, as he seemed to get to the right places at the right time. Sometimes you can think your players do well, but the opposition might not see it that way. But even Coventry's management thought he had a good game.'

THURSDAY, 4 APRIL
Nobody ever really thought relegation was a possibility after Tigana spent £1m a day in August. But how the mood had changed as confidence ebbed away. Edwin Van Der Sar admitted the Fulham boys had their eyes on the bottom of the table: 'Even if we win the FA Cup it will mean nothing if we are relegated. We must focus on the league, which is the most important thing. All our energy must go towards staying in the Premiership and getting the two wins that we need. We first started to look at what the other clubs were doing a few days ago. We have to win the two home matches at least, but it is no good waiting until then. We must get a result against Newcastle.' Rufus Brevett, who knows all about relegation after going down from the Premiership with QPR in 1996, echoed these fears: 'We are a good side, but you can't say we are too good to go down. When you're down at the bottom of the league you are bound to look over your shoulder. Of course what's happening behind you counts.' Jon Harley felt the team had to ditch its pretty football image now they were just three points above the drop zone: 'From now until the end of the season we have to focus on getting results, and it doesn't matter how we get them. We've been playing good football but getting nothing out of it. Everyone's frustrated but it's vitally important that we all stick together. Confidence is a major factor. If a goal goes against us, people will think, "Oh no, here we go again."'

FRIDAY, 5 APRIL
Steve Finnan, the only player to figure in every game this season, believed the Whites had to regain mental focus. 'Picking up just one point over the Easter weekend was a massive disappointment and I've got to admit our confidence has taken a bit of a nosedive recently. We are in deep trouble and desperately need a win. At this stage, I don't think any of us care how we get three points as long as we get back to winning ways. The style in which we play is irrelevant now and I'd happily settle for a deflected winner in injury time if it meant we

got the right result. It's hard to pinpoint why things have gone quite so wrong in the past couple of months but I think at least in part we've relaxed mentally. What we've learned in the past few weeks is that you've got to have the same level of focus in every single game, home or away, whether it be against Manchester United or one of the bottom three clubs. You just can't afford to ease off at any stage or against any opposition.'

SUNDAY, 7 APRIL

Mohamed Al Fayed promised to carry on funding the club in order to achieve his dream of making Fulham a major footballing power. While this seemed unlikely at the moment, Al Fayed was keen to emphasise that no matter what was happening on the pitch, he would stand by the club: 'I bought Fulham because I love the club. It is mine for life. I intend to hand it on to my children. I will continue to fund the club to the level required to realise my dream and the supporters' dream of making it one of the best in the world. Relegation is not in my thinking. You can expect us to enter the transfer market in the close season to strengthen the squad. This season has been tough, but I didn't expect it to be easy. I am satisfied with the players we have brought to the club this season and reaching the FA Cup semi-final is a big achievement. We have learned a lot this season and will improve even more as time goes on. Jean Tigana works harder than anyone. He has managed to help several players make the transition from First Division to Premiership standard.'

Skipper Andy Melville admitted that 'for the first time we talked about relegation. We know how difficult it is going to be at St James's Park. We have to go back to basics and by that I mean putting in the hard work. Perhaps we've been guilty of attempting to overplay and walk the ball into the net. What has happened is not down to tactics, but sometimes when you up the work rate things can change. But time is now running out. We are in a fight, and I would like to think everyone has taken on board just how serious the situation is. We are a team who have always enjoyed lots of possession and now we have to turn it into something positive, meaning more goals. It's obvious we are in a bad run and it must stop. Our poor run of results has silenced the crowd but now we need their full support more than ever.' Lee Clark, who will miss the chance of a return to his old stamping ground, pinpointed the start of the decline to the defeat at Boro: 'That was typical of the way we've played quite well without getting the end result. A few weeks ago, we were thinking about trying to nick one of the European places and the football was assured, but just as when you feel untouchable when you're winning, your self-belief takes a hit when you lose.' Since the turn of the year, the regular strikers have managed just eight goals between them. Newcastle boss Bobby Robson, however, had encouragement for the beleaguered Londoners: 'Tigana was a great player and Fulham's style is indicative of him. They've been unlucky, but I firmly believe they won't go down. They simply have too many good players to be relegated.'

MONDAY, 8 APRIL
NEWCASTLE UNITED 1 FULHAM 1

Finally, the storm clouds over Tigana's head lifted, with some spirit and fight in his side as they earned a point which put them one step closer to safety. After Dyer scored against the run of play, a wonderful deflection by Saha from a Davis shot sent the Fulham fans home happy and meant that the players could finally look forward to the FA Cup semi-final. Tigana said: 'It will be a fantastic game for us on Sunday and you can see the belief coming back. We showed a great improvement against Newcastle. We were strong and pressed and I think that is a good sign for the next game.' Given that Newcastle were pushing for a Champions League place, this result was outstanding. Tigana added: 'Saha's performance deserved a goal. He played very well and his only problem is in his head because he has a lot of quality. Even one off his knee will help, but it is the one time he has been lucky.' Lee Clark, still sidelined through injury, enthused: 'Everyone has to give credit to Fulham. We controlled the midfield and this enabled us to nullify Newcastle's attacking threat. The lads are disappointed we didn't win after the way we played.'

TUESDAY, 9 APRIL

Fulham physio Jason Palmer ruled out Lee Clark until the summer. Clark, whose season has been ruined by injury, admitted that missing the Newcastle game had been particularly disappointing: 'To have missed playing at St James's Park and not to be able to thank the people who supported me so well when I was there and who support me still when I go home is a real disappointment. Since leaving in the summer of 1997 I have never had the opportunity of playing at St James's. It's the first game I look for when the fixtures come out, so to miss that one was a bit of a kick in the teeth. It's a special place and I get up there as often as possible. I went to the Everton game on Good Friday and go to the Newcastle games whenever I can. If they are playing in London and I can see them, then I'll go. When I joined Fulham it meant coming to London, a place I never thought I would live. It's three years in June since I've been here and I'm still not used to it.' Nor are the fans used to Lee's Geordie accent on the ClubCall.

WEDNESDAY, 10 APRIL

Al Fayed spent £13,000 to send fans to the semi-final. Away travel for fans has been subsidised all season and the chairman has stepped it up for the club's big day out, booking 1,050 seats on two trains and filling 34 coaches, but charging just £15 for the train and £10 for the coach. The cheapest normal train fare was £50 return to Birmingham.

THURSDAY, 11 APRIL

Fulham have offered semi-final tickets to staff at Harrods. With 1,000 of their 16,000 allocation unsold, Al Fayed wanted to give them away to children and their parents, but the FA blocked the move because it might have affected segregation at Villa Park. A Fulham spokesman said: 'There is an annoyance with the FA because we did not agree to the 7 p.m. kick-off and our suggestion that the FA give concessions in terms of pricing for children was not accepted. We are a family club and have many families who are unable to go because of the cost of tickets.' Chelsea chairman Ken Bates accused the FA of 'No.10-style spin-doctoring' by writing to fans to inform them that Chelsea and Fulham agreed to the 7 p.m. kick-off time. He argued: 'We were not even consulted, let alone given the opportunity to agree the kick-off time.' Chelsea failed to sell all of their allocation for the first time as Bates called the choice of Villa Park 'stupid'.

FRIDAY, 12 APRIL
The build up to the semi-final really started at the media day at Motspur Park where journalists milled around the old mansion house and players started to get excited and looked forward to a weekend without thinking about relegation. Although Chelsea are hot favourites, the players know that anything can happen in a semi-final. Steve Marlet declared that he was ready to go to war with French World Cup star Marcel Desailly. Marlet, who is usually laid back, was not joking when he said: 'When I'm on the pitch I forget all about friendships. Marcel is a big player, he is the captain of France and Chelsea's best defender. But having him and Emmanuel Petit in the opposition will only serve as greater motivation for myself and Louis Saha.' With the question behind the scenes increasingly becoming whether Marlet had justified his transfer fee in the eyes of the chairman and fans, he went on: 'Of course the fans started to ask questions about my quality. I have not been able to show the real me in the first few months. I hope they will see the real me now. It has been a very difficult situation at Fulham because nobody expected us to be struggling in the Premiership. If we beat Chelsea and reach the final but go down, for the fans that would be a deception. Even if we won the FA Cup it would be no compensation for going down to the First Division. The perfect scenario would be to beat Chelsea on Sunday and then stay in the Premier League. The players are starting to get accustomed to the demands of English football and I feel we will be a much better team next year.'

Barry Hayles condemned the FA disciplinary system as a 'joke' and warned Tigana he could quit the club if a flood of big-money summer signings leave him stuck on the bench. Hayles was dropped at Newcastle and admitted it would be 'tough' to win back his place for the semi-final. As well as worries over his Fulham future, he was angry over the FA's decision to hit him with a three-match ban, starting on 29 April, for his bust-up with West Ham's Hayden Foxe. The suspension could rob Hayles of a fairy-tale appearance in the FA Cup Final. He fumed: 'To be honest, I think it's very harsh. Nearly five months have elapsed and it's strange how they've pushed it forward now and slapped down a three-match ban. The club are appealing and I'm hoping the FA will take into consideration that I pleaded guilty. It's taken so long to come through, while we've been doing well in the FA Cup.' Meanwhile Hayles faced another FA charge for his kick at Everton skipper David Weir, but the hearing, initially pencilled in for next week, was delayed again. Hayles can expect another three-match ban if found guilty of another offence of violent conduct.

In the middle of a goal drought and left out of the side for Fulham's last game, Hayles knows that if, as anticipated, Tigana brings in new faces over the summer, he would need to review his situation at the club: 'I'd have to decide whether to stay doing what I am doing – battling for a place – or move on. That will be a choice I make come the summer, and I'd also have to see what the club would have to say about it. I've got two years left on my contract after this season. I'm 30 in May, so I want to be starting as many games as possible next season.' But if any story sums up the magic of the FA Cup, it is Hayles' description of his career before being snapped up by Stevenage: 'I was a carpenter making partitions. I played football and had to pay three-pound subs to play every game – so it's a nice turn around now.'

Despite all the talk concerning Marlet, perhaps the canniest addition to the squad will prove to be Steed Malbranque. Damiano said about the young star: 'Steed can score or make goals, but he is just 22 and when you move to another country you face a lot of human challenges, then the challenge becomes to express yourself as a player. He will do that. The ball to him is like his girlfriend, and he has the capacity to change the flow of a game.'

SATURDAY, 13 APRIL

Tigana uttered those terrible words 'I could be sacked'. He could steer Fulham to only their second ever FA Cup Final and still be out of a job, because Al Fayed refused to consider relegation as an option. Only two points from their last nine Premiership games was not what the Harrods owner expected at such a critical time. With a furrowed brow and a slower chew on his toothpick Tigana said: 'The priority is to stay in the Premiership. If you do that, it is a good season. To play against Chelsea in an FA Cup semi-final is fantastic for Fulham and it would be a dream to play in the UEFA Cup next season. But we need to win more league games. This season has been difficult and frustrating for us. Many players are learning, and I am too. This is the first time I have lost so many games as a manager. Every chairman puts pressure on a manager for success and I have to deliver results for the chairman, I know that. If football managers are not successful they lose their heads. For me, it is not an achievement to reach the semi-final. The achievement is to win it and to be in the final. I like the compliment when people say we play good football, but I also want us to win. What we have needed this season is to score goals, we miss too many chances. But many of my players have not played at this level before and they have had to learn quickly because Premiership football is so different.'

Barry Hayles revealed that the atmosphere within the camp had changed from easy laughter and a calm air of sophistication to a more realistic one of tension and stress, saying: 'The manager always used to be bubbly, but now he is a lot more serious, maybe a bit more determined. He is perhaps more focused on certain aspects of our work, like set-pieces. But the same could be said for all the players as well. Maybe we were all getting a bit too comfortable.'

There was no way Al Fayed was going to let a little matter like an FA Cup semi-final pass without getting in on the media act and ruffling a few feathers. He held court at Harrods twice within a week, once for the daily press and then for the Sunday press. Each journalist was given a gold chocolate bar and a picture of Fayed playing football in Alexandria in his early twenties. He made it plain that he feels too much power is concentrated in the hands of a few influential clubs and claimed to be speaking on behalf of the smaller clubs when he said: 'The FA are kidnapped by the strong clubs. They have all the money and they don't care about the other clubs. They need a revolution to try to help the clubs which are suffering.' Al Fayed would like to see central marketing by the Premiership, so that Manchester United can't open 'Red Cafés' all around the world – they would have to be 'Premier Cafés', which all the clubs would benefit from. He would also like to be able to sack players if they are not performing, which is not a surprise considering the way some of the Fulham players have been playing. He added: 'The wages of the players are out of line. Some of the contracts around today are unbelievable. You pay a player £20,000, £30,000, £40,000 a week. You pay millions for him and then they belly dance on the pitch. They can't deliver. They don't want to deliver. You pay blood and it is not fair. If a player does not deliver he is just taking your money. It can be difficult for a manager to control his players at times. We don't know what they have been doing the day before a game. For some players the minute they start getting huge wages it goes to their heads. They get arrogant and think they are invincible, even if they don't deliver on the pitch. In any other job if you don't perform after, say, six months, then you're out. But in football you are handcuffed. In this game you have to sign a player for a few years, regardless of what he's like, because of the money it cost to get him and his wages on top of that. Then if it all goes wrong and the player goes out clubbing and womanising every night or isn't up to scratch, you can't do anything.' Al Fayed wanted performance-related pay: 'The whole game is a shambles and it's up to the FA and the Premier League to sort it out. They have the destiny of a great game in their hands and it is still the ultimate game of the ordinary people but it will be ruined if things carry on like this. We all have a responsibility, just look at the problems caused by the ITV Digital mess. So many clubs could go out of business as a result of that and where is the Government in it all? Where are the regulatory bodies? Where is the Lottery money? Every club is a community centre and should be treated as such.'

Al Fayed also explained why he was subsidising fans' travel expenses for the semi-final: 'Most Fulham fans are working-class, ordinary people. If you have a couple with two kids and they are on £15,000–£20,000 a year, and they have to pay £100 to travel, it is difficult for them. This shows someone cares about them and it is setting an example for other richer clubs.' Al Fayed also looked beyond the FA Cup competition to consider the club's chances of Premiership survival, saying: 'I am confident that we will stay up. Tigana has delivered. He's committed and he knows what he's doing. However, the players have let him down. They know that and they can't keep doing it because of the fans. They are the life-blood of this club. Yes, it is still Tigana's responsibility and I am sure those players can deliver. I haven't lost trust in anyone. In fact, I'm very confident.' However, while the rally call was Churchillian in its delivery, behind the scenes Al Fayed's patience was being stretched. Behind his air of confidence, one can only wonder what tensions lay between the chairman and the manager at a stage in the season when the club was hoping for FA Cup glory on the one hand and fighting for their Premiership survival on the other.

SUNDAY, 14 APRIL
CHELSEA 1 FULHAM 0
It was all about the Good, the Bad and the Ugly. The Good . . . the first FA Cup semi-final Fulham had been in for 27 years. Nearly twenty thousand Fulham fans set off on two special trains, 35 coaches and by the car-load for Villa Park. The atmosphere was brilliant. The Bad . . . the way Fulham played. The fans would have thought that their side could lift their performance for such an important game, but apart from a Legwinski shot after the best move of the match, Fulham never looked like scoring. The Ugly . . . Terry scored the winning goal after Fulham had failed to clear a corner. Tigana, whose side must now concentrate on avoiding relegation, admitted: 'This sums up our season. We are very disappointed and it's very sad for our fans. But we need to keep our focus on staying up. The main difference between the sides was experience of playing at the top level. We did not play too badly, were good in places and had our chances but we did not score. It is not just the strikers who should have to take all the pressure. It is up to all the players. It is everyone's problem. That's been our problem all season and that's why I'm very frustrated.' He added ruefully: 'This is why it's difficult for me to sleep.' Asked to compare Petit and Davis he said: 'Petit is a very, very clever player, knowing exactly when to break up the game, make the play, keep position. Davis has some possibilities but he needs to learn.' It was a sad way for the dream to end, but the fans needed to remember just how far Fulham had come. In 1997, while Chelsea were in an FA Cup semi-final, Fulham were playing Bury at Gigg Lane. A disappointed Tigana might switch off when the Cup Final is on TV: 'It will be a great final for you, but it is possible that I won't be watching it.'

Privately, Sarah Brookes said the game 'caused Jean a lot of pain and heart-ache', because it represented the one chance of success in the season: 'I had never seen such devastation on his face – it was the worst I had seen all season.'

MONDAY, 15 APRIL

'Stop feeling sorry for ourselves' was the direct message from Andy Melville. 'We have to make sure we pick ourselves up immediately. It's up to experienced players like myself to make sure we do. We thought we could get something against Chelsea, but we didn't and we have to get on with things. There just isn't time to get depressed or low. We still have a job to do and the Premiership was always our priority.' The challenge now was quickly to get over the hurt at missing out on the Cup Final and start fighting a relegation campaign in a season that started with such promise.

TUESDAY, 16 APRIL

Tigana demanded his players halt the team's unacceptable dip in league form: just 2 points from a possible 27. 'I put the FA Cup away last week, but now our league games are very important. I absolutely want my team to win the two games over the next week so that we stay up.'

Sarah Brookes commented: 'Jean was not surprised by the pressure from the press, but he was surprised by the fact that we slipped that low in the league and were not holding our own in the top eight. Both Jean and Christian were hugely demoralised by what went on with the team. To a great extent they put the blame on referees and their assistants and we spent a lot of time at the start of the season bringing referees into the club and talking with them. There was Luis Boa Morte's red card at Everton when he was accused of head-butting and it was going out on *The Premiership* like that but when I spoke to the programme makers the commentary was changed, since after the referee had seen the replay he changed his mind. They do blame the referees because the French believe the refs are there fundamentally to protect the game and they think the players who get penalised after an offence for retaliation are hard done by if they get booked or sent-off because they feel the foul should never have happened. It is a complete learning curve for them. They believe referees have cost them about seven points which would have made a huge difference. But during all the pressure Jean did not change his process and that is a great attribute. What happened was that he was concerned, though. There were only two big players' meetings during the season and they both came at the end. He was not one for crisis management. His philosophy was constant. It is about what the team will and can achieve. He gives them belief when they go out on the pitch. He does not shout and scream at them. The players are upset enough if they do not perform and Jean believes that is penance enough. Jean does not read the press so I have to tell him what's being written about him. When there was speculation over his job I would read it to him. He would just say it was normal. He would say the manager's job is only good when he is winning. He was totally philosophical about it and the way things may or may not go.'

THURSDAY, 18 APRIL

It had never seemed the sponsorship from heaven, although it was quite tasty. As Fulham scrabbled around for a shirt sponsor last summer Pizza Hut, who are owned by Whitbread, stepped into the void with £2m. Well, not any more. Fulham announced that its sponsorship deal would not be renewed for the 2002–03 season. Pizza Hut would not pay the asking price, even though the club came down to £1.5m. Whitbread offered a mere £750,000. Pizza Hut UK MD James O'Reilly said: 'We enjoyed working with Fulham and were considering renewing the sponsorship. We invested time in the deal and made an offer in line with what we believe the market value of sponsorships of this type is worth. However, as sometimes happens with sponsorships, it could not be extended. We wish Fulham every success for the future.' Fulham's Sales and Marketing Director Juliet Slot was reflective, saying: 'We're disappointed we could not reach an agreement.'

French boss Roger Lemerre had been at the semi-final to watch Steed Malbranque. Previously he had said that he did not really rate Malbranque too highly, but now Lemerre reckoned he was a different player, which is testimony to Damiano and the work he does with young players. As a result Malbranque was included in the French Under-21 team for the European Championship finals.

FRIDAY, 19 APRIL

As if exit from the FA Cup and a relegation battle were not bad enough, Sir Alex Ferguson now let it be known that he was chasing the talented Steve Finnan, who has gained a lot of admirers in an excellent season. A solid, reliable, pacy full-back, who gets forward well and is a good crosser of the ball, it was no surprise the highly consistent Finnan had caught Ferguson's eye. United were prepared to pay £8m for the 26-year-old, who was named in the Professional Footballers' Association Premiership Team of the Year. Finnan, however, put Fulham fans' minds at rest. 'Money doesn't always buy you success,' he said. 'And big-spending teams have gone back down before. It's flattering being linked with the biggest club in the world, but big things are going to happen at Fulham and I want to be part of that. I have heard the stories but I cannot afford to get carried away. I have been at Fulham for four years and seen the club come a long way. I am happy here and feel I can achieve a great deal.'

SATURDAY, 20 APRIL
LEEDS UNITED 0 FULHAM 1
The last time Fulham scored a goal at Elland Road was on 12 April 1966, when 'Pancho' Pearson scored a second-half winner to give the Whites a 0–1 victory in what was a considerable help in achieving what was probably Fulham's greatest ever escape from the threat of relegation from the top flight. This time it was Malbranque who grabbed the goal which could just be enough to keep

Fulham up. It wasn't the best goal in the world, but nobody at Fulham could care less. A delighted Damiano hailed this win as the best result of the season. He said: 'At this moment, based on the last six seasons, I feel we need one more point. We confirmed our quality in this game, but then every time we play home and away we play with spirit and we deserve this win. It's the result of the season for us, which has been an unlucky one in many respects. Today we were perhaps lucky given some of the chances Leeds had, but then the one we had was finished very well.' Sean Davis spoke of his delight at finally getting that sought-after win. 'We worked our socks off. Leeds could have punished us before half-time but they didn't and I thought we deserved the win. Normally this season, teams punish us but they didn't this time. We defended well and everyone, from the strikers to Edwin Van Der Sar in goal, had a good game. We were always up for this game. We've not had much luck and you are supposed to earn your luck and I thought we did that. Leeds missed chances, Robbie Keane had a one-on-one just before half-time and normally that goes in, but it hasn't and we have come back and Steed has got us the winner. To come to Leeds and get a result like this is a great achievement. We knew this was a big game and we have worked hard to get the win. Some of the lads said in the dressing room that they're not used to this feeling because we haven't won in a long time. It's a nice feeling and hopefully we can continue that on Tuesday.'

SUNDAY, 21 APRIL
Fulham officially dismissed rumours in the Sunday newspapers that former Chelsea boss Ruud Gullit is set to become the club's new team manager. Chester Stern told of Al Fayed's anger: 'I can say quite categorically that these rumours are complete and utter rubbish. The chairman is livid. Mohamed Al Fayed fully backs Jean Tigana, and there is positively no interest in any other manager in the world. We believe this is part of a long-running dirty tricks campaign devised to unsettle our players and manager at a crucial time of the season. Let me state quite clearly that Jean Tigana has always had the chairman's total support and nothing has changed.' While internally there were questions being asked about the players' attitudes and the manager's purchases, the club believed there were forces trying to 'destabilise' the club with a suspicion that a former employee might be behind it. 'The reports are scandalous and we haven't ruled out the possibility of taking legal action,' said Stern. But despite the categorical denials the speculation refused to go away: one article suggested that Tigana was wanted by Turkish club Besiktas.

MONDAY, 22 APRIL
The players could finally wake up to prepare for the first day of a week of training having won a game. Motspur Park was suddenly buzzing again and Tigana was in half an hour earlier than normal. Casting his eye ahead to the

last evening match at the Cottage, Sean Davis was cautious of a resolute Bolton side. With both sides having almost identical records so far in the Premiership, he warned that no one should be under any illusions that this will be an easy game. 'We have a big game tomorrow and hopefully we can repeat this performance in front of the home crowd and get the three points we need. The main thing for us this season is to stay in the Premiership. We have come a long way since I've been here and we were back in the Third Division. To come and stay in the Premiership in the first season is a good achievement.' Davis also had other issues on his mind. He was due to appear at Southwestern Magistrates' Court in Balham, south London, at 10.30 a.m., in connection with the 31 March incident when he was breathalysed by police in nearby Battersea. After attending the hearing he was hoping to line up in the Fulham midfield for the 8 p.m. scrap with Bolton.

Just as Fulham were starting to smile again Bolton manager Sam Allardyce stuck the knife into Tigana, claiming he faced the sack after the west London club revealed losses for the year to June 2001 of £24m – the biggest in British footballing history. 'If you don't achieve results, that is when the pressure rides on you,' he said. Fulham were level on points with Bolton, who spent only £1.4m on new players following promotion. Fulham, by contrast, shelled out £32m. The news of Fulham's finances made the front page of the *Evening Standard*, whose headline read: 'Fayed's Fulham Football Club loses a record £24m'. The losses were 30 per cent more than the previous record – Newcastle United's £18.9m loss in 2000. Much of the total was due to a jump in wages from around £8m to over £19m; and that was before the summer influx. Fulham's debts total over £61.7m, as opposed to £40.6m a year ago. Al Fayed bought the club in 1997 for £30m and vowed to make them 'bigger than Chelsea', and Allardyce admitted that in the long run his investment will probably pay off. 'Fulham have not won as many games as they would have liked,' he said. 'The team has functioned but they have not scored as many goals as they thought they would. Both of us are just interested in maintaining our Premiership status now and getting our plans ready for next season. They will probably be a better force next season because of the experience they have gained and the players will have learned a lot about the standard needed.' The good news was that turnover rose from £7.6m to £9m, largely on the back of increased ticket sales. The club listed their financial results at Companies House under the name Fulham Football Leisure Limited. Al Fayed had, in February, according to the papers lodged, used the big fees from Sky to secure £8m of debt finance for the club.

It was revealed that some season-ticket prices for next season would rise by 60 per cent, following a freeze on them for the first season in the Premiership. The top-priced ticket at the Cottage was £355, making it one of the cheapest of its kind in the country. Even a top price next season of £570 would be the most competitive in London, while the cheapest will go up to £437 from £304. A spokesman said: 'Many of our season-ticket holders have been benefiting from a price freeze and from watching Premiership football at First Division prices. Our aim is to make watching Fulham as accessible as possible but we also need to generate income to help fulfil our ambitions. We still think the costs involved are competitive and have carried out research to ensure that is the case.'

TUESDAY, 23 APRIL
FULHAM 3 BOLTON 0

This was the last time Fulham played under lights at the old Cottage and the team put on a performance they could be proud of. Kevin Keegan once said: 'There is something very special about night games at the Cottage. It is almost as if you can see Johnny Haynes running out.' This was certainly a special night for Fulham. Running the show on this occasion was Bjarne Goldbaek, a bystander for most of the season. He scored the first and helped set up Marlet before Hayles became the last Fulham player to score a goal at the Cottage. With the result confirming Premiership safety in style, Damiano reflected on the season and admitted that England's top division is much more competitive than people realise and that early predictions of a top-six finish were over-eager. 'When we arrived there were two players – Chris Coleman and Lee Clark – who had Premiership experience. They have both been injured this season, so it was presumptuous of people to think we would do better than we have. We signed Steve Marlet and everyone was talking about what we paid for him. But he was injured when he got here, then he got another knock in his first game, so that has been quite difficult. We have stayed in the Premier League and reached the semi-finals of the FA Cup, so it has been quite a good season.' Goldbaek reflected on the game: 'It was my first start since Ipswich in January, and that was only for 45 minutes, so I was very pleased with the way it went. In the first half there were a couple of occasions when I lost the ball but then got it back from a rebound, and then you start to think actually, this could be your day today. It was just fun to play with Steve Finnan as well, we know each other so well from last year; as soon as he plays the ball I know what he's going to do next, so it was just a question of me getting the ball to him in the right place at the right time. It's a big advantage when you get a good link-up like that. Finns is full of confidence as well; he's on the way to the World Cup and he's playing very well at the moment, so that makes things a little bit easier, of course. The way the crowd reacted was really nice. I could have stayed out there for hours – we haven't heard it like that for a while.'

But as the rest of the Fulham lads were celebrating staying up, Goldbaek was turning his attention to his future, and whether he has one with the club. His contract is up at the end of the season, and when asked if he would be happy to stay, he said: 'Of course. I like it here very much. We have a good team, and the training is now very similar to the way it was in other countries that I have played in. We try to play nice football here, which is important, and we have a lot of fun on the training ground and in the dressing room. You can see that everything is growing at the club. I can still remember when I first came here two and a half years ago and we had to wash all our clothes ourselves; everything is so different now. I have to admit that uncertainty does hang over your head a little bit. I've got to sort out a school for my son, and the renting of our house, that sort of thing, so it's difficult to make plans, but I would very much like to stay next season.'

Sarah Brookes noted the contrasting styles of the managers during the game: 'I was watching the Bolton game in the directors' box for some reason. And I saw Sam Allardyce run to the pitch when there was a bad tackle near the dug-out. He practically blew up like a kettle, and I remember watching and thinking he was going to have a heart attack one day. And then on my right side was Jean, also looking like he was about to explode but in that cool, calm, collected French manner. He was gesticulating wildly with his hands and then he looked to his left and saw Sam Allardyce, whose head was about to shoot off his shoulders. Jean looked at Allardyce, looked at Christian in the dug-out, shrugged his shoulders and just sat down.'

Before the game news filtered through that Sean Davis had been disqualified from driving for one year. He pleaded guilty at Southwestern Magistrates' Court to drink-driving. He was also fined £600 and ordered to pay £55 costs. The court heard that 22-year-old Davis, from Wimbledon, was driving his Y-reg BMW X5 on 31 March with his girlfriend and other friends after drinking vodka and cranberry juice at a West End club until 3.30 a.m. This was after the game against Southampton and only thirty-six hours before kick-off against West Ham. No wonder the club fined him two weeks' wages.

WEDNESDAY, 24 APRIL
Fulham will have to ground-share at QPR for two years instead of one after the High Court granted local objectors leave to appeal against the Government's decision not to call in the club's application to redevelop Craven Cottage. 'It is a disgrace that a tiny minority can spoil the enjoyment of the majority in this cynical way by employing delaying tactics,' said Mark Collins, the acting MD.

THURSDAY, 25 APRIL
Fulham were looking at qualifying for the UEFA Cup through the InterToto. Derby, Leeds, Villa, Chelsea, Newcastle, Ipswich and Everton had also applied earlier in the season. While there are mixed views about the competition, the opportunity to play some games against good-quality opposition, with European entry awaiting the winner, makes it something worth fighting for.

Van Der Sar looked back at the games against Leeds and Bolton: 'I think we played a little more defensively against Leeds. We only had one or two chances and scored from one of those, which is a very different story from most of the season. And not only did we score, we kept a clean sheet as well. And then against Bolton we kept another clean sheet and scored three goals as well, so that really was fantastic for everybody. We grew in confidence the longer the second half went on. In the first half they had a few chances and we didn't play all that well. I had to make a good save early on, and for the first twenty minutes we weren't that good, but we got better and gained confidence, and in the end we were happy about the way it went.' Van Der Sar was also enthusiastic about the InterToto Cup: 'Europe was our goal this season. We tried to go as far as we could in the FA and the Worthington cups,' he said. 'Unfortunately we had the slump in the league over the last couple of months, and that's cost us any chance of getting into the UEFA Cup that way, so now we have to work hard in the last two games to make sure we get a chance in the InterToto. I'm used to playing in Europe and it's good for you, it's a good way to gain experience and a good way of getting the club known. If we can reach that it will be a very good thing. I came to Fulham because it's a great story about the building of the club, and the possibilities here are enormous. Everybody has to start somewhere and it's sometimes more exciting to jump on a train that's at the station rather than one that's already down the line, because then you can enjoy the whole journey. We've got a long way to go, but the summer's coming and I don't know what the manager's ideas are regarding new players, but I think we need to strengthen our squad. We've played some good football this year, but for one reason or another we didn't get the points that we deserved, so we have to be better next year.'

He also quashed any ideas that he was regretting his move: 'It isn't the same level as Juventus, but it's more important that you enjoy yourself and enjoy life. I am very happy here in London and my wife and family are settled – my son speaks English already. I think there are excellent prospects here for everybody. It's going to take time, but if we can qualify for Europe via the InterToto that will be a big step. It would be some more good experience for the players.'

FRIDAY, 26 APRIL
The club's home for 105 years will soon be no more. Johnny Haynes, who played 658 times for the club, scoring 158 goals, will be the guest of honour for the final game at the Cottage against Leicester. One of those goals was against Leicester in 1966. He recalled: 'It was from 35 yards against Gordon Banks and we won 4–2. It would be lovely if the current team gave the Cottage a send-off like that.' Jimmy Hill looked back on his life at the club but also looked ahead: 'I have wonderful memories of Fulham and the Cottage but I am not sorry to see it go. I was behind football's first all-seater stadium at Coventry and nostalgia should not get in the way of progress. You must not hold back the future and without Mohamed Al Fayed there would be no Fulham. We can live without memories. Like how the groundsman Albert used to get up early on a Saturday morning to turn on the boiler so we could all have a hot bath after games. If he overslept he got a rollicking and we got a cold one.'

However, Leicester boss Mickey Adams did not have quite such fond memories. He conceded that Fulham were right to fire him after twenty months in charge when Al Fayed arrived. Adams said: 'At the time of leaving it hurt but I think it was the right decision for Fulham to make. Mr Al Fayed had a five-year plan and when you look at where they are now who can say he was wrong to bring in Kevin Keegan? And when you look at Mickey Adams, the new manager at Leicester City, who can say things have gone that badly for me as a consequence?' He admitted he was not ready to handle Al Fayed's millions at the time: 'I wasn't happy about spending it quickly but fortunately Kevin had no such inhibitions! I am looking forward to going back because I have a terrific rapport with the fans. I still get letters from supporters, so that will do me. If you can leave a club in a better position than when you joined, you have done your job and I think I did that at Fulham. I have nothing to be bitter about. Fayed left us in no doubt he wanted a Premiership club and so the sack for me was inevitable from the minute he came in. He wanted a big name and I can see why. The club started to become more professional when Fayed came in. But when you have worked with no money you don't necessarily know how to improve things when you are given £1m to spend. When I first arrived at Craven Cottage we had next to nothing and there was no manager's office. The treatment room was a Portakabin and we trained on rugby pitches from time to time and all took our own kit home and washed it. Because money was tight we used to have a scheme which involved taking up to six people on the team coach on Fridays if we had an overnight stay and an away game the next day. We had several regulars who more or less paid for our away travel. They got to go on the team bus, had a meal with me, a few drinks, a seat at the ground, fish and chips on the way home and a couple of cans of lager. We built on team spirit and I brought in decent players on free transfers who have gone on to have good careers. What we did on the budget we had was special.'

SATURDAY, 27 APRIL
FULHAM 0 LEICESTER 0

Tigana's hundredth game in charge was all about nostalgia, memories, days gone by. Just as well: because there was nothing about the game itself to celebrate. With relegation avoided, Fulham fans watched the final game at the old Craven Cottage with a sense of relief. This was the last time a Fulham team would emerge from the famous Cottage. And before they did, a few black-and-white legends took the field to walk on the hallowed turf they had once graced. The parade of stars included the incomparable Johnny Haynes, rightly announced as 'Mr Fulham himself', as well as record goalscorer Gordon Davies and FA Cup skipper Alan Mullery, Tosh Chamberlain, George Cohen, Roy Bentley, Maurice Cook and modern-day heroes like Simon Morgan. These were 'the Legends of Fulham' as 'Diddy' David Hamilton, matchday MC, put it. Some even discarded jackets at half-time and took penalties in their leather shoes. Big Al was on the pitch with the parade of legends before the start, and during the interval presented trophies to the Fulham Ladies team, before reappearing at the final whistle to lead the customary end-of-season lap of honour: 'It was a great occasion that will surely leave people with mixed emotions, myself included.' Pity about the match. 'Raise the roof,' urged 'Diddy', but for a club that will always be associated with Tommy Trinder, it was hard even to raise a laugh!

But a point did put Fulham within touching distance of the InterToto Cup. Van Der Sar said: 'You would normally expect three points against Leicester but we were apathetic and there was no passion. I played in the InterToto Cup for Juventus four years ago when we failed to qualify for Europe automatically so I know it would be very worthwhile for Fulham. Juventus won all three rounds and made the UEFA Cup after we had visited some strange places that used to be part of Russia.' Mickey Adams was apologetic: 'It wasn't the most entertaining game in the world. They gave me a great reception and it was more than I expected. We were aware of the carnival atmosphere and if there was a party or a cake to be cut, we wanted to blow the candles out.'

Tigana concluded with the obvious: 'The problem this year is only in the last 25 yards. I try all the time to get maximum points but I am not happy. Last year we scored many goals but this year was a big step and I have many things to work on this summer. There are many games that we could have won, but if you look at the players they have not played at this level before. Today was a very poor game. We started badly and although we improved a little, I am disappointed because it is our last game at this ground.'

Will he leave? Speculation continued, but Tigana ignored it and referred to his summer work as an indicator that he was staying. For the record, the last Fulham team to play at the Cottage was: Van Der Sar, Finnan, Brevett, Melville, Goma, Legwinski (Saha), Davis, Goldbaek (Collins), Malbranque, Marlet, Hayles.

Ever the salesman, the Harrods owner put up for sale unwanted stock. Turf was available at just £10 per square foot cut into 850 pieces (although the club 'cannot be held responsible for the condition of turf once it is removed from the ground and subsequently – due to the grass being live there will be a one-off collection'). Among the novel memorabilia were 116 Philips 2kw projector bulbs (from the floodlights for decoration purposes only), as well as fittings and a limited edition of 800 bricks from the soon-to-be-demolished Cottage itself.

MAY

Al Fayed 'helps' in signing of Sava ... Moves for Juninho ... Italian legend Baresi appointed ...

WEDNESDAY, 1 MAY

The journey from carpenter and non-league footballer to Premiership striker is one that very few have made. Barry Hayles did not have the luxury of being taught his trade in a football academy. Neither did he benefit from having full professional status until his mid-twenties. Yet Hayles is one of those players who can conjure up romantic football notions in us all. He is probably the best man to give his verdict on Fulham's season: 'To be honest I thought we would have done a lot better. Before the season started I thought that the gap from the First Division to the Premiership wasn't going to be that big. This season we've found out it's a massive leap. In every team you need a level of consistency, but the manager has brought different players into the team to do different jobs, so it's always hard when you come back into the side.'

As the close season approaches the cogs of the speculation machine slowly gear up for action. With much of the focus on the strikeforce, did Hayles feel that his time as a regular Premiership footballer could be coming to an end? 'Not really. I've been fearful of that from the time I got here. I'm always hearing that I'm not good enough to play at this level. I'm not worried about that any more, it's just the same story. When the other strikers joined I thought I was going to take a back seat but it didn't happen that way. I've got faith in my own ability so I'm just going to play the way I know I can play.'

Alain Goma denied reports that he wanted to join Parma after little more than a year with Fulham. Arsenal were linked along with Manchester United for Steve Finnan, while Millwall were reported to be on the trail of Hayles. Fulham, along with half a dozen other Premiership clubs, were linked with Rangers' midfield star Barry Ferguson, as well as Derby's under-21 international striker Malcolm Christie. And the papers also reported that Tigana wanted Kanu.

THURSDAY, 2 MAY

Steve Finnan has been voted Fulham's Player of the Season. Finnan produced a series of excellent performances at right-back and also earned the recognition of his fellow professionals by being listed in the PFA Team of the Season. Supporters in their thousands voted for him, with Goma finishing second and Malbranque coming third. Goma congratulated his team-mate on winning the award. 'For me Fin has been the Player of the Season. He's a top player, a top man and he deserves the award.'

Christian Damiano expressed concern about the short recovery time available for players in the congested English timetable. 'If a new calendar can be organised in the future that can be a lot wider, then that would be a big improvement. Perhaps the season could start at the beginning of August and finish at the end of May, or even early June. Then you could have a break of one or two weeks after perhaps 8 January which would be very beneficial for both the players and the pitches. Of course, sometimes you might have a World Cup or European tournament to think about, but a schedule could be adapted to take that into account. The most important thing in football is the players. At the moment the fans don't get the opportunity to see entertaining games and there is more chance of players getting injured.'

Reflecting on the two-week break with only a mid-table clash with Blackburn Rovers left, Damiano spoke about the difficulty of keeping players fit and focused with the way the season is currently structured: 'During the season they have to play fifty or fifty-five games and they have to do it in the best condition and in the best form. The big problem for all the managers is to keep their players in top form. If you have many games in a short period, it is impossible for the players to stay strong all the time.' This season's schedule is particularly hard to fathom, with teams having to wait two weeks to play their final game. For most clubs, these matches are meaningless fixtures, and, as Damiano says, it is not easy keeping players' minds on the job in these circumstances.

FRIDAY, 3 MAY

Lee Clark had surgery on the Achilles tendon injury which had kept him out for all but nine matches. This is after missing only one game in the promotion campaign. He will be out for five months.

SATURDAY, 4 MAY

Marlet and Finnan were told they will not have to play in the InterToto Cup if they end up going to the World Cup finals. Marlet's selection for France will go down to the wire since Roger Lemerre confirmed that Auxerre's Djibril Cisse would be going, leaving Marlet and Anelka to fight for the remaining place. Should Fulham qualify for the InterToto Cup, the second round would take place on 6 and 7 July, leaving little time for recovery. Damiano said players who'd been to the World Cup would be 'worn out before Christmas' if they were forced to play in the InterToto too.

SUNDAY, 5 MAY

Sean Davis struggled this season but found his feet eventually. Tigana was instrumental in that, given that he took time to give Davis extra tuition because he was playing in a position he had occupied himself for France. Davis reflected: 'It started off a bit slow but for the last fifteen games it's gone well. The manager has brought in a lot of players and it's been hard to gel but overall we've done well. Obviously we had a bad period when we didn't win for a long time but we deservedly stayed up this year. Our problem has been scoring goals. We'd dominate teams, make a mistake and they'd go straight down the other end and punish us. At Leeds we had the reverse scenario, where they dominated us but we snatched a goal and got the three points. I'm always confident,' Davis went on. 'If I'm playing well I expect to be starting so if the manager brings in new players it's not going to be a problem for me. If he brings in top-quality players and they're playing well when I'm not, I'd have no arguments.' With only one game of the current season remaining, it's perhaps most apt that Davis will be returning to the scene of the most memorable moment thus far in his career: Ewood Park.

'I'm looking forward to the last game of the season. Hopefully the Gaffer will put some of the young lads in and show the fans what we've got. If beating Blackburn means we'll be sure of getting into the InterToto Cup, then we'll have to go there looking for the win. I personally think the Gaffer might bring some of the young lads in just so we can see how they've progressed. We've got a lot of good young players like Zat Knight, Luke Cornwall, Calum Willock, Elvis Hammond, Mark Hudson and Tom Hutchinson. If he gives them a run-out, you never know, they might produce the goods.'

MONDAY, 6 MAY

A perfect season for the Fulham Ladies comes to a close. With their 2–1 defeat of the Doncaster Belles in the FA Cup on Monday, the Ladies have now won every game they have played this season, and have picked up the First Division Title, the FA Cup, the League Cup and the London County Cup along the way. Manager Gaute Haugenes, admitted there had been some celebrating and looked back at the game. 'It went pretty much the way we expected,' he said. 'They are a physical team, very strong, and they played very well. In the first half they hit their rhythm, hitting lots of long balls over the top and we were forced into doing the same thing. But in the second half we adjusted the way we were playing a little, got a bit more into our own rhythm, got the ball down on the floor and put some good passing moves together. We managed to get the wide players more involved and got some good crosses in, and we ended up having a very good second half. The main thing was that we won the trophy; that was our target right from the beginning of the season and it's a fantastic thing that we achieved it. The whole team played very well, but Katie Chapman had a fantastic game in the midfield and scored a great goal, and the other scorer, Rachel Yankey, also played very well; she was much more involved in the second half and really demonstrated all her skills; she ran well with the ball, put over some great crosses and had some good shots. It was a fantastic relief to win. There has been a lot of pressure on us to win the Cup after the defeat last season. We were the favourites and people expected us to win, and we put a lot of pressure on ourselves to win it. So it was a big relief – I was ten kilos lighter by the time the game ended! It was a fantastic feeling though. This win was very important for the club because women's football is taken very seriously here. We have the full support of everyone, fantastic support from the men's team and their staff, and fantastic support from the directors and everyone else who works here. So it's good to be the best so that we can reward them, and there's no doubt that after the season we've had, we can definitely say we are the best team in the country. This puts Fulham on the map, not only in England but in the rest of Europe as well, since there was a lot of media interest from outside this country. And of course the game was shown live on the BBC, which was fantastic.'

So were celebrations in order after the game? 'We had a very good time! We had a good celebration at Selhurst Park, and then we took the coach back to Craven Cottage and had a party, some food and a few drinks! It was a good evening. The season has ended now; we'll have the players back for some fitness testing before they go away on holiday, then we'll have a short break and report back for pre-season training on 1 July. And after that it is the big challenge of the Premier League. It will be a whole new experience for us playing against top-class opposition every week. I'm confident that we can challenge for the title straight away, but of course we won't know how we will do until we are actually there. But it is an experience that we need, and the only place we can get better is in the Premier League, so we are really looking forward to it. We will approach the challenge with confidence.'

TUESDAY, 7 MAY

An insider at Fulham revealed: 'As Jean and the players were going on holiday for a month, there were two strategy meetings involving the chairman and the manager. We know of all the rumours circulating about the manager's position, but the fact that a budget was discussed for new players and plans for next season put into operation made it clear that the manager was staying.' Chester Stern made a public statement about Tigana's position: 'Why on earth would Mr Al Fayed make statements in the press supporting the manager, and then sack him?' Stern stressed that Tigana was assured about his future at a meeting the previous month.

InterToto qualification rested on the result at Blackburn and Everton's result at Arsenal. That thoughts had turned from an FA Cup Final to the InterToto showed that realism had set in. Andy Melville made an excellent job of justifying the competition: 'The InterToto Cup is criticised a lot but, with the UEFA Cup at the end of it, it is a very important competition for us. We just need to put in one more good performance and we could end the season in Europe and possibly the top ten, which was what we have always been aiming for.' West Ham became all too aware of the pros and cons of the InterToto when they won it in 1999 and took their place in the UEFA Cup, before the extra travelling and matches involved finally caught up with them in the second half of the season as their early form faded. However, Melville countered that argument: 'We think of the InterToto as a route into Europe and that is where we want to be playing. We start our pre-season training before the end of June, which is earlier than a lot of clubs anyway. We still have something to play for and are really up for the game, a place in the top ten plus getting to the semi-finals of the FA Cup would mean our season was successful.' Realistically, at the start of the season, a place in Europe would have been gleefully accepted by the fans. Expectations, however, had got out of hand. Melville added: 'This season was all about learning as we went along. We are aware our success means there will be more pressure on us to perform next season but we are ready for that.'

WEDNESDAY, 8 MAY

Winger Eddie Lewis was called up to the USA World Cup squad but coach Bruce Arena attacked Tigana for refusing to release him until after the Blackburn match. The USA played World Cup warm-up games against Uruguay in Washington, Jamaica in New Jersey and Holland in Massachusetts, while Lewis had not played in Fulham's first team for eighteen months. Arena fumed: 'It is unfair on the player and it doesn't help us. There's nothing I can do. I think the guy Tigana is an absolute jerk.' The club were shocked by the outburst. Sarah Brookes said: 'We're very disappointed with what has been said. It really doesn't help the situation or the player. The fact is that we have suspensions and injuries for this weekend's game and Jean wants a full squad. He wants to include Eddie and we're quite happy for him to leave the next day.'

Steve Finnan was selected for the Republic of Ireland squad. Fresh from a hard training session, and unsure at first as to whether he had been called up or was the victim of yet another elaborate wind-up, Finnan spoke about what the news meant to him: 'It feels good, obviously, now the squad has been announced. I've not seen the full list, but I've just been told I'm on it, so I'm looking forward to meeting up now with the other players. All along you hope that you're going to be involved, and people say that you're going to go, but until it's actually announced and you see your name down there, you're never really sure. But now I can relax a little bit and really start looking forward to it. I think the news will start to sink in over the next few days. I've been involved in the Irish set-up for the last couple of years and I've played in all the recent games, and you always have half an eye on the World Cup. So I have been thinking about it, without letting myself get too carried away, but it's nice to be settled. I still find it hard to believe that it's happening, but it's a great honour for me and I'm really, really looking forward to it.'

THURSDAY, 9 MAY

Recent reserve matches saw one name crop up on the scoresheet fairly regularly. Elvis Hammond is one of a group of promising young players who are waiting to be given their chance in the first team. Tigana has privately been raving about the young striker who could find himself added to the first-team squad next season. Looking back over Hammond's season, frustration is the one word that would appear to sum up his campaign. A good start was cut short after Elvis fractured a bone in his foot, with the subsequent weeks of recovery hampering his promising progress. However, Hammond had fully shaken off any lingering adverse effects and was gearing up to challenge for a first-team spot. Not bad for a player who, initially, had no designs on becoming a professional footballer: 'Playing football professionally was something that just happened when I came out of school. Sean Davis was here already and he asked me to come down for a trial,' Hammond revealed. He joined straight out of school when he was 16. His CV reads like a footballing *Who's Who*. 'In Ghana I played with George Weah, Marcel Desailly, Roger Milla and Ibrahima Bakayoko. My agency knew Desailly and my family also knows him as well. So I was invited to play against Ghana and Burkina Faso in a few matches. I thought I did all right, it was pretty hot out there so I could only last forty-five minutes.' Hammond knows next year will be tough, but he is glad he hit form just as the season came to an end. 'If there were a few more games I'd like to think that I could get close to a first-team call-up. But seeing as it's so late in the season, I don't know what the Gaffer's going to do. It's entirely up to him who he picks but I think I'm ready. Next season I'm definitely looking to push for the first team. I'm 21 now and it's at this age when I need to be involved or just on the verge of being involved.'

FRIDAY, 10 MAY

The latest call-up to the World Cup finals was goalkeeping coach Gerry Peyton to join the Republic of Ireland and play a key part in preparing the team. 'I've been very fortunate to be asked by Mick McCarthy and the Irish FA to travel with the boys to the World Cup,' said Peyton. 'I'll meet up with them on 2 June after the Germany–Saudi Arabia game, which I'll be reporting on for them. We'll meet up then and I'll go through the game with them. I'll then stay with them for thirteen days, and I just hope that we can be successful there. The World Cup in Italy was a fantastic experience and I'm hoping Japan is going to be as good for us. Basically I'll be covering games for them, analysing their opponents, looking at players and tactics – to be honest, it'll be the same job that I do for Fulham. It's very exciting for me. I spent four years living in Japan, and I hope that my experience of the culture and how things work out there will help them be successful in the tournament. It would be very nice to be with them all the way through to the final!' Gerry made 33 appearances for the Republic in his distinguished goalkeeping career; it is fitting that once again he will enjoy another Irish adventure in the World Cup.

SATURDAY, 11 MAY
BLACKBURN ROVERS 3 FULHAM 0

There was no sign of last season's jubilation at Ewood Park. There could be little argument over the result as Rovers were simply the better side. Despite a series of first-half scares, Fulham reached the interval without conceding. However, with Rovers looking very dangerous on the attack, they had to produce a better display in the second period to avoid defeat. That didn't materialise. Rovers took the lead in the 52nd minute after Andy Cole tackled Maik Taylor to pass the ball into an empty net. Damiano admitted that the 'keeper approached the situation with a touch of over-confidence. Tigana had been forced to make a number of changes and Damiano acknowledged that Fulham's squad was not equipped to deal with these extensive changes: 'It was a game Blackburn deserved to win, as they had more chances. It was difficult for us as we were missing five important players and the other players could not cope.' Summing up Fulham's first season in the Premiership, Christian was not overly dis-appointed but still recognised the areas of weakness. 'If we had had one more striker we would have finished in the top eight but we were too weak up front, and in midfield only Steed Malbranque scored goals. We'll find out this week how much money we'll have to sign people and if we have to sell players.'

Despite the heavy defeat, Fulham qualified for the InterToto Cup. With Everton losing 4–3 in a thrilling match at Highbury, Fulham's one-point lead over the Toffees was maintained.

SUNDAY, 12 MAY

Troubled by persistent pain in his elbow over recent months, Van Der Sar underwent surgery. The operation was carried out as early as possible to ensure he was back to full fitness by the beginning of the next season. Physiotherapist Jason Palmer explained exactly what the problem was: 'Edwin has had an irritation to his left elbow for a number of weeks. We were able to manage it medically, but it wasn't really resolving itself. He had various scans and x-rays done, and they showed that he had some loose chips of bone that caused him pain and discomfort in certain movements of the joint. It wasn't something that required immediate surgery, so we waited until the team had secured its position in the Premiership next year and the management felt he could be released to have the loose bodies removed. He had the operation carried out in Amsterdam by a Dutch surgeon. I accompanied him to the surgery and actually went in and saw what was done. It was an arthroscopic surgical procedure that removed three fairly large loose bodies from the joint as well as doing a little bit of work on the wear and tear generally in the elbow. The pieces were effectively about half the size of a one-pence coin, so they were quite significant. It was a very successful operation, and he will now work with one of the Dutch national team's physios through the summer. If all goes to plan, and there's little that can go wrong, he will be back ready to go for pre-season. It's just a matter of getting the arm strong again and regaining his full range of movement.'

Steve Finnan received his award as Player of the Year at the Craven Cottage Gala Dinner.

MONDAY, 13 MAY

A final meeting between Al Fayed and his manager to discuss the summer recruitment plans took place. Tigana was linked to £4m-rated central defender Jean-Alain Boumsong, but there was a feeling that there were already sufficient signings from France, with five in the starting line-up, so clearly there was a change in direction on the purchase of players. Good news: Malbranque pledged his future to the club from the French under-21 training camp near Paris. The Frenchman was one of Tigana's stars and attracted attention from Premiership and European rivals. Malbranque, who scored eight goals in his first campaign, said: 'I see my next season being at Fulham. I feel good at this club and I'll stay.'

TUESDAY, 14 MAY

This was a season when all three promoted clubs stayed up after a struggle. Bolton led the Premiership in the early stages, but that proved highly deceptive, while Blackburn confirmed their survival only late in the season. Ipswich were relegated after earning a place in Europe the previous season. Ironically, despite going down, George Burley's side won a place in the UEFA Cup after winning the Fair Play League in the Premiership and being drawn out of the hat by UEFA. Based on Ipswich's demise in the Premiership, the biggest lesson is that the second season will be even more crucial for Fulham. The club successfully appealed against their £30,000 fine after originally being found guilty of misconduct in the Everton game. The go-ahead for the redevelopment of the Cottage came through after residents failed in a bid to force a public inquiry. QPR, whose Loftus Road ground will provide the club's temporary home during the redevelopment, came out of administration.

WEDNESDAY, 15 MAY

Al Fayed played a leading role in Tigana's first summer signing, Argentinian striker Facundo Sava. Chester Stern said: 'Al Fayed's family connections in South America tipped us off about the talents of this striker.' After two meetings with Al Fayed, Tigana has been allocated around £20m to ensure that Fulham continue to progress and Sava was the club's first signing since Tigana gained the backing of his chairman despite a turbulent end to the season. A representative of Sava's agent Juan Carlos Zamora confirmed talks were at an advanced stage, and only final details remained before the Argentinian completed his move. 'Sava has all but signed,' said the source. 'Final talks were going ahead today.' Target man Sava is a well-respected player in the Argentine league and his ability in the air is complemented by quick feet and an eye for goal. Although his club Gimnasia were hopeful of receiving around $4m for their star man, the price was ultimately set at £2m. Sava, Gimnasia's top scorer with 12 goals in 19 games, fits the bill for a target man. After being linked with Flo, Batistuta, Yorke and Andy Cole, Sava would seem to be a bargain buy and resolves Fulham's lack of height in attack. He agreed a four-year contract and said: 'The move is a big step for me and I will try to give my best for them.'

Next signing was Argentinian goalkeeper Martin Herrera on a free transfer from Alaves.

Fulham were offered the chance of bringing Juninho back to the Premiership. He made it clear he was thinking of a move when he said: 'Next season I'm going to be at Athletico Madrid, who are back in the First Division in Spain. I've got two years on my contract there, and I want it to work out. But in my heart I think I will play in England again.' Al Fayed's new policy is to abolish lavish salaries and after several days of talks it was decided Juninho's wage demands, plus the fee, made the financial package unrealistic for a 29-year-old.

FRIDAY, 17 MAY

England's opening tie in the Under-21 European Championships was only 34 minutes old when coach David Platt substituted Sean Davis for his own protection after he had been yellow-carded. Davis accepted that had he stayed on he would have probably been sent-off by whistle-happy Hungarian referee Attila Hanacsek. Davis said: 'The Gaffer has probably done me a big favour, because a sending-off would have ruled me out of at least one vital game. I've never been substituted after half an hour and I was shocked when my number came up, but having watched the rest of the game from the bench and seen the referee's attitude from a different perspective, I could understand the decision. If I'd made another tackle, I'd have probably gone.'

MONDAY, 20 MAY

Perhaps the most significant postscript to Tigana's first season in the Premiership was the appointment of Franco Baresi as director of football. Even more telling was that part of Baresi's role was as the chairman's advisor on football. Tigana will concentrate on working with the first team and on coaching, and although he will continue to be consulted on transfers, he will no longer be actively involved in the deals, as he has been in the past with a number of French agents. The former AC Milan and Italy sweeper has been given a wide brief, but in an advisory capacity only. Changes were sweeping through the club. Baresi is one of the most successful players in the modern game, with a World Cup-winner's medal, three European Cup triumphs and six Serie A titles. He captained AC Milan for 16 years and Italy for 4 years, winning 88 caps. Such was his impact at Milan that the club withdrew the No. 6 shirt when he retired. He missed a penalty in the semi-final shoot-out defeat by Argentina at Italia '90 and missed again four years later when Italy lost the final in the same heart-breaking manner to Brazil. But he was most definitely on the spot when Fulham needed him. Al Fayed said: 'This is the next step to realising my dream of making Fulham one of the foremost clubs in the world. Two years ago, I was fortunate to attract an international manager with the qualities of Jean Tigana. Now we have doubly strengthened our team with a man who is not only admired worldwide as a footballer but also widely recognised for his knowledge of the game at the highest level.'

Tigana's contract expires in June 2003, and although he has an option for a further two years he is highly unlikely to exercise it, and even if he does, the club might feel they need a change. Baresi clearly sees himself as the manager elect. And some observers believe it is a shrewd move to bring in the successor with time to adjust to a new country and its football. Baresi speaks almost no English but has the chance to learn the language and the demands of the Premiership. He was lured from his post as vice-president at Milan, for whom he played more than 750 times. This was largely an honorary role which carried little responsibility and Fulham's offer appealed to him. 'I won't be coach for at least the first year,' Baresi told Milan's website. 'The current coach, Tigana, will remain in his post and my eventual takeover will be up to Mohamed Al Fayed.' The club stressed that his arrival on 1 June would not affect the position of Tigana or his assistant manager Christian Damiano. Sources made it clear that Baresi's belief that he might succeed Tigana as manager was premature. He had been brought in simply to advise the chairman on the purchase of players.

Secret moves to secure the services of the 43-year-old Baresi began two months ago when there were concerns about Tigana's future at the club. But there appeared, at least on the surface, still to be a harmonious relationship between manager and chairman. A club source said: 'There is a mutual respect and a tremendous rapport. Christian speaks Italian and the three of them were talking about football like three excited children. Jean's reaction was not that of a man who feels he's being undermined.' Fulham had been less than satisfied with their scouting network and recently terminated the contract of chief scout Bernie Dickson. The new system will mean that Baresi and Tigana will discuss transfer targets, with Baresi negotiating and concluding deals once the manager gives the go-ahead.

John Collins observed: 'Baresi has a wealth of experience of playing at the top level. He has a terrific knowledge of European football. He will be looking out for the best talent available and the chairman is always looking to improve the club. If Franco can find top players for Jean Tigana, that's good news.' The only hitch was the premature announcement of Baresi's appointment. A source at the club admitted: 'There were one or two details in the contract that Baresi wanted to renegotiate. He had a meeting with Mohamed Al Fayed and was at Motspur Park the next day to try to complete the deal. The contract was redrafted overnight and it should all be signed in the morning.'

And so it came to pass.

Immediately Baresi switched the Tigana emphasis from little-known French acquisitions to his contacts in Italy. He put forward three names including Antonio Benarrivo from Parma.

West Ham's Paolo di Canio, who used to share a room with Baresi at Milan, said: 'He knows more about defending than anyone alive.'

Funny that, surely Fulham's problem was scoring goals!